Praise for *Heg*

"Like many powerful concepts, hegemonic masculinity has been deployed variously as a sharp tool that clarifies the workings of the social world, as a fuzzy term that means whatever an author wants it to mean, and as a simplistic foil against which a writer attempts to assert some other idea. James Messerschmidt—long a leading scholar in the field—contributes a clear road map to understanding the origins, development, and continuing importance of the concept. *Hegemonic Masculinity* is a welcome and valuable contribution to the maturation of gender theory in the social sciences."

—Michael A. Messner

"*Hegemonic Masculinity* is a comprehensive and informative overview of the history, critique, reformulation, and current theory of this core concept. It is sure to become a classic text in gender studies—an indispensable introduction for new students and a reliable resource for established scholars. I highly recommend it."

—Judith Lorber, professor emerita, Graduate School and Brooklyn College, CUNY; author of *Breaking the Bowls: Degendering and Feminist Change*

Hegemonic Masculinity

Formulation, Reformulation, and Amplification

James W. Messerschmidt
University of Southern Maine

ROWMAN & LITTLEFIELD
Lanham • Boulder • New York • London

Executive Editor: Rolf Janke
Editorial Assistant: Courtney Packard
Senior Marketing Manager: Kim Lyons

Published by Rowman & Littlefield
An imprint of The Rowman & Littlefield Publishing Group, Inc.
4501 Forbes Boulevard, Suite 200, Lanham, Maryland 20706
https://rowman.com

Unit A, Whitacre Mews, 26-34 Stannary Street, London SE11 4AB,
United Kingdom

British Library Cataloguing in Publication Information Available

Library of Congress Cataloging-in-Publication Data
Names: Messerschmidt, James W., author.
Title: Hegemonic masculinity : formulation, reformulation, and amplification / James W.
    Messerschmidt, University of Southern Maine.
Description: Lanham : Rowman & Littlefield, [2018] | Includes bibliographical references
    and index.
Identifiers: LCCN 2018004650 (print) | LCCN 2018006622 (ebook) | ISBN
    9781538114056 (ebook) | ISBN 9781538114032 (hardcover : alk. paper) | ISBN
    9781538114049 (pbk. : alk. paper)
Subjects: LCSH: Masculinity. | Men—Psychology. | Hegemony.
Classification: LCC BF692.5 (ebook) | LCC BF692.5 .M469 2018 (print) | DDC 155.3/
    32—dc23
LC record available at https://lccn.loc.gov/2018004650

∞ ™ The paper used in this publication meets the minimum requirements of American
National Standard for Information Sciences Permanence of Paper for Printed Library
Materials, ANSI/NISO Z39.48-1992.

Printed in the United States of America

For Raewyn, Cherished Friend, Perceptive Mentor, and
One of the Most Important Intellectuals of Our Time

Contents

Preface

Feminism has continually challenged the masculine nature of the academy by illuminating the patterns of gendered power that social theory had for centuries all but ignored. In particular, feminism secured a permanent role for sex, gender, and sexuality politics in popular culture and thereby moved analysis of sex, gender, and sexual power to the forefront of much social thought. The growth and maturation of explicit theoretical development and empirical research on masculinities followed logically from this feminist work.

The concept of *hegemonic masculinity*, formulated by Raewyn Connell (1987, 1995) more than three decades ago, has been the driving force behind the expanding field of masculinities studies. The concept has now established a long and considerable influence on the interdisciplinary understanding of gender, but in particular masculinity. In specifically the masculinities studies literature since the 1980s, the concept has become ubiquitous, it continues to serve as the principal touchstone for most research, and it is broadly used in a wide range of disciplines—the concept has proven to be crucial to conceptualizing masculinities worldwide. And the reason for the widespread popularity of the concept is that it contributes a significant understanding of how unequal gender relations are legitimated between men and women, masculinities and femininities, and among masculinities.

Although the concept maintains a distinctive status within gender studies across an abundance of disciplines, the concept simultaneously has often been criticized and terribly misunderstood by many scholars. This book then concentrates on the history of the concept and its unique applications. The aim of *Hegemonic Masculinity: Formulation, Reformulation, and Amplification* is to encourage the continued expansion and development of research and theorizing on hegemonic masculinities as well as to contribute a more exacting, careful, and meticulous understanding and utilization of the concept.

The bulk of the book concentrates on the "formulation," "reformulation," and "amplification" of the concept, and includes the "backstory" to

the development of the concept, the actual formulation and initial applications of the concept, the eventual reformulation and subsequent applications of that reformulation, and finally, the amplification of the reformulated concept of hegemonic masculinity. The book also includes a
chapter theorizing why and how hegemonic masculinities are constructed, and the concluding chapter chronicles the prospects for social
change toward more egalitarian gender relations. *Hegemonic Masculinity:
Formulation, Reformulation, and Amplification* brings together for the first
time in one volume the history of the concept as well as a discussion and
examination of some of the most important research accomplished on
hegemonic masculinity over the last thirty years. I am optimistic this
book will contribute to a more enlightened conceptualization of hegemonic masculinities.

The book is divided into six chapters. Chapter 1, "Backstory," summarizes and criticizes the two most popular academic feminist theories
prevalent just prior to and during the formulation of the concept of hegemonic masculinity—radical and socialist feminism. The concept emerged
in part during debates centering on the adequacy of the notion of *patriarchy*. In the 1960s and 1970s, existing social theory was either gender blind
or attributed gender inequality to the alleged "inferior nature" of women.
Theorizing patriarchy was the initial feminist focus in response to traditional androcentric social theory, and radical and socialist feminists
adapted different meanings of this term. However, not long after the
emergence of feminist theories of patriarchy it became obvious that there
existed significant problems with the concept. What grew out of the eventual criticisms of patriarchy was a major shift in theoretical focus in feminist theory—from "patriarchy" to "gender"—and the chapter closes by
outlining this significant change and its impact on the development of
hegemonic masculinity as a new feminist theoretical concept.

Chapter 2, "Formulation," discusses additional circumstances that
augmented the backstory, all of which crucially set the contextual stage
for the development of the concept of hegemonic masculinity. Following
this, the chapter summarizes Raewyn Connell's initial formulation of
hegemonic masculinity as well as notable early applications of the concept, in particular scholarly work that appeared from the late 1980s and
into the 1990s. The chapter furthermore discusses how, in various ways,
scholars expanded the concept during the 1990s and into the early 2000s.
Despite the considerable favorable reception of Connell's initial ap-

proach, the concept of hegemonic masculinity nevertheless attracted criticism during this time period. The chapter closes with an assessment of the major criticisms leveled against Connell's original formulation of hegemonic masculinity.

Chapter 3, "Reformulation," concentrates on Connell's and my (Connell and Messerschmidt 2005) reformulation of the concept of hegemonic masculinity. This reformulated model included certain aspects of the original formulation that empirical evidence over almost two decades of time indicated should be retained. Also well supported historically was the foundational idea that hegemonic masculinity legitimates unequal gender relations between men and women, masculinity and femininity, and among masculinities. The reformulated understanding of hegemonic masculinity additionally incorporated a more holistic grasp of gender inequality that recognizes the agency of subordinated groups as much as the power of hegemonic groups, and that includes the mutual conditioning or intersectionality of gender with such other social inequalities as class, race, age, sexuality, and nation. The reformulation furthermore included a more sophisticated treatment of embodiment in hegemonic masculinity, as well as conceptualizations of how hegemonic masculinity may be challenged, contested, and thus changed. Finally, instead of recognizing simply hegemonic masculinity at only the society-wide level, the reformulated model of hegemonic masculinity suggested that scholars analyze empirically existing hegemonic masculinities at three levels: the local, regional, and global. This chapter closes with a discussion of selected studies that illustrate various inceptive applications of the reformulated model of hegemonic masculinity.

Chapter 4, "Amplification," analyzes how recent scholarly work has enlarged upon and contributed to the further conceptualization of the reformulated model of hegemonic masculinity. In particular, the studies analyzed in this chapter demonstrate the omnipresent nature of hegemonic masculinities, yet simultaneously they show how these complex, specific masculinities are essentially hidden in plain sight. These studies further illustrate that particular hierarchical gender relationships between men and women, between masculinity and femininity, and among masculinities are legitimated—remarkably discerning certain of the essential features of the all-pervasive reproduction of unequal gender relations. The significance of distinguishing between "hegemonic" and "dominant" masculinities as well as recognizing the differences among hegemonic masculinities is emphasized. Given the fact that hegemonic masculinities necessarily constitute a relationship, femininities are vital and essential to the amplification of the reformulated model of hegemonic masculinities, and thus are a principal part of this chapter. The chapter furthermore highlights additional areas that have amplified the reformulated model, such as the recurring nature of "fleeting hegemonic masculinities," how hegemonic masculinities overall routinely are fluid, contingent, haphazard, provisional, and temporary, the hybrid nature of certain hegemonic masculinities, the importance of intersectionality and how hegemonic masculinities therefore differ by reason of their constitution with other inequalities, the prominence of the internet and the electronic complexion of hegemonic masculinities, and finally hegemonic masculinities in the global South.

Chapter 5, "Theory," presents a theoretical framework—what is labeled "structured action theory"—for conceptualizing the omnipresence of hegemonic masculinities throughout society and indeed worldwide. Structured action theory permits the exploration of how and in what respects hegemonically masculine embodied practices and thus unequal gender relations are constituted in certain settings at certain times. To understand the multifarious hegemonic masculinities discussed throughout the book, I argue that we must appreciate how structure and action are woven inextricably into the ongoing reflexive activities of constructing embodied unequal gender relations. The chapter discusses how this theory engages with the relationship among hegemonic masculinities and a variety of topics, such as structured action, intersectionality, embodiment, and masculinity challenges.

Finally, chapter 6, "Prospects," presents novel strategies for challenging unequal gender relations. Hegemonic masculinities are continually renewed, re-created, defended, and modified through social action. And yet they are at times resisted, limited, altered, and contested. Hegemonic masculinities can therefore be undermined through alternative practices that do not support unequal gender relations; in particular, counterhegemonic practices that contribute to the movement toward positive and progressive change in gender relations, and actually at times contribute to dismantling hegemonic masculinities and thus unequal gender relations. This chapter then points to the necessity of studying the diversity of masculinities and how that helps us to gain some grasp as to where energy should be directed to promote gendered social change; that is, those social situations where counterhegemonic practices are particularly possible or likely to materialize.

Concepts in the social sciences arise in response to specific intellectual and practical problems, and they are formulated in particular languages and intellectual styles. But they also have a capacity to travel and may acquire new meanings as they do. This has certainly happened with the concept of hegemonic masculinity, and that journey is documented throughout this book—from formulation, to reformulation, to amplification. As a theoretical construct, over the last three decades the concept of hegemonic masculinity has been applied to new research settings, resulting in the concept mutating in novel directions. There is nothing wrong with this process in itself—it is a common way that knowledge in the social sciences develops. But it means that new usages must always be open to critique, and I engage with some of these developments by showing how certain formulations lack substance and justification with regard to the optimal utilization of the concept for understanding unequal gender relations today.

In dialogue with new and diverse scholarship, the renovated conception of hegemonic masculinities suggested herein has, I believe, a growing relevance in the present moment. The making and contestation of unequal gender relations is historically changing societies—locally, regionally, and globally—and is a process of enormous importance for which we need conceptual tools like *hegemonic masculinity*.

* * *

Parts of this book have appeared elsewhere in different form. I thank Raewyn Connell and Sage Publications for permission to reproduce the following in revised and expanded form: Raewyn Connell and James W. Messerschmidt, "Hegemonic Masculinity: Rethinking the Concept," *Gender & Society* 19, no. 6 (2005): 829–59, reprinted by permission of Sage Publications. I also thank Sage Publications for permission to publish a revised version of James W. Messerschmidt, "Engendering Gendered Knowledge: Assessing the Academic Appropriation of *Hegemonic Masculinity*," *Men and Masculinities* 15, no. 1 (2012): 56–76, reprinted by permission of Sage Publications. The book also includes a revised version of chapter 2 in James W. Messerschmidt, *Masculinities and Crime: Critique and Reconceptualization of Theory* (Lanham, MD: Rowman & Littlefield,

1993), as well as a revised version of chapter 2 in James W. Messerschmidt, *Masculinities in the Making: From the Local to the Global* (Lanham, MD: Rowman & Littlefield, 2016).

Some of the material discussed in this book was presented in various stages of development as keynote addresses or lectures at: Ruhr University, Bochum, Germany, 2012; Durham University, Durham, England, 2013; University of Vienna, Vienna, Austria, 2013; Aalborg University, Aalborg, Denmark, 2014 and 2017; Palacky University, Olomouc, Czech Republic, 2014; University of Freiburg, Freiburg, Germany, 2015; Colby College, Waterville, Maine, USA, 2016; University of Southern California, Los Angeles, California, USA, 2016; Occidental College, Los Angeles, California, USA, 2016; University of Akron, Akron, Ohio, USA, 2016; University of Ljubljana, Ljubljana, Slovenia, 2016; Rome University of Tor Vergata, Rome, Italy, 2016; University of Oslo, Oslo, Norway, 2017; and Stockholm University, Stockholm, Sweden, 2017. I thank the participants at each of these events for their extremely thoughtful remarks and reflections.

I also would like to mention academic friends who have provided keen insight during numerous and constructive intellectual conversations over recent years about many of the topics covered in this book—all have helped to improve my arguments in important and beneficial ways: Raewyn Connell, Mike Messner, Pat Martin, Tristan Bridges, Jeff Hearn, Oystein Holter, Stephen Tomsen, Ann-Dorte Christiansen, Mimi Schippers, Lucas Gottzen, and Dusan Bjelic. I thank all of these people and hope that I have justified in these pages the time, intellectual assistance, and support they so generously provided.

As always, the Access and Interlibrary Loan Services librarians at the University of Southern Maine's Glickman Family Library have been an essential component of my research. I thank in particular Pat Preito—who has always been unwavering in helping me obtain important sources of scholarship—as well as Zip Kellogg, John Plante, and Loraine Lowell.

Finally, I wish to extend considerable appreciation to the entire staff at Rowman & Littlefield—my favorite publisher!—but especially to Sarah Stanton (acquisitions editor), Carli Hansen (assistant editor), Janice Braunstein (production editor), and April LeHoullier (copyeditor).

Most of all thanks to Ulla, Erik, and Jan—the most important people in my life!

ONE

Backstory

The concept of hegemonic masculinity emerged in part during debates centering on the adequacy of the feminist theoretical notion of *patriarchy*. In the 1960s and 1970s, existing social theory was either gender blind or attributed gender inequality to the alleged "inferior nature" of women. Theorizing "patriarchy" was the initial feminist focus in response to traditional androcentric social theory, and feminists adapted different meanings of the concept. However, not long after the emergence of feminist theories of patriarchy it became obvious that the concept presented significant problems.

In this chapter I summarize first the two most notable feminist theories utilizing the concept of patriarchy in the 1970s: radical feminism and socialist feminism. Radical feminists deployed the concept of patriarchy to refer exclusively to power relations between men and women while socialist feminists attempted to analyze not simply patriarchy but rather how patriarchy and capitalism interact to construct specific power relations between men and women. Following this, I discuss the eventual criticisms of both attempts to theorize patriarchy that were articulated in the late 1970s and throughout the 1980s. What grew out of these criticisms was a major shift in theoretical focus in feminist theory—from "patriarchy" to "gender." I conclude by outlining this change. The shift from patriarchy to gender as the primary theoretical object in feminist theory is the most significant event in the *backstory* to understanding the eventual conceptualization of *hegemonic masculinity* by Raewyn Connell (1987, 1995).

1

PATRIARCHY

Prior to the emergence of the concept of *hegemonic masculinity* in the 1980s, feminist theories of the 1970s illuminated the patterns of gendered power that social theory to that point had all but ignored. In particular, it was both "radical feminism" and "socialist feminism" that actually put second-wave feminism on the academic map. Both theories secured for sexual politics a permanent role in popular culture and the academy, and they moved analysis of gendered power to the forefront of feminist thought and analysis. Permit me to begin with a discussion of radical feminism, and then I will turn to socialist feminism.

Radical Feminism

The goal of radical feminism was to understand masculine power and to develop appropriate strategies for its elimination. Radical feminism viewed masculine power and privilege—what came to be known as *patriarchy*—as the root cause of all forms of social inequality; patriarchy is primary, all other social relations (such as class, race, age, and sexuality) derive from relations between men and women. For radical feminists, women were, historically, the first oppressed group and thus patriarchy—allegedly existing in every known society—is the most widespread and deepest form of oppression. According to radical feminism, history is an ever-changing struggle of men for power and domination over women, this being the dialectic of sex (Firestone 1970). Radical feminism made distinctive and original contributions to feminist theory, yet got entangled with biological arguments as the foundation of "patriarchy." In what follows, I briefly discuss the development of radical feminism because this hitherto history is significant for understanding the eventual formulation of the concept of hegemonic masculinity.

Second-wave feminism was stimulated by Simone de Beauvoir's ([1949] 1972) well-known argument in *The Second Sex*: "One is not born but rather becomes a woman." As de Beauvoir pointed out: "biological fate" does not "determine the figure that the human being presents to society; it is civilization as a whole that produces this creature indeterminate between male and eunuch which is described as feminine" (295). De Beauvoir argued that the social—not the biological—determines women's situation; that is, women are embedded socially in unequal patriarchal relations where they are compelled "to assume the status of Other"

(29). It is not biology that determines women's destiny, "but the manner in which her body and her relation to the world are modified through the action of others than herself" (734).

It was Kate Millett (1970), writing in *Sexual Politics* more than twenty years later, who was one of the first academic feminist theorists to take de Beauvoir's words seriously. Millett theorized power relations between women and men as "patriarchy," which she maintained did not dissolve with the emergence of a market economy. Rather, Millet held that gendered power relations were "sturdier than any form of segregation, and more rigorous than class stratification, more uniform, certainly more enduring"; patriarchy is "the most pervasive ideology of our culture and provides its most fundamental concept of power" (25). Millett continued: "Our society, like all other historical civilizations, is a patriarchy," a form of societal organization whereby "that half of the populace which is female is controlled by that half which is male" (25). For Millett, patriarchy is a universal phenomenon, and every avenue of power within contemporary society—the military, the economy, the educational system, the state, and so on—is seen as entirely under the control of men. In short, masculine power permeates the entire society, and patriarchy is the social structural base of all power relations—racial, political, and economic.

Millett further argued that though patriarchy manifests itself throughout society, the family is its chief institution. Through sex-role socialization, the family encourages members to adjust and conform to patriarchal ideologies and practices. Human personality is formed along lines of masculine and feminine, lines that entail an elaborate, dichotomous, and oppressive code of conduct through which men are viewed as possessing superiority and, accordingly, are allocated public and private power. As Millett (26) further pointed out, the creation of such "sex roles" constructs a binary involving aggression, intelligence, force, and efficacy in the male; passivity, ignorance, docility, "virtue," and ineffectuality in the female. And with regard to specific practices, such sex roles "assign domestic service and attendance upon infants to the female, the rest of human achievement, interest, and ambition to the male" (26). Millett rejected biological reductionism, arguing that men and women are *trained* to accept a social system that is divided into "male" and "female" spheres, encompassing unequal power relations.

Millett emphasized power in the private realm because, for her, the foundation of patriarchy is the private and interpersonal power by which

men dominate women. Whereas all previous social analyses had concentrated on the public nature of power in terms of class, caste, and status,
Millett argued that personal relations between men and women were
soundly political, similar to domination and subordination in politics
generally; that is, relations between men and women involved a "power-
structured relationship" whereby women are controlled by men. This
domination by men is not enforced by naked violence, Millett argued, but
occurs through sex-role socialization and the personal nature of gendered
power in the home. It was radical feminists who popularized the slogan
that "the personal is political," the idea that there exists a political dimension to personal life. Insofar as inequality is institutionalized throughout
society, sex-role socialization occurs in all "walks of life."

Classic radical feminist works, such as Millett's, did not afford violence by men a central place in their theories of masculine dominance.
Early radical feminists argued that the normal functioning of masculine-
dominated institutions sufficed to maintain the social control of women
and to reproduce patriarchy. Nevertheless, Millett did point out that control in patriarchal society would be imperfect and even inoperable without the rule of force. In patriarchal society, then, men were perceived by
Millett as being equipped psychologically and technically to perpetuate
physical violence against women, if necessary, to maintain power, authority, and control.

Millett's argument that patriarchy is a *cultural* phenomenon, reproduced through socialization, had wide support in the early 1970s. But in
addition to patriarchal sex-role socialization, many radical feminists
argued that in patriarchal society sexuality is socially constructed in
men's interests, thereby hindering women's assertion of their own sexual
needs. For example, Anne Koedt's (1973, 199) influential article "The
Myth of the Vaginal Orgasm" argued that although orgasm originates in
the clitoris, women have "been fed a myth of the liberated woman and
her vaginal orgasm" because "women have been defined sexually in
terms of what pleases men." Koedt (199) advised women to redefine their
sexuality by discarding "the 'normal' concepts of sex and create new
guidelines which take into account mutual sexual enjoyment." Early on,
then, radical feminists were reappraising women's sexual pleasure by
rejecting the double standard that denied sexual assertiveness in women
while celebrating it in men. The subjects of sexual pleasure and assertiveness were at the heart of the radical feminist critique of "normal" hetero-

sexual practice in the early 1970s (Segal 1988). As the discussion of Millett's work indicates, early radical feminists specifically addressed sexual danger, but sexual danger was not central to radical feminist theory.

By the mid-1970s, however, the radical feminist emphasis on the social nature of patriarchy and the learning of gender, sexuality, and violence was considered an unsatisfactory idealist explanation of masculine dominance, and radical feminists began to search for root causes of patriarchy (Jaggar 1983). Millett's concentration on men's *social* power quickly became the biological essentialism of subsequent feminist scholars. In particular, radical feminists assigned strictly dichotomous and intrinsic natures to men and women as the "root cause" of patriarchy. In the mid-1970s, the materialist alternative of biological reductionism became fashionable in much radical feminist thought (H. Eisenstein 1983).

Susan Brownmiller (1975) was in the forefront of adding this new twist to radical feminist theory. In *Against Our Will: Men, Women and Rape*, Brownmiller advanced the idea that rape is the actual foundation of patriarchy and, therefore, propagates gender inequality by viciously subordinating women to men and limiting, indeed policing, women's social behavior. For Brownmiller, rape is not a sociological question, but a biological one. Because humans enjoy a unique form of sexuality not based entirely on reproduction, the sexual urge can occur virtually at any time, and not simply in response to a reproductive cycle.

In addition to the unique nature of human sexuality, human anatomy also plays a critical and determinant role in rape. Brownmiller (14) argued that had it not been for an accident of biology, "an accommodation requiring the locking together of two separate parts, penis into vagina, there would be neither copulation nor rape as we know it." Finally, Brownmiller argued that because men possess raw physical strength in relation to women, they make use of this physical ability to overcome their biological sexual urge. It is the combination of this biological and physical capacity to rape that leads men to construct an "ideology of rape." In short, "when men discovered that they could rape, they proceeded to do it" (14).

This ability and resulting ideology to rape became simultaneously the mechanism of controlling women and a weapon of force against them. From prehistoric times to the present, rape, according to Brownmiller (15), has played a crucial role in reproducing patriarchy: "It is nothing more or less than a conscious process of intimidation by which *all men* keep *all women* in a state of fear." The fear created by rape has, according to Brownmiller, acted historically and cross-culturally as a means of social control. For Brownmiller, although all men are potential rapists, all men need not engage in rape for patriarchy to be sustained. The men who do rape provide the necessary means for maintaining patriarchy. Brownmiller (209) concluded that on the shoulders of rapists "there rests an age-old burden that amounts to an historic mission: the perpetuation of male domination over women by force." Rapists are seen by Brownmiller as the "front-line shock troops . . . in the longest sustained battle the world has ever known" (209). Rape is the personal political weapon that sustains patriarchy and thus the subordination of women, and it was Brownmiller who popularized the idea that "rape is violence, not sex."

Brownmiller's perspective differs from Millett's and other early 1970s radical feminists in the sense that patriarchy is not a sociological phenomenon, but rather is founded in men's alleged biological ability and resulting ideology to rape. Brownmiller argued that because rape and women's subordination seemed to exist in every known society, patriarchy is a universal system that stems from biological causes and, thus, "male" and "female" are no longer social categories constructed through socialization.

Brownmiller differs from early radical feminists in yet another important way: in her work, violence against women (rape) was seen, for the first time, as central to radical feminist theorizing. It was now clearly asserted by radical feminists that violence against women is the foundation of patriarchy and, therefore, sexual danger replaced sexual pleasure as the central component of radical feminist thought. Despite such differences, Millett and Brownmiller did show a similar perspective in the sense that men and women are depicted as distinctly different *categories* from each other.

In traditional social thought, women were the Other, the different, inferior, and deviant species. For many radical feminists of the mid- to late 1970s (and throughout the 1980s), "femaleness" was increasingly theorized as normative, and "maleness," the Other. Rather than viewing women's difference from men as a source of their subordination, radical feminists began considering these differences as a source of pride and reason for confidence. Eventually, this position led to a celebration of an alleged essential "femaleness" and a denunciation of an avowed essential "maleness." For such radical feminist theorists as Mary Daly, Robin Mor-

gan, Adrienne Rich, Andrea Dworkin, and Catharine MacKinnon, everything—from the workplace to the bedroom—that is "female" is good and
everything "male" is bad (Echols 1989; H. Eisenstein 1983). For example,
Rich (1976, 39, 72) argued that there are superior powers inherent in
women that do not exist in men and, consequently, these powers bond
women with the "natural order"; women's special powers associate her
"more deeply than man with natural cycles and processes." As Hester
Eisenstein (1983, 112) states, for these radical feminists "women embody
the force of light and men the force of darkness."

By the mid-1970s and into the 1980s, the issue of violence against
women moved to center stage for radical feminism. This focus on "male"
violence merged with a denunciation of "maleness" as the "force of darkness" and a new criticism of heterosexuality, creating a condemnation of
what became known as "male sexuality." In other words, heterosexuality
was now explicitly theorized as the underpinning essence of patriarchy
and linked with violence against women. For example, Robin Morgan
(1978, 165) claimed as early as 1978 that "rape exists any time sexual
intercourse occurs when it has not been initiated by the woman, out of
her own genuine affection and desire." Andrea Dworkin (1980a, 288)
connected "male sexuality" with murder by arguing "that sex and murder are fused in the male consciousness, so that one without the other is
unthinkable and impossible" and that "the annihilation of women is the
source of meaning and identity for men." Dworkin (1979, 15, 59) insisted
further that "the penis" is the "hidden symbol of terror," even more
significant than "the gun, the knife, the fist, and so on," and rape is "the
defining paradigm of sexuality"—heterosexuality is "the stuff of murder,
not love" (1980b, 152). Dworkin (1980b, 148–49) continued:

> Men love death. In everything they make, they hollow out a central
> place for death, let its rancid smell contaminate every dimension of
> whatever still survives. Men especially love murder. In art they cele-
> brate it, and in life they commit it. They embrace murder as if life
> without it would be devoid of passion, meaning and action, as if mur-
> der were solace, stilling their sobs as they mourn the emptiness and
> alienation of their lives. . . . In male culture, slow murder is the heart of
> the eros, fast murder is the heart of action, and systematized murder is
> the heart of history.

In her book *Intercourse*, Dworkin (1987, 128) repeated that heterosexuality
is the basis of women's social and sexual subordination; intercourse and

inequality are "like Siamese twins, always in the same place at the same time pissing in the same pot."

This fusion of violence and heterosexuality as the mainstays of patriarchy was most theoretically developed in the work of Catharine MacKinnon. MacKinnon (1989) argued that sexuality is a natural attribute and the primary sphere of masculine power, encompassing the expropriation of women's sexuality by men. It is the exploitative nature of heterosexuality that structures men and women as social beings in society. MacKinnon further claimed that the universal system of patriarchy is maintained through heterosexuality and sexual violence. For MacKinnon, sexuality is crucial to women's subordination, and she theorizes it as a dynamic of inequality: gender derives from sexual dominance, not vice versa. The formula reads as follows: "sexuality equals heterosexuality equals the sexuality of (male) dominance and (female) submission" (137). MacKinnon (137) added that "sexuality is the dynamic of control by which male dominance—in forms that range from intimate to institutional, from a look to rape—erotizes and thus defines man and woman, gender identity and sexual pleasure," and it "maintains and defines male supremacy as a political system." Following Dworkin, MacKinnon (174) argued that intercourse is not that different from rape: "it is difficult to distinguish the two under conditions of male dominance"—as heterosexuality is simply coercive and violent sex. MacKinnon (172) concluded that if "sexuality is central to women's definition and forced sex is central to sexuality, rape is indigenous, not exceptional, to women's social condition." Following the logic of MacKinnon's argument, *all* heterosexual women are victims and *all* heterosexual men are rapists.

A significant change in radical feminist thought then emerged in the 1970s and 1980s: the emphasis shifted from the social nature of patriarchy through sex-role socialization to biological essentialism as the base of patriarchy. This necessitated a return to assigning strictly dichotomous and intrinsic natures to men and women—but also to a celebration of "femaleness" as the ultimate virtue and a condemnation of "maleness" and heterosexuality. For these radical feminists, women make up the good category and men constitute the bad category, plain and simple. And it is this essential categorical difference that leads to patriarchy, which seeks to "subjugate and colonize" the "relative and powerful essence" of femaleness (Budgeon 2015, 247).

Socialist Feminism

During the early stages of second-wave feminism, other feminists working within the Marxist tradition did not follow the essentialist path and developed an alternative feminist perspective. In the mid-1960s, Juliet Mitchell (1966, 13) focused on "asking feminist questions but trying to come up with some Marxist answers." Marxist feminists—as they would become known—subsequently attempted to explain women's oppression through the use of Marxian categories. Marxism was viewed as the scientific explanation of subordination, yet that explanation had historically ignored women's labor. In particular, Marxism failed to acknowledge women's work in the home, much less comprehend how this acknowledgment would lead to a conflict theory of gendered inequality as part of the very structure of capitalist societies. Marxist feminists then began to more seriously theorize Friedrich Engels's ([1884] 1942, 76) claim that "the determining factor in history is, in the last resort, the production and reproduction of immediate life," which involves "the production of the means of subsistence" and "the production of human beings themselves."

In 1969, Margaret Benston sought to uncover the material conditions of "reproduction" that in capitalist societies define the group "women." According to Benston, women's work in the home entails the production of "use-values," not the production of marketable commodities. In other words, the products and services produced by women in the home are to be consumed in the home. As such, they never reach the market. This production of use-values in the home, according to Benston (1969, 20), is the defining cornerstone of women, women's labor, and inequality between men and women. Benston argued that in a society in which money determines value, women are a group who work outside the money economy in the form of reproductive labor and thus their work is valueless; it is "not even real work," and in "structural terms, the closest thing to the condition of women is the condition of others who are or were also outside of commodity production, i.e., serfs and peasants" (20). Under the capitalist system of commodity production, Benston maintained, the material basis of women's subordination is found in the fact that women's reproductive labor in the home is not considered real work.

Benston stimulated a lengthy debate on the Marxist conception of reproductive domestic labor. Of particular importance in this debate was Wally Seccombe's (1973) article "The Housewife and Her Labour under

Capitalism." Extending Benston's idea, Seccombe attempted to show that the primary purpose of the family in a capitalist mode of production is to reproduce labor power that is eventually sold to capital in the labor market. Under such economic conditions, inasmuch as the housewife does not produce surplus value, she is an "unproductive laborer." Nevertheless, as Seccombe (7) put it, when the housewife "acts directly upon wage-purchased goods and necessarily alters their form, her labour becomes part of the congealed mass of past labour embodied in the labour power. The value she creates is realized as one part of the value labour power achieves as a commodity when it is sold." For Seccombe (7), this simply involves the "application of the labour theory to the reproduction of labour power itself, namely that all labour produces value when it produces any part of a commodity that achieves equivalence in the market place with other commodities." Such acts of daily maintenance and socialization as preparing meals, cleaning house, doing laundry, and caring for children are forms of reproductive labor and therefore create value because that very labor eventually is incorporated into capital through the husband's and children's labor power. And the result is that men do not have to concern themselves with anything other than work *outside* the home, which in turn benefits their employer. Women's "value," then, from Seccombe's perspective, is additionally employed to enhance individual men's value on the labor market as it allows the latter to dedicate more time to their job.

Clearly, then, Benston, Seccombe, and others were attempting to introduce women's reproductive labor in the home into an androcentric Marxist framework in order to demonstrate that domestic labor could be analyzed as productive work. Women's domestic segregation in a capitalist economy could actually be explained, it was argued, through Marxist theory. The implication was that Marxism provided the conceptual tools for establishing not only that women's work in the home is a form of labor, but also that this type of labor is central in the explanation of the unique forms of subordination from which women suffer within capitalist societies. According to these theorists, then, the oppressor is capitalism that exploits and benefits from women's labor.

The domestic-reproductive-labor literature initially marked an advance over traditional Marxism but quickly fell into disfavor as an explanation of inequality between women and men. In particular, this reasoning was criticized for its failure to confront the most salient issue—social relations between men and women in the home. In other words, women's domestic labor was understood by Marxist feminists in its relation to capital, but not in its relation to men. As Sylvia Walby (1986, 20) pointed out, "The most important question is settled *a priori*. The interests that men, and in particular husbands, may have in the continuation and shaping of domestic work, are almost totally neglected." The distinct premise of the domestic-reproductive-labor argument was that capitalism is the problem, not men.

The domestic-reproductive-labor focus on the housewife and her apparent connection to capitalism proved an important development in the evolution of socialist feminist theory. Nevertheless, in the feminist literature of the early 1970s, an explanation for masculine dominance that did not focus solely on patriarchy was still lacking. Criticizing Marxist theory for its inability to recognize and conceptualize inequality between men and women, certain Marxist feminists appropriated the concept of patriarchy from radical feminism, and attempted to use it in a nonreductionist manner to explain masculine dominance and women's subordination under capitalism. For some Marxist feminists writing in the early 1970s, the term "patriarchy" seemed adequate to address the profundity and pervasiveness of masculine dominance.

One of the first Marxist feminist writings to employ this concept and to juxtapose capitalism with patriarchy was Sheila Rowbotham's (1973) *Women's Consciousness, Man's World*. According to Rowbotham (117), "Patriarchal authority is based on male control over women's productive capacity, and over her person." Although patriarchy existed prior to capitalism, Rowbotham argued, under a capitalist mode of production patriarchy develops a historically specific configuration. While capitalism has "whittled away" at certain aspects of masculine dominance (e.g., women's labor in the market weakens the economic hold of men over women in the family), patriarchy has, Rowbotham continues, still "retained the domination of men over women in society. This domination continues to pervade economic, legal, social, and sexual life" (122). In this way, Rowbotham theorized patriarchy as transhistorical, with contemporary iterations as refracted through the economic system. Although Rowbotham theorized patriarchy as an autonomous system of inequality, under capitalism this system becomes "an ever present prop in time of need" (120). For Rowbotham, then, capitalism remained primary and thus structures patriarchy in her theoretical understanding of masculine dominance.

It was this continued concentration on the primacy of capitalism, as represented by Rowbotham's work, that eventually produced a break from Marxist feminism. Certain feminist theorists simply refused to accept the argument that relations between men and women were somehow of secondary importance to production relations. Their goal was to construct a theory that was truly socialist and truly feminist—one that undeniably required the avoidance of overstating an economic analysis at the expense of inequality between men and women.

A theoretical understanding of patriarchy provided the means by which to analyze relations between men and women outside Marxist categories and became the first step in formulating a cohesive socialist feminist theory. Expanding upon Rowbotham's initial conceptualization, patriarchy eventually was theorized as a "system" with its own history and its own form of subordination that is independent of capitalism. Socialist feminists now viewed contemporary Western societies as a composite of two equally important and discrete systems, patriarchy and capitalism, in which neither prevailed over the other but equally interacted. Socialist feminists attempted to synthesize some aspects of radical feminism and Marxism into a theory that gave priority to neither capitalism (production) nor patriarchy (reproduction), but viewed them as equal, interacting and co-reproducing. Socialist feminists viewed capitalism and patriarchy as so inextricably intertwined that they are inseparable. They argued further that the social experiences of men and women are different just as are their class experiences. This differing social experience shapes and limits the lives of both men and women. Zillah Eisenstein (1979) and Heidi Hartmann (1981) were notable forerunners in an attempt to connect capitalism and patriarchy, as equal interacting "dual systems," in an effort to understand masculine dominance. The goal of these self-proclaimed socialist feminists was to explain theoretically the relationship between what seemed to be two relatively autonomous systems of exploitation and oppression.

Zillah Eisenstein (1979) asserted that capitalism and patriarchy have an elective affinity such that they depend on each other for survival. The two systems do not merely operate adjacent to each other but, according to Eisenstein, are in fact so intertwined as to form a mutually constituted interdependent system—"capitalist patriarchy." Eisenstein (21) argued that both capitalism and patriarchy "embody *relations of power* which define them." To understand capitalism and patriarchy in any given historical context, Eisenstein maintained that feminist theory must grasp the power relations that give them shape. Eisenstein attempted to analyze power relations in patriarchy as part of power relations in capitalism and vice versa, rather than cut off from each other, to understand how interdependent and interconnected these differing power relations are.

Heidi Hartmann's (1981) "The Unhappy Marriage of Marxism and Feminism: Toward a More Progressive Union" likewise attempted to overcome the weaknesses of both traditional Marxism and radical feminism. Hartmann argued that throughout its history, Marxist theory had clearly remained gender blind and that radical feminism is ahistorical, insufficiently materialist, and ignores production relations or subsumes them under patriarchal relations. Hartmann theorized that patriarchal relations are both distinct from and independent of capitalist relations and that both capitalism and patriarchy consist of their own systems of power and hierarchy. Hartmann's theory attempted to recognize both systems without prioritizing one over the other. Patriarchy, Hartmann argued, like capitalism, has its own material base—masculine control over women's labor power—and this historically changing system of male-female relations interacts with, but is not subsumed by, capitalist class relations. It is this interaction that leads to historically specific forms of masculine dominance and women's oppression. Capitalist class relations are theorized as gender neutral, yet when they interact with patriarchal relations, the result is a particular form of masculine dominance.

THE SHIFT FROM PATRIARCHY TO GENDER

Despite the different usages of the concept of patriarchy by radical and socialist feminists, by the mid-1980s serious problems regarding the concept were discussed in the feminist literature. For example, Raewyn Connell (1985, 264) referred to the radical and socialist feminist use of the concept as "categoricalism," or theorizing that the categories of "women" and "men" "are taken as being in no need of further examination or finer differentiation" because these theories "operate with the categories as given" and do not concern themselves "with how they come to be what they are." Radical and socialist feminists were criticized specifically for their concentration on two uniform opposed and contrasting categories rather than recognizing the diversity embedded within these dualist classifications and seeking to explain and understand this diversity as well. A major result of this radical and socialist feminist focus on alleged differences between the categories "women" and "men" has been to direct theory away from issues that complicate and obscure differences *among* men and *among* women, such as race, age, sexuality, and nationality.

It was additionally argued that the concentration on patriarchy blurred the fact that men exercise unequal amounts of control over their own lives as well as the lives of women. Emphasizing men and women as single categories results in a great deal of the actual experiences of real men and women being subsumed under experiences said to *represent* their categories. By focusing on the alleged differences between two categories, radical and socialist feminists failed to consider variations among men, concentrating instead on an alleged "typical male," as if such a male could be empirically found to represent all men. As A. Mark Liddle (1989, 762) put it, this theoretical focus on the "typical male" leads to a "model of male agency which is at best one-dimensional."

Regarding the radical feminist versions of patriarchy, these theorists were specifically criticized for characterizing the alleged "typical male" "as more or less unrelieved villainy and all men as agents of the patriarchy in more or less the same degree" (Carrigan, Connell, and Lee 1987, 140). Men's violence against women as a consciously chosen "male" instrument for purposes of maintaining patriarchal power was likewise criticized. Scholars argued that although radical feminists correctly claimed the effect of violence against women as social control, it was nevertheless invalid to assume all men behave violently for the purpose of controlling women. Again I turn to Liddle (1989, 762–69) who convincingly argued in the 1980s that this instrumentalism confuses the *effects* of violence with the *motivations* of individual perpetrators. Although some men are clearly motivated to control women through violence, not all violent men share this specific goal, and the vast majority of men are not violent against women. Radical feminism was thus denounced for simply bulldozing away the complexity in which masculinity is situationally and therefore differently accomplished throughout society.

Research at the time also challenged the radical feminist view that "femaleness" is the ultimate virtue and "force of life." In such a view one is hard put to explain why, for example, white "mistresses" (normally the wives of plantation owners or "masters") in the US antebellum South engaged in some of the most barbaric forms of punishment, resulting in permanent scarring of African American female slaves (Fishman 1993).

As a group, white mistresses were notorious for the "veritable terror" they perpetrated on African American women. Consider the following examples (Fox-Genovese 1988, 309):

> Ida Henry's unpredictable mistress could be either tolerant or mean. One day the cook was passing potatoes at the table and "old Mistress . . . exclaimed to de cook, 'what you bring these raw potatoes out here for?' and grabbed a fork and stuck it in her eye and put her eye out." Once Anna Dorsey, failing to hear her mistress call her, continued with her work until the mistress "burst out in a frenzy of anger over the woman not answering." Despite Anna Dorsey's protestations, her mistress "seized a large butcher knife and struck at Anna," who, "attempting to ward off the blow . . . received a long gash on the arm that laid her out for some time." Hannah Plummer's mother's mistress "whipped her most every day, and about anything. Mother said she could not please her in anything, no matter what she done and how hard she tried." Once, the mistress returned from town especially angry and "made mother strip down to her waist, and then took a carriage whip an' beat her until the blood was runnin' down her back."

Moreover, radical feminism was seen as unable to account for what was labeled African American female slave "criminal resistance," such as "Sally, who hit her master over the head with a poker and put his head in the fireplace," or another female slave who, after being whipped, knocked the overseer from his horse and proceeded to pounce upon him, eventually chopping off his head, mutilating his body, and killing the horse (Fishman 1993, 21). And if we jump to the 1980s, violence by a member of the Turban Queens, a female gang in New York City, was reported as follows (A. Campbell 1991, 262):

> But once you're in a fight, you just think—you've got to fuck that girl up before she does it to you. You've got to really blow off on her. You just play it crazy. That's when they get scared of you. It's true—you feel proud when you see a girl you fucked up. Her face is all scratched or she got a black eye, you say, "Damn, I beat the shit out of that girl, you know."

These historical examples of violence by women were reported in research during the time period under discussion and became incomprehensible in an analysis that concentrates on men as exclusively the "force of darkness" and women as exclusively the "force of light."

The radical feminist focus on the absolute primacy of sexuality was likewise seen as deeply problematic. Given that rape is not solely a violent act but also a sexual one—"you cannot, by fiat, take sex out of a sexual act, it will creep back in at every point" (Smart 1989, 44)—for many feminist scholars, it did not follow that the enactment of heterosexuality in itself bestows on men power over women. After reviewing research on men and sexuality, Segal (1990, 212) argued that it is precisely through sex that many men "experience their greatest uncertainties, dependence and deference in relation to women—in stark contrast, quite often, with their experience of authority and independence in the public world." Additionally, research showed at the time that rape correlates with a specific type of socially constructed heterosexuality rather than with heterosexuality per se. As with gender, so too with sexuality—feminist scholars began to see the complexity with categories (like "woman" and "man," but also "heterosexuality" and "homosexuality"). For example, Barbara Lindemann's (1984) analysis of rape in eighteenth-century Massachusetts revealed that rape was extraordinarily uncommon in comparison to the 1980s. Although in this period Massachusetts was securely dominated by men (81),

> the cultural expectations about sexual behavior probably minimized the occurrence of rape. Extramarital sexual activity by men and women alike was severely condemned and frequently punished. Ministers enjoined women not to flaunt their sexual attractiveness. Men were not extolled for the sexual conquest of many women. Women were understood to be as interested in sex as men. Thus neither in marriage nor in courtship would a man believe that a woman really meant yes when she said no. The rape prototype of female enticement, coy female resistance, and ultimate male conquest was not built into the pattern of normal sexual relations.

According to historical scholarship of the time, it was not until the early 1800s that masculinity began to be associated with seeking sexual pleasure through conquest and its feminine equation with sexual "passionlessness." Women's sexual appetites were no longer comparable with those of men. Women were increasingly seen as lacking sexual aggressiveness, and lustfulness was considered uncharacteristic of women (Cott 1979, 163). However, this idea of "sexual passionlessness" was applied primarily to white, middle-class women. Working-class women and women of color continued to be identified as sexually passionate and thus sexually available (D'Emilio and Freedman 1988, 46). And according to scholars writing in the late 1970s and throughout the 1980s, there emerged a new emphasis on the physical attractiveness of women; notions of femininity shifted from meekness and spirituality to beauty and sexual appeal (Ulrich 1983, 115–16; D'Emilio and Freedman 1988, 43). A new type of heterosexuality then evolved in which women were now required to conform to "male" tastes and wait to be chosen, but "resist seduction or suffer ostracism for capitulating; men, meanwhile, were free to take the first step, practice flattery, and escape the consequences of illicit sexual relations" (Cott 1979, 172).

This new type of heterosexuality continued into the 1980s. Yet research during this time also demonstrated that other heterosexual practices existed as well. For example, Wendy Hollway (1984) showed that many women and men simply desired a "one night stand" for sexual pleasure from sex and neither expected a "relationship" to develop. Similarly, Dalma Heyn's (1992, 163) study of the "erotic silence" of white, middle-class, heterosexual, married women in the United States revealed that many had an extramarital affair in which the "only goal is mutual pleasure, without which it has no reason for being." Sharon Thompson's (1990, 277) examination of African American teenage mothers revealed that they never described themselves as passive victims, but rather "as strong women who take their pleasure and defend their bodies and their rights." These young women described sexual appetites "as insatiable as their need for affirmation and opportunity," and this insatiability drove them "to break taboos—having oral, anal, and group sex—and being slick" (274).

In all of these situations exploitation is clearly possible, but not inevitable. And not surprising, to many men of the 1970s and 1980s "good sexuality" was not simply force and conquest, but warmth, love, trust, the desire to be loved and to love as a whole person (Prieur 1990, 145). Unfortunately, radical feminists rendered these men, as well as men who have supported women in their struggles for equal rights and liberation (see Kimmel and Mosmiller 1992), hidden from history.

Finally, if truly consensual heterosexual relations were impossible in the 1970s and 1980s, it follows that all heterosexual men were victimizers and all heterosexual women were victims during this time period. Such a view, however, was seen by many feminist scholars as extremely condescending not only to victims of actual rape (who are judged no worse off than all other heterosexual women) and to heterosexual women (who have the ability to say no to a man), but also, as Rosemary Tong (1989,

130) pointed out, to heterosexual women who have "the ability to say 'yes' — to engage in a nonexploitative relationship with a man."

Quite simply, radical feminists failed to put into historical perspective their assumption that "male sexuality" is *essentially* and therefore *unchangeably* coercive and insatiable. It was reported at the time that contemporary industrialized societies had "thrust sex to the forefront of society" as never before, and popular culture — from prime-time TV to feature films to pornography — had become saturated with the image of masculinity as sexually unlimited and coercive (Porter 1986, 220). This form of heterosexuality, however, is historically and socially constructed — sexuality is simply one practice through which men express and confirm a specific type of masculinity. The radical feminist position on "male sexuality" as uncontrollable and preordained with violence whereas "female sexuality" is nurturant and serene was consequently understood as reproducing, rather than challenging, current gender arrangements: "radical feminists are buying into the male-dictated dichotomies they are trying to avoid" (Tong 1989, 135).

Although recognizing the sex-blind nature of Marxism, socialist feminist theory was faulted for being uncritical of the core elements of Marxist theory. The result was postulation of a capitalist system where genderless capitalists exploit genderless workers and a patriarchal system where men exploit women (Jaggar 1983). Consequently, socialist feminist theory was conceptualized as merely attempting to tack patriarchy onto an unaltered androcentric Marxism (Beechey 1987). In other words, socialist feminists failed to demonstrate that capitalism and patriarchy were *intersecting* "dual systems."

Other scholars argued that socialist feminism was deterministic in the sense that behavior — including gender behavior — was seen as simply resulting from a social system — patriarchal capitalism — that is external to the actor. In such a view, individuals display little or no agency but, rather, their social practices directly result from the structure of patriarchal capitalism. Socialist feminism, in this view, failed to account for the intentions of actors and for how social action is a meaningful construct in itself (Smart 1987).

As discussed above, socialist feminism embraced the concept of patriarchy in an attempt to conceptualize what Marxist theory omitted; namely, inequality between women and men. By the mid-1980s, however, most socialist feminists admitted that, despite its many insights, this theoretical effort was a dismal failure (Beechey 1987; Acker 1989b). In particular, the concept of patriarchy was criticized for restricting the theoretical exploration of historical variation in masculine dominance. As we have seen, Sheila Rowbotham (1981, 365) once accepted the validity of the concept, yet later argued that the term actually obscured "the multiplicity of ways in which societies have defined gender" and implies "a structure which is fixed, rather than the kaleidoscope of forms within which women and men have encountered one another." Similarly, Beverly Brown (1988, 410) wrote that "the criticism of patriarchy *per se* tends to focus upon its character as a timeless, universal tautology that always works to reduce all gender relations to an identity of male dominance that in turn cannot be explained but simply posited."

Sylvia Walby (1986) attempted to save the concept of patriarchy for socialist feminist theory by arguing that a "patriarchal mode of production" is the foundation of a patriarchal "system." For Walby, and as discussed earlier by Marxist feminists, the site of the patriarchal mode of production was the household: "The producing class is composed of housewives or domestic laborers, while the non-producing and exploiting class is composed of husbands" (52–53). Housewives produce labor power—the generational production of children and the day-to-day maintenance of the husband—but do not have control over the product of their labor, labor power. This results in the husband's expropriation of surplus value from the housewife (53–54):

> He sells this labour power to an employer and receives a wage which is less than the value of the goods he has produced. He gives a portion of this wage to the wife for the maintenance of the family, and retains some for himself. The portion allocated to the wife's use on herself is typically less than the part of the wage allocated for the use of the husband on himself. In addition the housewife typically works longer hours than the man. Thus she performs more labour and receives less than he does.

Although this analysis clearly describes exploitation as it exists in many households—in the 1980s as well as today—it was questionable at the time whether such exploitation was as uniform and systematic as Walby seemed to claim. For example, Crompton and Sanderson (1990, 16–17) argued that because of this probable variability, the contrast more appropriately "lies between 'market' and 'non-market' *workers*, rather than male and female." Despite the fact that men do at times combine in numerous ways to exploit and exclude women, it was argued that gender relations in the home are not simply analogous to class relations. Walby, in similar fashion as radical feminists, was criticized for portraying men in a one-dimensional way. As Roper and Tosh (1991, 10) pointed out in their critique of Walby:

> At work or home, men are simply agents of oppression. Masculinity is seen as unitary, fixed in time, and oppressive in equal degree. Without a more complete understanding of why men sought to control and exploit women, we risk returning to theories of an inherent male tendency towards domination.

It was also suggested that to view the production of things and the reproduction of people as representing two distinct "systems"—a common feature in socialist feminist theories during this time—is to miss how "reproductive labor" is simultaneously "productive labor," and vice versa. For example, much reproductive labor falls within the paid-labor market. As Alison Jaggar and William McBride (1985, 192) noted in 1985, the production of food and clothes has been industrialized, laundering and food preparation continue to move outside the home, health care is performed increasingly by paid workers, and so is the care and education of children.

It was also asserted at this time that the production of goods is for species survival and therefore this production is simultaneously reproductive. Goods are produced not only for consumption, but to reproduce the human species as well. For example, the production of a children's book, the chair that a parent and child sit in to read that book, the house that they both live in, and so on, simultaneously represent productive and reproductive labor. Production and reproduction then are not separate systems; rather, they constitute each other by forming a continuous process of species survival and enhancement—it is impossible to separate them. To be sure, these criticisms were the first to recognize—however unwittingly—the notion of *intersectionality*, although the term was not used during this time. In other words, unequal relations between men and women are not confined to the so-called private sphere and class relations to the so-called public sphere. Feminists increasingly acknowledged that gender and class relations had been, and continued to be, produced and reproduced in all societal institutions. Yet socialist feminists had assumed, but not demonstrated, that the two "systems" were linked.

This of course held true for race and sexuality as well. Both radical and socialist feminist theory spoke from an unacknowledged but race- and heterosexist-specific position and thus tended to write out of history the existence of racial minorities, lesbians, and gay men. These theories claimed to be relevant to all women and men but in fact were grounded in the specific experience of white heterosexual women and men. Radical and socialist feminism constricted the possibilities of understanding how gender, class, race, sexuality, age, and nationality intersect (Dill 1988; Mohanty 1988; Spellman 1988). To be sure, feminists of color in the late 1980s began to articulate how gender *intersects*—not simply *interacts*— with race, class, sexuality, and nationality (Crenshaw 1989; King 1988; Dill 1988; Mohanty 1988; Spellman 1988). In short, during this time period the concept of patriarchy came to be regarded as "a-historical, a-political, homogenizing, lacking cultural specificity, too abstract, and too broad—an imprecise category not useful in understanding the gender order" (Ozyegin 2018, 235).

Unable to overcome the difficulties with the concept of patriarchy as utilized in both radical and socialist feminist theories, most attempts in the social sciences to more thoroughly conceptualize patriarchy came to an abrupt end in the mid- to late 1980s (Beechey 1987). Many feminists thought the concept could not be further developed in an analytically useful way and that a new approach was needed (Acker 1989b). As should be obvious from the criticisms of both radical and socialist feminist theories, that shift involved a change from "patriarchy" to "gender" as *the* central and primary object of feminist theory. Ann Oakley (1972) was one of the first feminist scholars to distinguish between "sex" and "gender." In her book *Sex, Gender, and Society* (1972), Oakley defined "sex" as the biological differences between men and women (genitalia and reproductive capacities that are allegedly universal and immutable) and "gender" as the social differences associated with each sex ("masculinity" and "femininity" that are variable and culturally mutable). And as Budgeon (2015, 246) notes, it was culture—rather than the body—that by the mid-1980s became determinate regarding the alleged differences between men and women.

This shift from "patriarchy" to "gender" involved asking new questions, such as how gender is embedded in areas previously seen as having nothing to do with gender, such as science, the military, organizations, and men (Acker 1989b). A new feminist paradigm was forming

that avoided any concentration on an independent structure like patriarchy (radical feminism), or continually attempting to link the "dual systems" of patriarchy and capitalism (socialist feminism). Instead, feminists
began to develop a framework that was able to conceptualize how social
relations are gendered, how "gender shapes and is implicated in all kinds
of social phenomena" (Acker 1989a, 77).

Raewyn Connell was one of the first to place emphasis on *gender
relations* rather than patriarchy. As early as 1982, Connell and colleagues
(Connell et al. 1982; Kessler et al. 1982) produced two books that analyzed gender relations in families and schools. And Connell (1985,
266–67) began to formulate a theory that had the capacity of "grasping
the interweaving of personal lives and social structure" without collapsing toward categoricalism and biological determinism. She suggested
that such a theory must concentrate on the constraining power of *gender
relations,* "something that people fetch up against" (267). Connell (267)
suggested that the problems associated with radical feminism and socialist feminism can be solved by a theory of gender practice, centering on
what people do to shape the *gender relations* they live in as well as being
attentive "to the structure of relations as a condition of all practice." For
Connell, "structure" was internally complex yet maintained patterns of
gender relations. For example, Connell (Kessler et al. 1982, 10) argued in
the early 1980s that

> particular kinds of behavior, particular ways of being, are made cultu-
> rally dominant [and] come to be seen as the pattern of masculinity or
> femininity in general, [while] other kinds of behavior and character are
> defined in relation to them as deviant or inferior, and attract derision,
> hostility, and sometimes violence. For lack of any snappier term, we
> have come to refer to the culturally dominant patterns as "hegemonic
> masculinity" and "hegemonic femininity."

The shift from patriarchy to gender then included the emergence of the
concept of "hegemonic masculinity" alongside a theoretical conceptualization of *gender relations* as one of the most important theoretical projects
feminists undertook in the 1980s.

CONCLUSION

In this opening chapter I presented the changing nature of feminist theory during the 1970s and 1980s as the first part of the backstory to the

development and formulation of the concept of hegemonic masculinity. This historical information is essential to grasping a full understanding of the genesis of hegemonic masculinity in feminist thought. The backstory involves first the comprehension of radical and socialist feminist theories—the two most popular feminist perspectives during this time period—and their differing utilization and application of the concept of *patriarchy*. Radical and socialist feminist scholars highlighted patriarchy as a way to overcome and critique androcentric social theory that proffered problematic explanations of masculine dominance or simply were gender blind.

Eventually feminist scholars recognized the limitations of both of these approaches, concluding that patriarchy could not be useful analytically as a concept for feminist thought and inquiry. Feminist scholars subsequently began to move theoretically in a different direction, a route that significantly altered the discourse in feminist theory. Many feminists shifted their theoretical focus from "patriarchy" to "gender" and how gender relations are implicated in all walks of life. This was a monumental shift that ultimately resulted in the emergence of feminist theories of gender that remain significant today—such as the work of Candace West and Don Zimmerman (1987) and Raewyn Connell (1987, 1995)—but also led to the appearance of the concept of "hegemonic masculinity." The shift then from patriarchy to gender forms *the* first but essential fragment of the backstory to understanding the initial formulation of the concept of hegemonic masculinity. I turn to the rest of the backstory and that initial formulation in chapter 2.

TWO

Formulation

In chapter 1 the shift from "patriarchy" to "gender" as the theoretical object of feminism was highlighted as a major part of the backstory leading to the formulation of the concept of hegemonic masculinity. In this chapter I first discuss additional circumstances that augmented that backstory, all of which crucially set the contextual foundation for the development of the concept. Following this, second, I summarize notable applications of the initial concept of hegemonic masculinity, specifically scholarly work that appeared from the late 1980s and into the early 1990s. Third, I turn to how in various ways scholars expanded the concept during the 1990s and into the early 2000s. Finally, I close the chapter with an assessment of the initial criticisms leveled against the concept of hegemonic masculinity.

AND NOW, THE REST OF THE BACKSTORY . . .

The concept of hegemonic masculinity was first proposed in reports from a field study of social inequality in Australian high schools (Kessler et al. 1982). However, it was also advanced in a related conceptual discussion of the making of masculinities and the experience of men's bodies (Connell 1983), and in a debate over the role of men in Australian labor politics (Connell 1982). The high school project provided empirical evidence of multiple hierarchies—in gender as well as in class terms—interwoven with active projects of gender construction (Connell et al. 1982).

These beginnings were systematized in the paper "Toward a New Sociology of Masculinity" (Carrigan, Connell, and Lee 1985), which extensively critiqued "male sex role" literature, and proposed a model of multiple masculinities and power relations. In turn, this model was integrated into a systematic sociological theory of gender (Connell 1987). The resulting six pages in Connell's hugely influential book *Gender and Power* (Connell 1987) on "hegemonic masculinity and emphasized femininity" (note the change from "hegemonic femininity") became the most cited source for the concept of hegemonic masculinity. The concept articulated by the research groups in Australia represented a synthesis of ideas and evidence from apparently disparate sources. But the convergence of ideas was not accidental because closely related issues were addressed by researchers and activists in other countries; the time was, in a sense, ripe for a synthesis of this kind.

As discussed in chapter 1, some of the most basic sources for the development of the concept were radical and socialist feminist theories of patriarchy, the limitations of patriarchy as a theoretical construct, and the subsequent shift to gender in feminist theory. Additionally important were related debates over the role of men in transforming unequal gender relations (Goode 1982; Snodgrass 1977). Some men in the New Left had tried to organize in support of feminism, and the attempt had drawn attention to class differences in the expression of masculinity (Tolson 1977). Moreover, women of color—such as Maxine Baca Zinn (1982), Angela Davis (1983), and bell hooks (1984)—criticized the race bias that occurs when power is solely conceptualized in terms of sex difference, thus laying the groundwork for investigating intersectionality but also for questioning any universalizing claims about the category of "men."

The Gramscian term "hegemony" was current at the time in attempts to understand the stabilization of class relations (Connell 1977). In the context of socialist feminist (dual systems) theory (Z. R. Eisenstein 1979), the idea was easily transferred to the parallel problem of gender relations. However, this transfer risked a significant misunderstanding. Antonio Gramsci's writing focused on the dynamics of structural change involving the mobilization and demobilization of whole classes. Without a very clear focus on this issue of historical change, the idea of "hegemony" would be reduced to a simple model of cultural control. And in a great deal of the debate about gender, large-scale historical change is not in focus. Here is one of the sources of later difficulties with the concept of hegemonic masculinity.

Even before the "second wave" of the women's movement, a literature in social psychology and sociology about the "male sex role" had recognized the social nature of masculinity and the possibilities of change in men's conduct (Hacker 1957). During the 1970s there was an explosion of writing about "the male role," sharply criticizing role norms as the source of oppressive behavior by men (Brannon 1976). Critical role theory provided the main conceptual basis for the early antisexist men's movement. The weaknesses of sex-role theory were, however, increasingly recognized (Lopata and Thorne 1978; Kimmel 1987; Pleck 1981). They included the blurring of behavior and norm, the homogenizing effect of the "role" concept, and its difficulties in accounting for power.

Power and difference were, on the other hand, core concepts in the gay liberation movement, which developed a sophisticated analysis of the oppression of men as well as oppression by men (Altman 1972). Some theorists saw gay liberation as bound up with an assault on gender stereotypes (Mieli 1980). The idea of a hierarchy of masculinities grew directly out of homosexual men's experience with violence and prejudice from straight men. The concept of "homophobia" originated in the 1970s and was already being attributed to the conventional male role (Morin and Garfinkle 1978). Theorists developed increasingly sophisticated accounts of gay men's ambivalent relationships to unequal gender relations and conventional masculinity (Broker 1976; Plummer 1981).

An equally important source in the formulation of the concept was empirical social research. A growing body of field studies was documenting local gender hierarchies and local cultures of masculinity in schools (Willis 1977), in male-dominated workplaces (Cockburn 1983), and in village communities (Herdt 1981; Hunt 1980). These studies added the ethnographic realism that the sex-role literature lacked, confirmed the plurality of masculinities and the complexities of gender construction for men, and gave evidence of the active struggle for power that is implicit in the Gramscian concept of "hegemony."

Finally, the concept was influenced by psychoanalysis. Freud himself produced the first analytic biographies of men, and in the "Wolf Man" case history showed how adult personality was a system under tension, with countercurrents repressed but not obliterated (Freud [1917] 1955). The psychoanalyst Stoller (1968) popularized the concept of "gender identity" and mapped its variations in boys' development, most famously those leading to transsexualism. Others influenced by psychoanalysis picked up the themes of men's power, the range of possibilities in gender development, and the tension and contradiction within conventional masculinities (Friedman and Lerner 1986; Zaretsky 1975).

CONCEPTUALIZATION

What emerged from this matrix in the mid-1980s was an analogue, in gender terms, of "power structure research" in political sociology—focusing the spotlight on a powerful group. Hegemonic masculinity was understood as the pattern of practice (i.e., things done, not just a set of role expectations or an identity) that allowed men's power over women to continue. Hegemonic masculinity was conceptualized by Connell (1987, 1995) as a specific form of masculinity in a given historical and society-wide social setting that *legitimates* unequal gender relations between men and women, between masculinity and femininity, and among masculinities. As Connell (1987, 183, emphasis added) points out in *Gender and Power*: "Hegemonic masculinity is always constructed in *relation* to various subordinated masculinities as well as in *relation* to women." Both the *relational* and *legitimation* features were central to Connell's argument, involving a certain form of masculinity in unequal relation to emphasized femininity and nonhegemonic masculinities. Arguably, hegemonic masculinity has no meaning outside its *relationship* to emphasized femininity—and nonhegemonic masculinities—or those forms of femininity that are practiced in a complementary, compliant, and accommodating subordinate relationship with hegemonic masculinity. And it is the legitimation of this relationship of superordination and subordination whereby the meaning and essence of hegemonic masculinity are revealed. The emphasis on *hegemony* in gender relations underscored the achievement of hegemonic masculinity largely through cultural ascendancy—discursive persuasion—encouraging all to consent to, coalesce around, and embody such unequal gender relations between men and women, between masculinity and femininity, and among masculinities.

For Connell, then, *gender relations* were seen as structured through power inequalities between men and women, masculinity and femininity, and among masculinities. Accordingly, the concept of emphasized femininity is essential to Connell's framework, underlining how this feminized form adapts to masculine power through compliance, nurturance, and empathy as "womanly virtues" (1987, 188). More specifically, emphasized femininity is defined through "the display of sociability rather than technical competence, fragility in mating scenes, compliance with men's desire for titillation and ego-stroking [and] acceptance of marriage and childcare" (187). But Connell (183–84) recognized additional femininities, such as those defined "by strategies of resistance or forms of non-compliance" and others identified "by complex strategic combinations of compliance, resistance and co-operation."

Hegemonic masculinity is also constructed in relation to what Connell establishes as four specific nonhegemonic masculinities: first, *complicit* masculinities do not actually embody hegemonic masculinity yet through practice realize some of the benefits of unequal gender relations and consequently when practiced help sustain hegemonic masculinity; second, *subordinate* masculinities are constructed as lesser than or aberrant and deviant to hegemonic masculinity, such as effeminate men; third, *marginalized* masculinities are trivialized and/or discriminated against because of unequal relations external to gender relations, such as class, race, ethnicity, and age; and finally, *protest* masculinities are constructed as compensatory hypermasculinities that are formed in reaction to social positions lacking economic and political power.

For Connell, these concepts were abstract rather than descriptive, defined in terms of the logic of unequal gender relations. They assumed that gender relations were historical, so gender hierarchies were subject to change. Hegemonic masculinities, therefore, came into existence in specific circumstances and were open to historical change. More precisely, there could be a struggle for hegemony, and older forms of masculinity might be displaced by new ones. This was the element of optimism in an otherwise rather bleak theory. It was perhaps possible that a more humane, less oppressive, means of being a man might become prevalent, as part of a process leading toward an abolition of gender hierarchies.

APPLICATION

Connell's initial formulation found prompt, significant, and enthusiastic application, being utilized in a variety of academic areas. In the late 1980s and throughout the 1990s, research on men and masculinity was being consolidated as an academic field, supported by a string of conferences, the publication of textbooks (e.g., Brod 1987), several journals, and a rap-idly expanding research agenda across the social sciences and human-ities.

The concept of hegemonic masculinity was used in education studies to understand the dynamics of classroom life, including patterns of resis-tance and bullying among boys (Messerschmidt 2000). It was used to explore relations to the curriculum and the difficulties in gender-neutral pedagogy (Martino 1995). It was used to understand teacher strategies and teacher identities, among such groups as physical education instruc-tors (Skelton 1993).

The concept also had influence in criminology. All data reflect that men and boys perpetrate more of the conventional crimes—and the more serious of these crimes—than do women and girls. Moreover, men hold a virtual monopoly on the commission of syndicated, white-collar, and po-litical forms of crime. The concept of hegemonic masculinity helped in theorizing the relationship among masculinities and a variety of crimes (Messerschmidt 1993), and was also used in studies on specific crimes committed by boys and men, such as rape in Switzerland, murder in Australia, football "hooliganism" and white-collar crime in England, and assaultive violence in the United States (Newburn and Stanko 1994).

The concept was also employed in studying media representations of men, for instance, the interplay of sports and war imagery (Jansen and Sabo 1994). Because the concept of hegemony helped to make sense of both the diversity and the selectiveness of images in mass media, com-munication and media researchers began mapping the relations between representations of different masculinities (Hanke 1992). Commercial sports are a focus of media representations of masculinity, and the devel-oping field of sports sociology also found significant use for the concept of hegemonic masculinity (Messner 1992). It was deployed in under-standing the popularity of body-contact confrontational sports—which function as an endlessly renewed symbol of masculinity—and in under-standing the violence and homophobia frequently found in sporting mi-lieus (Messner and Sabo 1990).

The social determinants of men's health had been raised earlier, but the "sex role" concept was too diffuse to be of much use. The concepts of multiple masculinities and hegemonic masculinity were increasingly used to understand men's health practices, such as "playing hurt" and risk-taking sexual behavior (Sabo and Gordon 1995). The concepts of hegemonic and subordinated masculinities not only helped in under-standing men's exposure to risk, but also in understanding men's diffi-culties in responding to disability and injury (Gerschick and Miller 1994).

The concept of hegemonic masculinity also proved significant in or-ganization studies, as the gendered character of bureaucracies and work-places was increasingly recognized. And ethnographic and interview studies traced the institutionalization of hegemonic masculinities in spe-cific organizations (Cheng 1996; Cockburn 1991) and their role in organ-izational decision-making (Messerschmidt 1995). A particular focus of this research was the military, where specific patterns of hegemonic mas-culinity had been entrenched but were becoming increasingly problemat-ic (Barrett 1996).

Discussions on professional practices concerned with men and boys also found the concept helpful. Such practices include psychotherapy with men (Kupers 1993), violence prevention programs for youth (Den-borough 1996), and emotional education programs for boys (Salisbury and Jackson 1996).

Finally, the concept was used in studies of war and international rela-tions. In particular, feminist scholars began to problematize masculinities generally, and the hegemonic masculinity of certain men specifically, within the theories and practices of international relations and war (Za-lewski and Parpart 1998; Hooper 1998; Cohn and Enloe 2003).

These then are the primary fields where the concept of hegemonic masculinity was applied in the decade immediately following its formu-lation. But there was also a wider range of application, for instance, in discussions of art (Belton 1995), in such academic disciplines as geogra-phy (Berg 1994) and law (Thornton 1989), and in general discussions of men's gender politics and its relation to feminism (Segal 1990). Accord-ingly, we may reasonably conclude that the analyses of multiple mascu-linities and the concept of hegemonic masculinity served as a framework for much of the developing research effort on men and masculinity, re-placing sex-role theory and categorical models of patriarchy.

EXPANDING THE CONCEPT

Eventually, from the 1990s to the early 2000s, the growing research effort tended to expand the concept itself. The picture was fleshed out in four main ways: by documenting the consequences and costs of hegemony; by uncovering mechanisms of hegemony; by showing greater diversity in masculinities; and by tracing changes in hegemonic masculinities.

Costs and Consequences

Regarding costs and consequences, research in criminology showed how particular patterns of aggression were linked with hegemonic masculinity, not as a mechanical effect for which hegemonic masculinity was a cause, but through the pursuit of hegemony (Bufkin 1999; Messerschmidt 1997). Moreover, the pioneering research of Messner (1992) showed that the enactment of hegemonic masculinity in professional sports, while reproducing steep hierarchies, also comes at considerable cost to the victors, in terms of emotional and physical damage.

Mechanisms

Research was also fruitful in revealing mechanisms of hegemony. Some are highly visible, such as the "pageantry" of masculinity in television sports broadcasts (Sabo and Jansen 1992) and the social mechanisms Roberts (1993) calls "censure" directed at subordinated groups—ranging from informal name-calling by children, to the criminalization of homosexual conduct. Yet other mechanisms of hegemony were found to operate by invisibility, removing a hegemonic form of masculinity from the possibility of censure (D. Brown 1999). Consalvo (2003), examining media reporting of the Columbine High School massacre, noted how the issue of masculinity was withdrawn from scrutiny, leaving the media with no way of representing the shooters except as "monsters."

Diversity

International research strongly confirmed the initial insight that gender orders construct multiple masculinities. Valdés and Olavarría (1998) showed that even in a culturally homogeneous country such as Chile there is no unitary masculinity, because patterns vary by class and generation. In another famously homogeneous country, Japan, Ishii-Kuntz (2003) traced the "emergence of diverse masculinities" in recent social history, with changes in childcare practices a key development. Diversity of masculinities was also found in specific institutions, such as the military (Higate 2003).

Gutmann (1996), in the most artfully observed modern ethnography of masculinity during this time period, studied a culture where there is a well-defined public masculine identity—Mexican "machismo." Gutmann showed how the imagery of machismo developed historically and was interwoven with the development of Mexican nationalism, masking enormous complexity in the actual lives of Mexican men. Gutmann teased out four patterns of masculinity in the working-class urban settlement he studied, insisting that even these four are crosscut by other social divisions and are constantly renegotiated in everyday life.

Change

Finally, a considerable body of research showed that masculinities are not simply different, but also are subject to change. Challenges to hegemony are common, and so are adjustments in the face of these challenges. Morrell (1998) assembled evidence about gender transformations in southern Africa associated with the end of apartheid, a system of segregated and competing unequal gender relations. Ferguson (2001) traced the decline of long-standing ideals of masculinity in Ireland—the celibate priest and the hardworking family man—and their replacement by more modernized and market-oriented models. Dasgupta (2000) sketched out the tensions in the Japanese "salaryman" model of masculinity, especially after the "bubble economy" of the 1980s: a cultural figure of the "salaryman escaping" had appeared. Taga (2003) documented diverse responses to change among young middle-class men in Japan, including new options for domestic partnership with women. Meuser (2003) outlined generational change in Germany, partly driven by men's responses to changes among women. Many (though not all) young men, now expecting women to reject unequal gender relations, were found to be crafting a "pragmatic egalitarianism" of their own. Morris and Evans (2001), studying images of rural masculinity and femininity in Britain, discovered a slower pace of change, but an increasing subtlety and fragmentation in the representation of hegemonic masculinity.

From the mid-1980s to the early 2000s, then, the concept of hegemonic masculinity passed from a conceptual model with a fairly narrow empirical base, to a widely used framework for research and debate about men and masculinities. The concept was applied in diverse cultural contexts and to a considerable range of practical issues. It is not surprising, then, that the concept attracted criticism during this time period, and to this I now turn.

CRITICISMS

Five principal criticisms of hegemonic masculinity were advanced during debate about the concept from the early 1990s and into the 2000s. This section evaluates each criticism in turn.

The Underlying Concept of "Masculinity"

That the underlying concept of "masculinity" and/or "masculinities" is flawed was argued from primarily a realist and a poststructuralist view. Hearn (1996; 2006, 44) noted a number of difficulties with the concepts, such as the wide variety of uses of the terms, the imprecision in these uses, and their "use as a *shorthand* for wide range of social phenomena that appear to be located in the *individual*." To Petersen (1998, 2003), Collier (1998), and MacInnes (1998), the concept of masculinity was flawed because it essentializes the character of men or imposes a false unity on a fluid and contradictory reality. Some versions of this argument criticized masculinity research because it had not adopted a specific poststructuralist tool kit—which would, for instance, emphasize exclusively the discursive construction of identities (Whitehead 2002). The concept of masculinity was criticized for being framed within a heteronormative conception of gender, one that essentializes male/female difference and ignores difference and exclusion within the gender categories. The concept of masculinity was said to rest logically on a dichotomization of sex (biological) versus gender (cultural), and thus marginalizes or naturalizes the body.

No responsible mind can deny that in the huge literature concerned with "masculinity" there is a great deal of conceptual confusion, as well as a great deal of essentializing. This certainly was common at the time in accounts of masculinity in pop psychology, in the "mythopoetic" men's movement, and in journalistic interpretations of biological "sex-difference" research. It is another matter, however, to claim that the concept of masculinity *must* be confused or essentialist, or even that researchers' use of the concept typically *is*.

The reason that social science and humanities research on masculinities has flourished during the last thirty years is precisely that the underlying concept employed is *not* reified or essentialist. The notion that the concept of masculinity is essentialized or homogenized is quite difficult to reconcile with the tremendous multiplicity of social constructions that ethnographers and historians have documented with the aid of this concept (Connell 2003). Even further removed from essentialism is the fact that researchers during this time period had explored masculinities enacted by people with female bodies (Halberstam 1998; Messerschmidt 2004). "Masculinity" is not a fixed entity embedded in the body or personality traits of individuals. Masculinities are configurations of practice that are accomplished in social action and, therefore, can differ according to the gender relations in a particular social setting.

The idea that a recognition of multiple masculinities necessarily turns into a static typology likewise was not borne out by the development of research during the 1990s and early 2000s. A paradigmatic example is Gutmann's (1996) Mexican ethnography, mentioned earlier. Gutmann was able to tease out different categories of masculinity—for example, the macho and the *mandilón*—while recognizing, and showing in detail, that these were not monadic identities but always are relational, and constantly are crosscut by other divisions and projects. Warren's (1997) observations in a British elementary school provide another example. Different constructions of masculinity were found, which generated effects in classroom life, even though many boys did not fit exactly into the major categories; indeed, the boys demonstrated complex relations of attachment and rejection to those categories.

The idea that the concept of gender embeds heteronormativity was a familiar criticism (Hawkesworth 1997), but it was a contested criticism (Scott 1997). Although it correctly identified a problem in categorical models of gender, it is not a valid criticism of relational models of gender (e.g., Connell 2009; Walby 1997) nor of historical approaches where the construction of gender categories is the object of inquiry. In the development of the concept of hegemonic masculinity, divisions among men—especially the exclusion and subordination of homosexual men—were quite central issues (Carrigan, Connell, and Lee 1985). Moreover, during this time period the policing of heterosexuality was a continuous and major theme in discussions of hegemonic masculinity.

The idea that the concept of masculinity marginalized or naturalized the body (because it is supposed to rest on a sex/gender dichotomy) was perhaps the most startling of the claims in this critique. Startling, because the *interplay* between bodies and social processes has been one of the central themes of masculinity research from its inception. One of the first and most influential research programs in the new paradigm was Messner's (1992) account of the masculinity of professional athletes, in which the use of "bodies as weapons" and the long-term damage to men's bodies were examined. The construction of masculinity in a context of disability (Gerschick and Miller 1994), the laboring body of working-class men (Donaldson 1991), men's health and illness (Sabo and Gordon 1995), and boys' and girls' interpersonal violence (Messerschmidt 2000, 2004) were among the themes found at this time in research on how bodies are affected by social processes. And theoretical discussion had explored the relevance of the "new sociology of the body" to the construction of masculinity (e.g., Connell 1995).

Critiques of the concept of masculinity make better sense when they point to a tendency, in research as well as in popular literature, to dichotomize the experiences of men and women. As Brod (1994) accurately observed, there was a tendency in the men's studies field to presume "separate spheres," to proceed as if women were not a relevant part of the analysis, and therefore to analyze masculinities by looking only at men and relations among men. As Brod also argued, this is not inevitable. The cure lies in taking a consistently relational approach to gender— not in abandoning the concepts of gender or masculinity.

Ambiguity and Overlap

Early criticisms of the concept raised the question of who actually represents hegemonic masculinity. It was familiar at this time that many men who hold great social power do not necessarily embody a hegemonic masculinity. On the other hand, Donaldson (1993) remarked that there did not seem to be much masculine substance to those men identified by researchers as hegemonic models. He discussed the case of the Australian "iron man" surf-sports champion described by Connell (1990), a popular exemplar of hegemonic masculinity. But the young man's regional hegemonic status actually prevented him from doing the things his local peer group defined as masculine—going wild, showing off, drunk driving, getting into fights, and defending his own prestige.

Martin (1998) criticized the concept for leading to inconsistent applications, sometimes referring to a fixed type of masculinity, on other occasions to whatever type is dominant at a particular time and place. Similarly, Wetherell and Edley (1999) contended that the concept fails to specify what conformity to hegemonic masculinity actually looks like in practice. Hearn (2004) asked whether hegemonic masculinity referred to cultural representations, everyday practices, or institutional structures. And Whitehead (1998, 58; 2002, 93) suggested there was confusion over who actually is a hegemonically masculine man—"Is it John Wayne or Leonardo DiCaprio; Mike Tyson or Pele? Or maybe, at different times, all of them?"—as well as confusion about who can enact hegemonic practices.

The above critics correctly pointed to ambiguities in usage during this time period. Accordingly, it was desirable to eliminate any usage of hegemonic masculinity as a fixed, transhistorical model. This usage violates the historicity of gender and ignores the massive evidence of change in social definitions of masculinity. Hegemonic masculinities often are constructed in ways that provide models of relations with women and solutions to problems of gender relations. Further, they articulate loosely with the practical constitution of masculinities as ways of living in everyday local circumstances. To the extent they do this, they contribute to hegemony in society as a whole. It is neither surprising nor inconsistent that men who function as exemplars at the regional level, such as the "iron man" discussed by Donaldson, exhibit contradictions.

At the local level, hegemonic patterns of masculinity are embedded in specific social environments, such as formal organizations. There were, for instance, at this time well-defined patterns of managerial masculinity in the British corporations studied by Roper (1994) and Wajcman (1999). Socially legitimated hegemonic models of masculinity were also found to be in play in families. For instance, men's gender strategies shaped negotiations around housework and the "second shift" in the US families studied by Hochschild (1989). Hegemonic patterns of masculinity are both engaged in and contested as children grow up. Gender is made in schools and neighborhoods through peer group structure, control of school space, dating patterns, homophobic speech, and harassment (Mac an Ghaill 1994; Thorne 1993). In none of these cases examined during this time would we expect hegemonic masculinity to stand out as a sharply defined pattern separate from all others. And a degree of overlap or blurring between hegemonic and nonhegemonic masculinities is extremely likely if hegemony is effective.

The overlap between masculinities was also seen in terms of the social agents constructing masculinities. Cavender (1999) showed how hegemonic masculine models were constructed differently in feature films of the 1940s compared with those of the 1980s. This was not just a matter of the characters written into the scripts. Practice at the local level—that is, the actual face-to-face interaction of shooting the film *as an actor*—ultimately constructs hegemonic masculine fantasy models (in this case, "detectives") at the society-wide or regional level (this question of the relations between levels will be explored in chapter 3).

The Problem of Reification

The idea that the concept of hegemonic masculinity reduces, in practice, to a reification of power or toxicity was also argued from different points of view. Holter (1997, 2003), in the most conceptually sophisticated of all critiques during this time period, argued that the concept constructs masculine power from the direct experience of women rather than from the structural basis of women's subordination. Holter believed that we must distinguish between "patriarchy," the long-term structure of the subordination of women, and "gender," a specific system of exchange that arose in the context of modern capitalism. It is a mistake to treat a hierarchy of masculinities constructed within gender relations as logically continuous with the patriarchal subordination of women. Holter (1997) tellingly pointed to Norwegian survey evidence showing that the gender identities of men do not map directly onto such equality-related practices as attitudes toward violence.

Holter certainly is correct that it is a mistake to deduce relations among masculinities from the direct exercise of personal power by men over women. At the least, we also must factor in the institutionalization of gender inequalities, the role of cultural constructions, and the interplay of gender dynamics with race, class, and region.

At the time period under discussion, research on these issues showed that the concept of hegemonic masculinity was not trapped in reification. Among the fruitful studies of institutional masculinities were those that revealed quite subtle variations, for instance, between the different branches of a single military force, the US Navy (Barrett 1996). There were studies of locally specific hegemonic masculinities constructed in spaces such as a New Zealand country pub, that show the interweaving of masculinity with rural identity (H. Campbell 2000). Other research at the time, especially studies of school classrooms (Martino 1995; Warren 1997), showed the fine-grained production and negotiation of masculinities (and femininities) as configurations of practice.

Collier (1998) criticized the concept of hegemonic masculinity through its typical use in accounting for violence and crime. In the "masculinity turn" in criminology, Collier suggested, hegemonic masculinity came to be associated *solely* with negative characteristics that depict men as unemotional, independent, non-nurturing, aggressive, and dispassionate—which are seen as the *causes* of criminal behavior. Martin (1998, 473) similarly observed a drift toward a view of hegemonic masculinity not just as a type, but as a *negative* type, for instance, in "saying that defending gun ownership is a defense of hegemonic masculinity."

This criticism had force. It drew on McMahon's (1993) accurate analysis of the psychologism in many discussions of men and masculinity. Men's behavior was reified then in a concept of "masculinity" that, in a circular argument, becomes the explanation (and the excuse) for the behavior. This was also seen in many discussions of men's health and problems of boys' education—indeed, any of the contemporary troubles assembled under the banner of a "crisis in masculinity." In pop psychology the invention of new character types was endemic (the alpha male, the sensitive new-age guy, the hairy man, the new lad, the "rat boy," etc.). In this environment, hegemonic masculinity became a scientific-sounding synonym for a type of rigid, domineering, sexist, "macho" man (in the Anglo usage, e.g., Mosher and Tomkins, 1988).

Because the concept of hegemonic masculinity was conceptualized at this time as a practice that permits men's collective power over women to continue, it is not surprising that *in some contexts* hegemonic masculinity actually does refer to men engaging in toxic practices—including physical violence—that stabilize gender power in a particular setting. However, violence and other noxious practices are not always *the* defining characteristics, in that hegemony has numerous configurations. As Wetherell and Edley (1999) ironically observed, one of the most effective ways of "being a man" in certain *local* contexts may be to demonstrate one's distance from a *regional* hegemonic masculinity.

Collier (1998) discerned that a crucial defect in the concept of hegemonic masculinity is that it excludes "positive" behavior on the part of men—that is, behavior that might serve the interests or desires of women. This hardly is a problem once we get beyond a rigid trait theory of personality. Most accounts of hegemonic masculinity during this time period *did* include such "positive" actions as bringing home a wage, sustaining a sexual relationship, and being a father. The concept of hegemony would be irrelevant then if it only referred to, for example, violence, aggression, and self-centeredness; hegemony is constituted through consent and active participation in a wide range of ways.

Collier (1998, 21) was right in remarking that what actually is being discussed in many accounts of hegemonic masculinity and crime (and, we may add, health and education) is "a range of popular ideologies of what constitute ideal or actual characteristics of 'being a man.'" What Collier missed, however, is that sophisticated research of this time period consistently went on to explore the relationship of those ideologies to the daily lives of boys and men—including the mismatches, the tensions, and the resistances.

It is men's and boys' practical relationships to collective images or models of masculinity, rather than simple reflection of them, that is central to understanding gendered consequences in violence, health, and education. This has been evident since Messerschmidt's (1993) formulation of the idea that different crimes are *used* by different men in the construction of masculinities. Collier found this idea unacceptable, either tautological and universalizing, or too multitudinous in what it explains. But there is nothing surprising about the idea of diverse practices being generated from common cultural templates; and there is nothing *conceptually* universalizing in the idea of hegemonic masculinity. Coordination and regulation occur in the live social practices of collectivities, institutions, and whole societies. The concept of hegemonic masculinity was not intended by Connell as a catchall or as a prime cause; it was seen as a means of grasping a certain dynamic within the social process.

The Masculine Subject

Several authors argued during this time period that the concept of hegemonic masculinity was based on an unsatisfactory theory of the subject. Wetherell and Edley (1999) developed this critique from the standpoint of discursive psychology, arguing that hegemonic masculinity cannot be understood as the settled character structure of any group of men. We must question "how men conform to an ideal and turn themselves into complicit or resistant types, without anyone ever managing to exact-ly embody that ideal" (337).

Wetherell and Edley suggested we should understand hegemonic norms as defining a subject position in discourse that is taken up strategi-cally by men in particular circumstances. Hegemonic masculinity certain-ly has multiple meanings—a point that some authors offered as a criti-cism, but that Wetherell and Edley take as a positive point of departure. Men can dodge among multiple meanings according to their interaction-al needs. Men can adopt hegemonic masculinity when it is desirable. But the same men can distance themselves strategically from hegemonic mas-culinity at other moments. Consequently, "masculinity" does not repre-sent a certain *type* of man but, rather, a way that men position themselves through discursive practices.

Whitehead (2002, 93) argued that the concept of hegemonic masculin-ity can "see" only structure, making the subject invisible: "The individual is lost within, or, in Althusserian terms, subjected to, an ideological appa-ratus and an innate drive for power." To Whitehead, the concept failed to specify how and why some heterosexual men legitimate, reproduce, and generate their power, and do so as a social minority vis-à-vis women and other men. Consequently, use of the concept results "in obfuscation, in the conflation of fluid masculinities with overarching structure and, ulti-mately, in 'abstract structural dynamics'" (Whitehead 2002, 93–94). For Whitehead, it was preferable to concentrate on discourse as the means by which men come to know themselves, to practice "identity work," and to exercise gender power and resistance.

A related criticism derived from psychoanalysis. According to this view, the model of hegemonic masculinity presumed a unitary subject, but depth psychology reveals a multilayered or divided subject (Collier 1998; Jefferson 1994). Jefferson (2002) criticized the "over-socialized view of the male subject" in studies of masculinity, which resulted in a lack of attention to how men actually relate psychologically to hegemonic mas-culinity. Given multiple masculinities, Jefferson argued that researchers should ask "how actual men, with their unique biographies and particu-lar psychic formations, relate to these various masculinities" (73). Jeffer-son suggested that boys and men choose those discursive positions that help them ward off anxiety and avoid feelings of powerlessness.

The argument from discursive psychology is well taken, and was well integrated with a fruitful research approach. A good example of this time period is Lea and Auburn's (2001) study of the story told by a convicted rapist in a sex-offender program, which showed how the narrating offender moves between conflicting discourses of sexual interaction in a way that reduces his responsibility for the rape. Another example is Louise Archer's (2001) exploration of the identity talk of young Muslim men in Britain, showing how they use a specific model of hegemonic masculinity ("powerful, patriarchal") to position themselves in relation to Afro-Caribbean men, white men, and Muslim women. From this work we can learn not only how masculinities are constructed in discourse but also how they are used in discourse. Specifically we learn how a locally hegemonic version of masculinity can be used to promote self-respect in the face of discredit, for instance, from racist denigration.

Discursive perspectives emphasize the symbolic dimension, whereas the initial notion of hegemonic masculinity was formulated within a multidimensional understanding of gender. Although any specification of hegemonic masculinity typically involves the formulation of cultural ideals, it should not be regarded *only* as a cultural norm. Gender relations also are constituted through nondiscursive practices, including wage labor, violence, sexuality, domestic labor, and childcare, as well as through unreflective routinized actions.

Recognizing the nondiscursive and nonreflexive dimensions of gender gives us some sense of the limits to discursive flexibility. That there are such limits is a point powerfully made in Rubin's (2003) study of female-to-male transsexual men. One is not free to adopt any gender position in interaction simply as a discursive or reflexive move. The possibilities are constrained massively by embodiment, by institutional histories, by economic forces, and by personal and family relationships. The costs of making certain discursive choices can be extremely high—as shown by the rate of suicide among people involved in transsexual moves.

Constraint also may arise from within the person. Rubin's respondents act as they do, and face the costs, because of an unshakable conviction of being men—despite starting out with female bodies and being brought up as girls. They are convinced of being unitary subjects, though they live a contradiction that seems to exemplify Jefferson's argument for the divided subject. Although one can agree with Jefferson that psychoanalytic practice and theory are important resources for understanding the complex subject of gender practice, Jefferson's particular psychoanalytic approach is not without problems (Messerschmidt 2005), and it is important to recognize the diversity and wealth of the psychoanalytic tradition. Approaches such as Sartre's existential psychoanalysis are helpful for understanding masculinities *as projects*, and a masculine identity as always being a provisional accomplishment within a life course. Adlerian psychoanalysis, with its emphasis on the emotional consequences of gendered power relations in childhood, gave rise to the idea of the "masculine protest" that still resonates with contemporary discussions of marginalized youth.

The concept of hegemonic masculinity originally was formulated with a strong awareness of psychoanalytic arguments about the layered and contradictory character of personality, the everyday contestation in social life, and the mixture of strategies necessary in any attempt to sustain hegemony (Carrigan, Connell, and Lee 1985; Connell 1987). Although it is somewhat ironic that the concept was criticized for oversimplifying the subject, it is of course true that the concept often had been employed during this time period in simplified forms.

Does the concept *necessarily* erase the subject? Whitehead's claim that the concept of hegemonic masculinity reduces to structural determinism is flatly wrong. Masculinity is defined as a configuration of practice organized *in relation to* the structure of gender relations. Human social practice creates gender relations in history. The concept of hegemonic masculinity embedded at the time a historically dynamic view of gender in which it was *impossible* to erase the subject. This is why life-history studies have become a characteristic genre of work on hegemonic masculinity.

The initial conception of hegemonic masculinity homogenized the subject only if it was reduced to a single dimension of gender relations (usually the symbolic) and only if it was treated as the specification of a norm. As soon as one recognizes the multidimensionality of gender relations (Connell 2009) and the occurrence of crisis tendencies within gender relations (Connell 1995), it is impossible to regard the subject constituted within those relations as unitary. There are of course different ways of representing the incoherence of the subject. The conceptual language of poststructuralism is but one way of doing that; psychoanalysis and the model of agency within contradictory social structures provide others.

The Pattern of Gender Relations

In social theories of gender there has often been a tendency toward functionalism—that is, seeing gender relations as a self-contained, self-reproducing system, and explaining every element in terms of its function in reproducing the whole. Hawkesworth (1997) detects this tendency in most modern theories of gender, and Bourdieu's (2001) late intervention to explain masculine domination has given a new lease on life to functionalism in gender analysis. And not surprisingly, a concern was expressed by Hearn (2004, 63) who, although appreciating the salience of the concept of hegemonic masculinity, argued that "the hegemony of men in relation to women, children and other men needs to be addressed more directly."

The hierarchical relations of men and women constitute a historical process, not a self-reproducing system. Moreover, gender hegemony is open to challenge and requires considerable effort to maintain. Though this point was made in early statements on the hegemonic masculinity concept, it is not just a theoretical idea. There was considerable detailed work during this time period that shows the tactics of maintenance through the exclusion of women, ranging from Bird's (1996) work on homosociality to the organizational research by Collinson, Knights, and Collinson (1990), Cockburn (1991), Martin (2001), and Collinson and Hearn (2005).

Further, there likewise existed substantial evidence that hegemonic masculinity is not a self-reproducing form, whether through "habitus" or any other mechanism. To sustain a given pattern of hegemony requires the *policing of men* as well as the *exclusion and/or discrediting of women*. Evidence of such mechanisms ranges from the discrediting of "soft" options in the "hard" world of international relations, security threats, and war (Hooper 2001), to homophobic assaults and murders (Tomsen 2002), and even to the teasing of boys in school for "sissiness" (Kimmel and Mahler 2003; Messerschmidt 2000).

In Demetriou's (2001) careful critique of the concept of hegemonic masculinity, the historicity of gender is acknowledged. Demetriou, however, suggested that a kind of simplification occurred. He identified two forms of hegemony, internal and external. "External hegemony" refers to the institutionalization of men's dominance over women; "internal hegemony" refers to the social ascendancy of one group of men over all other men. Demetriou argued that the relationship between the two forms is unclear in the original formulation of the concept and unspecified in current usages. Moreover, internal hegemony typically was understood in an "elitist" way. That is, nonhegemonic masculinities were seen as having no impact on the construction of hegemonic masculinity. Nonhegemonic masculinities exist in tension with, but never penetrate or impact, hegemonic masculinity. There is, then, a dualistic representation of masculinities.

Such a conceptualization, Demetriou argued, misses the "dialectical pragmatism" of internal hegemony, by which hegemonic masculinity appropriates from other masculinities whatever appears to be pragmatically useful for continued domination. The result of this dialectic is not a unitary pattern of hegemonic masculinity, but rather a "historic bloc" that weaves together multiple patterns whose hybridity is the best possible strategy for external hegemony. By such means, a constant process of negotiation, translation, and reconfiguration occurs.

This conceptualization leads to a different view of historical change in masculinities. In other words, hegemonic masculinity does not simply adapt to changing historical conditions. Rather, the hegemonic masculine bloc is a hybridization whose appropriation of diverse elements makes it "capable of reconfiguring itself and adapting to the specificities of new historical conjunctures" (Demetriou 2001, 355). For example, Demetriou discussed the increasing cultural visibility of gay masculinity in Western societies. This made it possible for certain heterosexual men to appropriate "bits and pieces" of gay men's styles and practices, and to thus construct a new hybrid configuration of gender practice. Such an appropriation blurs gender difference but does not undermine unequal gender relations.

Demetriou's conceptualization of dialectical pragmatism in "internal hegemony" is useful, and he makes a convincing case that certain representations of masculinity and some heterosexual men's everyday gender practices have appropriated aspects of gay masculinities. Clearly, specific masculine practices may be appropriated into other masculinities, creating a hybrid, and I will have more to say about hybrid hegemonic masculinities in chapter 4.

The concept of a hegemonic "bloc" brings into focus the issue of multiple hegemonic masculinities, and others have indeed criticized the tendency to speak of just *one* pattern—"hegemonic masculinity is always used in the singular" (Jefferson 2002, 71). There is a paradox here. Because every ethnography discovers a distinctive gender culture, every life-history study uncovers unique trajectories of men's lives, and every structural analysis defines new intersections of race, class, gender, and generation, it is logically possible to define "a thousand and one" variations of masculinity (Meuser and Behnke 1998). This surely is also true of claimants to hegemony. Considering the empirical diversity of masculinities, the implication that there are multiple hegemonic masculinities—whether local, regional, or global—is one of the subjects further explored in chapter 3.

CONCLUSION

Connell's initial conception of hegemonic masculinity concentrated on how hegemonic masculinity in a given historical and society-wide setting *legitimates* unequal gender *relations* between men and women, masculinity and femininity, and among masculinities. Both the *relational* and *legitimation* features were central to her argument, involving a particular form of masculinity in unequal relation to a certain form of femininity—that is, "emphasized femininity," which is practiced in a complementary, compliant, and accommodating subordinate relationship with hegemonic masculinity—as well as in relation to nonhegemonic masculinities; what Connell labeled complicit, subordinate, marginalized, and protest masculinities. And the achievement of hegemonic masculinity, according to Connell's initial formulation, occurs largely through discursive legitimation (or justification), encouraging all to consent to, unite around, and embody such unequal gender relations. Connell's initial model found significant and enthusiastic application and expansion from the late 1980s to the early 2000s, being utilized in a variety of academic disciplines and areas. Despite this considerable favorable reception of Connell's approach, however, the concept of hegemonic masculinity nevertheless attracted criticism that was solidly responded to in this chapter.

Given the threads outlined in this chapter, Connell and I (Connell and Messerschmidt 2005) collaborated in 2005; we recognized and appreciated certain criticisms of the concept, and then we specifically recommended how the concept of hegemonic masculinity might be rethought and thus reformulated. This reformulation currently is the signature statement on hegemonic masculinity, and it is the subject of chapter 3.

THREE

Reformulation

Thirteen years ago Raewyn Connell and I (Connell and Messerschmidt 2005) responded to the criticisms of Connell's initial formulation of hegemonic masculinity, and then we reformulated the concept in numerous ways. In chapter 3 I specifically discuss which features of the original concept Connell and I concluded have held up well in light of research and criticism, those features that should be discarded, and (in greater detail) those areas where the concept is in need of reformulation. Following this I close the chapter by summarizing selected studies to illustrate various initial applications of the reformulated model of hegemonic masculinity.

WHAT SHOULD BE RETAINED AND REJECTED

The fundamental feature of the concept of hegemonic masculinity remains a combination of the plurality of masculinities and of a hierarchy among hegemonic masculinity and emphasized femininity as well as nonhegemonic masculinities. This basic idea has well withstood more than thirty years of research experience and continues to do so. Moreover, multiple patterns of masculinity have been and continue to be identified in numerous studies, in a variety of countries, and in different institutional and cultural settings. And it is a widespread research finding that certain masculinities are hegemonic, necessarily in *relation* to emphasized femininity and nonhegemonic masculinities. That the concept of hegemonic masculinity presumed the subordination of femininities and nonhegemonic masculinities is a process that has been documented in a wide range of studies internationally. And the original key feature and component of hegemonic masculinities—the *legitimation* of unequal gender *relations*—continues to be uncovered as the essence of gender hegemony.

The idea that the hierarchy of gender relations is a pattern of *hegemony*, and not a pattern of simple domination, has also been well supported. Cultural consent, discursive centrality, institutionalization, and the marginalization or de-legitimation of alternatives continue to be widely documented features of hegemonic masculinities. Also well supported is the original idea that hegemonic masculinity need not be the commonest and/or the most powerful pattern of masculinity in everyday life.

The original formulation placed some emphasis on the possibility of change in gender relations, on the idea that a particular hegemonic masculinity was open to challenge—from women's resistance to gender inequality, and from men as bearers of alternative masculinities. And research continues to fully confirm the idea of the historical construction and reconstruction of hegemonic masculinity. Thus, both at *local* and at broad societal or *regional* levels, the situations in which masculinities are formed change over time, and these changes require new strategies in gender relations and will redefine the meaning of hegemonic masculinity.

Connell and I also argued thirteen years ago that three features of applications of the early formulation of hegemonic masculinity have not withstood criticism, and should be discarded. The first was a too-simple model of the social relations surrounding hegemonic masculinities. The formulation in *Gender and Power* attempted to locate all masculinities (and all femininities) in terms of a single pattern of power: the "global dominance" of men over women (Connell 1987, 183). Although this was useful at the time in preventing the idea of multiple masculinities from collapsing into an array of competing lifestyles, by 2005 it clearly was seen as inadequate to our understanding of relations among groups of men and forms of masculinity, and of women's relations with hegemonic masculinities. For instance, hegemony in gender relations involves an interplay of costs and benefits; challenges to hegemonic masculinity arise from the "protest masculinities" of marginalized ethnic groups; and girls and women may appropriate aspects of hegemonic masculinity in constructing gender relations. Clearly, the *relationship* between hegemonic masculinity and femininities and nonhegemonic masculinities is essential to retain, yet better ways of understanding gender hierarchy are now required.

We also argued that despite the critique of trait psychology in *Gender and Power* and the appeal to psychoanalytic ideas about unconscious motivation, early statements on hegemonic masculinity, when they attempted to characterize the actual content of different configurations of masculinity, often relied on trait terminology—or at best, failed to offer an alternative. The notion of masculinity as an assemblage of traits created the path to treatment of hegemonic masculinity as a fixed character type, a notion that has given considerable trouble to properly applying the concept of hegemonic masculinity. We therefore argued that not only the essentialist concept of masculinity, but also more generally the *fixed* character trait approach to gender, should be thoroughly transcended.

Finally, we argued that *dominant* forms of masculinity are not necessarily analogous to *hegemonic* forms of masculinity, because the former may not always legitimate unequal gender relations and they often center only on actual groups of men. For example, in chapter 2, I pointed out that there has been considerable conceptual confusion around the concept, and that ambiguities in the usage of hegemonic masculinity have indeed transpired over the years. Additionally, Connell and I confronted this confusion and ambiguity by, in part, specifically distinguishing the "dominant" from the "hegemonic." For instance, consider our discussion of toxicity practiced in certain *dominant* forms of masculinities (Connell and Messerschmidt 2005, 840):

> It is difficult to see how the concept of hegemony would be relevant if the only characteristics of the dominant group were violence, aggression, self-centeredness. Such characteristics may mean dominant but hardly would constitute hegemony—an idea that embeds certain notions of consent and participation by the subaltern groups.

In short, our emphasis was on the significance of distinguishing masculinities that legitimate a hierarchical relationship between men and women, masculinity and femininity, and among masculinities (hegemonic), from those that do not (dominant). Therefore, it is important not to equate one with the other.

WHAT SHOULD BE REFORMULATED

In light of the research and critiques discussed in chapter 2, Connell and I reasoned that the concept of hegemonic masculinity required reformulation in four principal areas: the nature of gender hierarchy, the geography of masculine configurations, the process of social embodiment, and the dynamics of masculinities. In the following subsections I summarize our line of thought at the time and our specific research suggestions on each.

Gender Hierarchy

Compared with the original formulation of the concept of hegemonic masculinity, research had shown the complexity of the relationships among different constructions of masculinity. For example, research in discursive psychology indicated how different constructions of masculinity at the local level may serve as tactical alternatives. Structured relations among masculinities were found to exist in all local settings, motivation toward a specific hegemonic version varied by local context, such local versions inevitably differed somewhat from each other, and we found that there exists a variety of hegemonic masculinities in one localized setting. Demetriou's notion of dialectical pragmatism captures the reciprocal influence of masculinities: hegemonic masculine patterns may change by incorporating elements from others as well as elements of femininities.

Analyses of relations among masculinities also at the time more clearly recognized the agency of nonhegemonic groups—often conditioned by their specific location (as discussed below). "Protest masculinity" was understood in this sense: a pattern of masculinity constructed in local working-class settings, sometimes among ethnically marginalized men, that embodies the claim to power typical of regional hegemonic masculinities, but that lacks the economic resources and institutional authority that underpins regional and global patterns.

Research had also documented the durability or survivability of nonhegemonic patterns of masculinity, which may represent well-crafted responses to race/ethnic marginalization, physical disability, class inequality, or stigmatized sexuality. Hegemony may be accomplished, then, by the incorporation of certain aspects of such masculinities rather than by active oppression in the form of discredit or violence. In practice, both incorporation and oppression can occur together. By 2005, for instance, the above was recognized as the position of particular masculinities in gay communities, whereby a spectrum of experience ranging from homophobic violence and cultural denigration to toleration and even to cultural celebration and political representation occurs. Similar processes of incorporation and oppression were also at the time occurring among girls and women who construct masculinities (Messerschmidt 2004).

The concept of hegemonic masculinity was formulated originally in tandem with a concept of "hegemonic femininity"—soon renamed "emphasized femininity"—to acknowledge the asymmetrical position of masculinities and femininities in unequal gender relations. In the development of research on men and masculinities, this relationship has dropped out of focus. We saw that occurrence as regrettable for more than one reason. Gender is always *relational*, and patterns of hegemonic masculinity are *always already* socially defined in contradistinction from some model (whether real or imaginary) of femininity.

Perhaps more important, we argued that focusing solely on the activities of men occludes the practices of women in the construction of gender among men. As is well shown by life-history research, women are central in many of the processes that construct masculinities—as mothers; as schoolmates; as girlfriends, sexual partners, and wives; as workers in the gender division of labor; and so forth. The concept of "emphasized femininity" in the initial formulation focused on compliance to masculinity, and is still highly relevant in contemporary mass culture. Yet, gender hierarchies are also impacted by new configurations of women's identity and practice, especially among younger women—which continue to be increasingly acknowledged by younger men. Research on hegemonic masculinity we thus argued *must* more closely consider the practices of women and the historical interplay of femininities and masculinities. In chapter 4, I emphasize research that amplifies this crucial and essential aspect of hegemonic masculinities.

Accordingly, we suggested that understandings of hegemonic masculinity must incorporate a more holistic grasp of gender hierarchy, one that recognizes the agency of subordinated groups as much as the power of hegemonic groups, and recognizes the mutual conditioning of gender and other social dynamics. This reformulation will over time, we argued, reduce the isolation of "men's studies" and will emphasize the relevance of gender dynamics to existing problems—ranging from the effects of globalization to issues of violence and peacemaking—now being explored in other fields of social science.

The Geography of Masculinities

We noted that change in locally specific constructions of hegemonic masculinity had been a research theme for the last two decades. And with growing attention to globalization, the significance of transnational arenas for the construction of masculinity had also been argued. For example, Hooper (1998, 2000, 2001) described the deployment of hegemonic and other masculinities in the arenas of international relations, and Connell (1998) proposed a model of "transnational business masculinity" among corporate executives that was connected with neoliberal agendas of globalization.

Whether, or how far, such processes override more local and regional gender dynamics was still being debated. Pease and Pringle (2001), in an international collection of the time, argued for a continued focus on understanding masculinities regionally and comparatively. Connell and I (Connell and Messerschmidt 2005) pointed out that at the least we must understand that regional and local constructions of hegemonic masculinity are shaped by articulation of these gender systems with global processes. In this vein, Kimmel (2005) had examined how the effects of a global hegemonic masculinity are embedded in the emergence of regional (white supremacists in the United States and Sweden) and global (Al-Qaeda in the Middle East) resistant forms of masculinities.

Considering that these issues were now unavoidable for studying masculinity, Connell and I (Connell and Messerschmidt 2005) suggested the following basic framework. Empirically existing hegemonic masculinities should be analyzed at three levels:

1. Local: constructed in the arenas of face-to-face interaction of families, organizations, and immediate communities, as typically found in ethnographic and life-history research
2. Regional: constructed at the level of the "culture" or the nation-state, as typically found in discursive, political, and demographic research
3. Global: constructed in such transnational arenas as world politics and transnational business and media, as studied in what was then the emerging research on masculinities and globalization

Moreover, we pointed to the fact that links between these levels not only exist, but can be important in gender politics. Global hegemonic masculinities pressure regional and local hegemonic masculinities; regional hegemonic masculinities provide cultural materials adopted or reworked in global arenas, and provide models of masculinity that may be important in local gender dynamics.

Consider specifically the relation between regional and local hegemonic masculinities. At the regional level, hegemonic masculinities are represented symbolically through the interplay of specific local masculine practices that have regional significance, such as those constructed by feature-film actors. The exact content of these practices varies over time and across societies. Yet, regional hegemonic masculinities shape a society-wide sense of masculine reality and, therefore, operate in the cultural domain as "on-hand" material to be actualized, altered, or challenged through practice in a range of different local circumstances. Regional hegemonic masculinities, then, provide cultural frameworks that may be materialized in daily practices and interactions.

It is tempting to posit a basic hierarchy of power or authority, running from global to regional to local—but we argued that this could mislead. In discussions of globalization, the determining power of the "global" is often overestimated, whereas the resistance and capacity of what was labeled the "regional" goes unrecognized (Mittelman 2004). The limited research conducted at the time on masculinities in global arenas (e.g., Connell and Wood 2005; Hooper 2001) did not suggest a powerful formation with the capacity to overwhelm regional or local masculinities. Yet, the evidence of global dynamics in gender was growing, and it was clear that such processes as economic restructuring, long-distance migration, and the turbulence of "development" agendas have the power to reshape local patterns of masculinity and femininity (Connell 2005; Morrell and Swart 2005). In other words, we had every reason to believe that hegemonic and nonhegemonic masculinities would become increasingly important to global politics, and because of that we suggested that this should be a key arena for future research on hegemonic masculinities.

We therefore concluded that adopting an analytical framework that distinguishes local, regional, and global hegemonic masculinities (in *relation* to femininities and nonhegemonic masculinities at each level) allowed researchers to recognize the importance of place without falling into a monadic world of totally independent cultures or discourses. Although local models of hegemonic masculinity may differ from each other, they often overlap; the interplay with society-wide gender dynamics is part of the explanation. Further, because hegemonic masculinities are always already constituted in men's interaction with women and femininities, the commonalities in women's gender practices also produce convergence. Accordingly, local constructions of hegemonic masculinity often—but not always—have a certain "family resemblance," to use Wittgenstein's term, rather than a logical identity. In this sense, although local plurality may be compatible with particular hegemonic masculinities at the regional or society-wide level, we argued that scholars should likewise recognize that there exist multiple models of hegemonic masculinity at all three levels—local, regional, and global—and not simply one monolithic type.

Social Embodiment

That hegemonic masculinity is related to particular ways of representing and using bodies had been recognized from Connell's early formulation of the concept. Yet, Connell and I (Connell and Messerschmidt 2005) pointed out that the pattern of embodiment involved in hegemony had not been convincingly theorized. We noted, for instance, that the importance of masculine embodiment for identity and behavior emerges in many contexts. In youth, skilled bodily activity becomes a prime indicator of masculinity, and this is a key means by which heterosexuality and masculinity become linked in many societies: prestige conferred on boys with heterosexual partners, and sexual learning imagined as exploration and conquest. Such body practices as eating meat and taking risks on the road also become linked with masculine identities. This logically results in health promotion strategies that work by de-gendering—contesting hegemonic masculinity, or moving men in a more androgynous direction. But the *difficulties* of de-gendering strategies also are partly based in embodiment, for instance, in the commitment to risk-taking practices as means of establishing masculine reputation in a peer group context.

The common social-scientific reading of bodies as objects of a process of "social construction" was during this time widely considered inadequate. Bodies are involved more actively, more intimately, and more intricately in social processes than theory had traditionally allowed. Bodies participate in social action by delineating courses of social conduct: the body is a participant in generating social practice. So we argued that it is important not only that masculinities be understood as embodied, but also that the interweaving of embodiment and social context be addressed.

The need for a more sophisticated treatment of embodiment in hegemonic masculinity is made particularly clear by the issue of transgender practices, which are difficult to understand within a simple model of social construction. This issue had been reframed by the rise of queer theory, which had already treated gender crossing as a subversion of the gender order, or at least as a demonstration of its vulnerability. Sharp debates over transsexualism were abundant, with some psychiatrists questioning the very possibility of gender change. Consequently, it was not easy to be confident about the implications of transgender practice for hegemony. With Rubin (2003) and Namaste (2000), we suggested that scholars consider that the masculinities constructed in female-to-male transgender life courses are not inherently counterhegemonic. "Self-made men" can pursue gender equality or oppose it, just like nontransgender men. What the transgender experience highlights is modernity's treatment of the body as the "medium through which selves interact with each other" (Rubin 2003, 180).

To understand embodiment and hegemony we asserted Connell's (2009) conceptualization of the importance of understanding bodies as both objects of social practice and agents in social practice. We pointed to the fact that there are circuits of social practice linking bodily processes and social structures—many such circuits—that represent the historical process in which society is embodied. These circuits of social embodiment may be direct and simple, or they may be long and complex, passing through institutions, economic relations, cultural symbols, and so forth—but always involving material bodies. This is easily illustrated by thinking about the gender patterns in health, illness, and medical treatment.

Among hegemonic groups of men, the circuits of social embodiment constantly involve the institutions on which their privileges rest, and in a pioneering study by Donaldson and Poynting (2004) on the daily lives of ruling-class men this was dramatically revealed. This study demonstrated, for instance, how their characteristic sports, leisure, and eating practices deploy their wealth, and establish relations of distance and dominance over other men's bodies. Herein lies a rich field of research, especially when we consider how expensive technologies—computer systems, global air travel, secure communications—amplify the physical powers of elite men's bodies.

The Dynamics of Masculinities

Although long acknowledged, the internal complexity of masculinities had only gradually come into focus as a research issue. As indicated by the earlier discussion (in chapter 2) of the "subject" in gender practice, we argued that scholars should explicitly recognize the layering, the potential internal contradiction, within all practices that construct masculinities. Such practices cannot be read simply as expressing a unitary masculinity. They may, for instance, represent compromise formations between contradictory desires or emotions, or the results of uncertain calculations about the costs and benefits of different gender strategies.

In addition, life-history research had by this time period pointed to another dynamic of masculinities: the structure of a project. Masculinities are configurations of practice that are constructed, that unfold, and that change over time. A small literature on masculinity and aging, and a larger one on childhood and youth, emphasized this issue by the mid-2000s. Further, the careful analysis of life histories may detect contradictory commitments and institutional transitions that reflect different hegemonic masculinities, and may also hold seeds of change.

Hegemonic masculinities are likely to involve specific patterns of internal division and emotional conflict, precisely because of their association with gendered power. Relationships with fathers are one likely focus of tension, given the gender division of labor in childcare, the "long hours culture" in professions and management, and the preoccupation of wealthy fathers with managing their wealth. Ambivalence toward projects of change on the part of women are likely to be another, leading to oscillating acceptance and rejection of gender equality by the same men. Any strategy for the maintenance of power is likely to involve a dehumanizing of other groups and a corresponding withering of empathy and emotional relatedness within the self (Schwalbe 1992). Without treating privileged men as objects of pity, we reasoned that hegemonic masculinity does not necessarily translate into a satisfying experience of life.

In fact, we pointed out that change over time, while certainly shaped by contradictions within masculinities, may also be intentional. Children as well as adults share a capacity to deconstruct gender binaries and criticize hegemonic masculinity, and this capacity is the basis of many educational interventions and change programs. At the same time, bearers of hegemonic masculinity are not necessarily "cultural dopes"; they may actively attempt to modernize gender relations and to reshape masculinities as part of the deal. An example of the time was the "new public management" in public-sector organizations, which rejected old-style bureaucracy and believed in "flatter" organizations, equal opportunity, and family-friendly employment policies. Yet, we indicated that even the modernization of masculinities may not solve certain problems. This too, as Meuser (2001) argued, generates contradictions that may lead to further change. After all, life is dynamic, not static.

Gender relations are always an arena of tension. A given pattern of hegemonic masculinity is hegemonic to the extent that it provides a potential solution to these tensions, tending to stabilize unequal gender relations or reconstitute them in new conditions. A pattern of practice (i.e., a version of masculinity) that provided such a solution in past conditions but not in new conditions is open to challenge—is in fact certain to be challenged.

Such contestation occurs continuously through the efforts of the women's movement (at the local, regional, and global levels), among generations in immigrant communities, between models of managerial masculinity, among rivals for political authority, among claimants for attention in the entertainment industry, and so on. The contestation is real, and gender theory does not predict which or who will prevail—the process is historically open. Accordingly, hegemony may fail: the concept of hegemonic masculinity does not rely on a theory of social reproduction.

Put another way, the conceptualization of hegemonic masculinity should acknowledge explicitly the possibility of *democratizing* gender relations and of abolishing power differentials—not just of reproducing hierarchy. A transitional move in this direction requires an attempt to establish a version of masculinity open to equality with women. In this sense it may be possible to define masculinities that are thoroughly "positive." Recent history, however, has shown the difficulty of doing this in practice. Nevertheless, positive masculinities remain a key strategy for contemporary efforts at reform, and I discuss this further in chapter 6.

APPLICATION

Since 2005 scholars have keenly applied this reformulated model of hegemonic masculinity in a number of ways. In this section I outline through
examples four major paths such *initial* applications followed in scholarly
research. First, gender researchers specifically began to examine hegemonic masculinities at the local, regional, and global levels. Second, research demonstrated how women under certain situations may actually
contribute to the cultivation of hegemonic masculinity. Third, studies
appeared that demonstrated how hegemonic masculinities may be open
to challenge and possibly reproduced in new form, resulting in new strategies of unequal gender relations and redefinitions of hegemonic masculinities. Finally, scholarly work analyzed how neoliberal globalization
impacts the construction of hegemonic masculinities in several countries
in Asia, Africa, and Central and Latin America, as well as how new
nonhegemonic masculinities may arise under such conditions in these
countries. I begin with a discussion of a few examples of hegemonic
masculinities at the local, regional, and global levels.

Local, Regional, and Global

An excellent example of research on the local level is the work of
Edward Morris (2008), who studied gender difference in academic per-
ceptions and outcomes at a predominantly white and lower-income rural
high school in Kentucky. Appropriating the concept of hegemonic masculinity as a specific contextual pattern of practice that discursively legitimates the subordination of women and femininity to men and masculinity, Morris utilized a mixed methodology by observing in-school interaction, interviewing students (eight boys and seven girls), and analyzing
school records and documents. Morris found that girls generally outper-
formed boys academically and that they had higher ambitions for post-
secondary education. Morris demonstrated that in-school interaction positioned masculine qualities as superior to the inferior qualities attached
to femininity as well as to certain forms of subordinate masculinity,
thereby providing an in-school justification for unequal gendered social
action. The article highlighted how in the localized, face-to-face settings
of a rural Kentucky high school, gender inequality was legitimated
through the construction of hierarchical relations between a particular
classed, raced, and sexualized hegemonic masculinity and emphasized

femininity. Morris concluded that the boys' academic underachievement was embedded in these unequal gender relations.

In an important paper by Ronald Weitzer and Charis Kubrin (2009), these authors appropriated the concept of hegemonic masculinity as the discursive subordination of women to men and used the concept to examine all the rap albums that attained platinum status (sales of at least one million copies) from 1992 to 2000. Weitzer and Kubrin chose platinum albums because their numerical success ensured analysis of a rap-music sample that reached a large segment of the US population, thus justifying regional status. Their methodology involved content analysis of a random sample that consisted of 403 songs from 130 different albums. Analysis of the data identified five themes that emphasized unequal gender relations: (1) degradation of women, praise of men; (2) sexual objectification of women, sexual empowerment of men; (3) women as distrustful, men as invulnerable: (4) normality of violence by men, normality of women as victims; and (5) women as prostitutes, men as pimps.

Weitzer and Kubrin's study revealed how much of this rap music constructed a regional form of hegemonic masculinity by depicting men and women as inherently different and unequal and by espousing a set of superior/inferior related gendered qualities for each, for their "appropriate" behavior toward each other, and for the necessity of sanctions if anyone violated the unequal gender relationship. This study demonstrated how within popular culture, through the widespread distribution of rap music, gender inequality was legitimated at the regional level, thereby providing a society-wide cultural rationalization for unequal gender relations. Weitzer and Kubrin showed how rap music initially had local roots but came to exercise a society-wide regional influence on youth of all racial and ethnic groups.

An example of hegemonic masculinity constructed at the *global* level is Elizabeth Hatfield's (2010) examination of the popular US-based television program *Two and a Half Men*. Hatfield concentrated her scrutiny on the way gender is constructed by the two main characters—Charlie and Alan—who are white, middle-class, professional brothers living together. Hatfield also examined the changing gender constructions by Alan's son, Jake. Since its debut broadcast in 2003, the program led for many years the US sitcom ratings in popularity, being the second most popular (behind *Family Guy*) US television show for males eighteen to twenty-four, averaging approximately fifteen million US viewers per week, and it continues to be screened worldwide in at least twenty-four different countries (which approximately triples the number of weekly viewers). Thus, this show proceeds in having extensive regional and global influence.

Hatfield employed a content analysis in reviewing 115 episodes of the show, concluding that *Two and a Half Men* offers a media representation of hegemonic masculinity through the gender performance of, and the relationship between, the two main characters. Appropriating hegemonic masculinity as a specific form of masculinity that subordinates both femininity and alternative masculinities, Hatfield found that Charlie constructs hegemonic masculinity and Alan femininity, and in the process Alan's femininity consistently is subordinated to Charlie's hegemonic masculinity.

Hatfield's study admirably demonstrates how a particular sitcom — which has widespread transnational distribution — is an important example of the global legitimation and rationalization of unequal gender relations through the depiction of a superior/inferior hierarchical relationship between the two main characters. A salient aspect of this sitcom then is how it primarily represents and legitimates an unequal masculine/feminine relationship in and through two assumed male bodies.

In sum, then, these three articles demonstrate that empirically existing hegemonic masculinities exist at local, regional, and global levels; that hegemonic masculinities are formed through an unequal and hierarchical relationship between masculinities and femininities (even though femininities may be constructed in and through male bodies); and that through this relationship hegemonic masculinities circulate a legitimating justification for unequal gender relations.

Cultivation

Following the reformulation of the concept of hegemonic masculinity, research emerged that featured how the agency of women contributes to the *cultivation* of hegemonic masculinity. For example, Kirsten Talbot and Michael Quayle (2010) argued that the production of hegemonic masculinities requires "at least some kind of 'buy-in' from women" and that thus under certain circumstances and in specific situations women construct "emphasized femininities" whereby they "contribute to the perpetuation of oppressive gender relations and identities" (256). Through in-depth interviews and an extensive focus group session with five heterosexual, middle-class, university undergraduate South African women,

Talbot and Quayle explored interviewee involvement in a variety of localized contexts—work, social, romantic, and family—and found that the five women uniformly grouped these four contexts into two parts: "work and social" versus "romantic and family" situations. In each part the women reported supporting specific and unique types of gender relations; that is, they identified certain inviolable masculine and feminine qualities that each considered essential to each situation.

In romantic and family situations, the women argued that men should be in control and dominant, should financially provide for family members, and should protect those in their care. In work and social settings, however, the women desired their male workmates and male friends to possess masculine characteristics centering on platonic, friendly, equal relationships. In work and social relationships with men, masculine passivity was valued and agency was undesirable; in romantic and family relationships, masculine agency was valued and passivity was undesirable. In work and social contexts, then, the women expected to be treated in an egalitarian and gender-progressive manner, they considered romantic and family masculine features as "violations," and they valued those masculine features that "violated" hegemonic masculine qualities.

Although not a representative sample, the interviewees in this study supported and expected different types of gender relations in different local contexts. Accordingly, this study demonstrated how various forms of gender relations might be produced contextually and validated by both men *and* women and how women might construct differing forms of femininities—emphasized and liberated—in differing contexts as they recognize and support situational masculinities. And in regard to the specific cultivation of hegemonic masculinity, the women in this study were "particularly willing to accept subjugation to engage in ideals of romantic partnership congruent with emphasized femininity" (255).

As a second example, in an article on hegemonic masculinity and the profession of veterinary medicine, Leslie Irvine and Jenny Vermilya (2010) demonstrate that, despite contemporary veterinary medicine being numerically dominated by women, it is the women in this profession who often sustain, justify, and preserve hegemonic masculinity. Through interviews with twenty-two women who were practicing veterinarians or veterinary students, Irvine and Vermilya found that certain "inferior" gendered qualities, such as nurturance, compassion, and emotionality, traditionally were attached to female veterinarians. The women veteri-

narians interviewed actually placed little value on these particular characteristics, and, in fact, they distanced themselves from these traits
through their on-the-job practices. The women veterinarians instead constructed practices traditionally viewed by the profession as "superior,"
such as emphasizing science rather than nurturance, insensitivity in place
of compassion, and control instead of emotionality. Irvine and Vermilya
demonstrated how women veterinarians participated in "the patterns of
practice that sustain and justify the status quo, and thus preserve hegemonic masculinity" (74). These women appropriated the same practices
that men had long used to keep women out of the profession and therefore exemplified how hegemonic masculinity might be cultivated by
those deemed subordinate and with interests at odds with that hegemonic masculinity. The consequences of hegemonic masculinity in this profession actually lower salaries for women relative to men, underrepresent
women in the administration of veterinary schools, concentrate women
in companion-animal services, and maintain low numbers of women
who own veterinary practices.

These two articles on cultivation show that in studies of hegemonic
masculinities, the focus can no longer center exclusively on men and
instead must give much closer attention to both the practices of women
and the social interplay of femininities and masculinities.

Contestation

Always open to challenge when contested, hegemonic masculinities
often inspire new strategies in gender relations and result in new configurations of hegemonic masculinities. For example, in an examination of
autobiographical accounts of British soldiers involved in peacekeeping
duties in Bosnia in the 1990s, Claire Duncanson (2009) explored whether
or not a subsequent peacekeeping masculinity challenged the local hegemonic masculinity of the British military. Duncanson identified the British military hegemonic masculinity as consisting of brave, strong, and
tough masculine soldier/protectors in contrast to the timid, weak, and
tender feminine wife/mother in need of protection.

Through an analysis of four autobiographical accounts of British sol-
diers/officers involved in peacekeeping missions (formal and informal
activities designed to prevent, halt, or resolve conflicts) in Bosnia, Duncanson found first that each of these soldiers experienced both *emasculating* and *masculinizing* aspects of peacekeeping: regarding the former, each

soldier considered peacekeeping inferior, frustrating, and less masculine than "real fighting"; concerning the latter, each attempted therefore to position peacekeeping as 100 percent masculine behavior. For Duncanson, the former (emasculation) reinforced the local military hegemonic masculinity, but the latter (masculinist) both disrupted that hegemonic masculinity and attempted to position peacemaking masculinity as a new form of localized hegemonic masculinity in the British military. As Duncanson (69) explained, "When soldiers valorize peacekeeping tasks as masculine, they are not only asserting that there is another way to be a 'real man'; they are asserting that it is *the* way." Although the soldiers/officers regarded peacekeeping as often emasculating, they simultaneously constructed peacekeeping as masculine by claiming that actually it was tougher, more dangerous, and more challenging than participating in war.

At the same time, these soldiers/officers did not challenge the notion of women solely as wives and mothers in need of protection, and they feminized Balkan male soldiers as weak, irrational, and emotional while masculinizing themselves as controlled, civilized, and intelligent. Peacekeeping masculinity then challenged traditional British localized military hegemonic masculinity yet simultaneously was constructed in relation to subordinate racialized and feminized "Others." The end result was a new form of hegemonic masculinity that discursively legitimated hierarchical gender relations between men and women, between masculinity and femininity, and among masculinities.

A second example of the contestation of hegemonic masculinity is a study of high school rugby in Australia by Richard Light (2007), who appropriated hegemonic masculinity as a localized discourse in the particular setting of the high school and operated "at an unquestioned, common-sense level" (323). Light argued that this particular hegemonic masculine discourse shaped the performance of the high school rugby team members by emphasizing physical force and power during play instead of skills and tactical knowledge. Through interviews with team members and the coach, as well as observations of practices and games, Light found that the majority of players described this discursive approach to the sport as "no mistakes rugby," which was "highly structured, predictable, and heavy" (329). The hegemonic masculine discourse encouraged players to take an instrumental view of their bodies as weapons to dominate and actually injure opponents. Value was placed on employing powerful and purposeful physical contact, bodily force, and mastery to overcome the opposition; to take control of "enemy" territory on the field; and to move the team forward throughout the season. Players were thus compelled to embody "heavy contact" so as to establish superior power position over opponents—there was little room allowed for player autonomy, independence, and creativity in generating and utilizing space. And the consequence was the embodiment of hegemonic masculine relations on the field.

Within the confines of the high school setting, then, a powerful discourse emphasized a characteristic hard and tough hegemonic masculinity that the boys on the rugby team felt obliged to reproduce in practice. No boy wanted to "let down the tradition" of the school, and this credo made it difficult for any player to challenge the contextual hegemonically masculine discourse in any explicit way. And because of its power, the boys reproduced this particular pattern of hegemonic masculinity over generations.

Nevertheless, and despite the struggle, the boys did attempt to contest the no mistakes form of rugby through a much less structured and more creative style of play. During a two-week break at school the team participated in a rugby tournament, and it was here that the players decided collectively to change their style of play in a way that allowed more risk taking on the field and more support for each other when mistakes occurred. The new style also involved much less structure, better communication, respectful understanding among players, and increased excitement—enthusiasm for the new "open" rugby as opposed to the "no mistakes" rugby was dramatic. And because of the success with the new style of play, following the tournament the coach decided to allow the team to play open rugby in the remaining games of the season. Yet owing to an important loss to a regular season team, school administrators and coaches quickly dropped the new style of play. Again, Light attributed this to how deeply embedded the hegemonic masculine discourse was in the culture of the school. In other words, although the players attempted to mount a new form of masculinity that contested the established no mistakes rugby, the traditional hegemonic masculine discourse was far too entrenched in the school culture for any new hegemonic masculinity to emerge. Accordingly, Light insightfully documented the social processes involved in a localized struggle over hegemony and the reinstallment of a traditional hegemonic masculinity that had been contested and briefly displaced.

In sum, then, these two pieces document various ways hegemonic masculinities have been contested, resulting in the construction of new strategies of unequal gender relations and thus redefinitions of hegemonic masculinities.

Globalization

Immediately following the reformulation of the concept of hegemonic masculinity, research also began appearing that highlighted how neoliberal globalization influences the construction of hegemonic and nonhegemonic masculinities in countries such as those in Asia, Africa, and Central and Latin America. An excellent example is a study that utilized a mixed methodology—a survey, focus group discussions, and interviews. In this article, Christian Groes-Green (2009) examined the impact of neoliberal globalization on both urban middle-class and urban working-class young men (ages sixteen to twenty-three) in Maputo, Mozambique. Groes-Green found that in the local arena of Maputo, an established form of hegemonic masculinity involved men providing economically for their female partners and families, a practice that primarily defined hierarchical relations between them. Although both the middle-class and working-class young men Groes-Green studied intended to construct such hierarchical gender relations, with the arrival of neoliberal globalization only the former were able to live up to this particular hegemonic masculinity.

In 1987 the Mozambican government, through economic support from the World Bank and the International Monetary Fund, allowed considerable foreign business investment into the country. This policy subsequently heralded a growing middle class with access to higher education, steady and secure jobs, and excellent incomes. Nevertheless, the downside of this development was economic impoverishment of the majority of the population, mass unemployment among primarily working-class youth, and an increasing gap between the middle and working classes.

During his fieldwork, Groes-Green observed how middle-class and working-class young men constructed different hegemonic masculinities, and he attributed these contrasting masculinities to the neoliberal economic changes impacting Maputo. In particular, the middle-class young men had easy access to higher education, stable employment, and high incomes. Consequently, they were able to easily attract young women as partners who also supported hierarchical gender relations—these young men effortlessly constructed this particular type of localized hegemonic masculinity.

In contrast, the working-class young men, who experienced much less access to higher education as well as escalating unemployment rates, were unable to live up to the standards of hegemonic masculinity in this localized environment. And as Groes-Green (299) put it, these men developed "a masculinity that takes the body and its physical powers as its sources." In the absence of higher education, stable jobs, and an adequate income, these working-class men engaged in two specific "corporeal performances" to construct masculine power relations over their female partners. The first corporeal performance involved their becoming preoccupied with particular "sexual techniques" (such as consuming large quantities of aphrodisiacs), allegedly to increase their sexual skills and sexual stamina and thereby provide "a gateway to staying in power" by preserving a sense of superiority over their partner by managing her sexual satisfaction (298). The second corporeal performance involved some of these men increasingly engaging in physical violence against their female partner primarily to "make her respect you" (294). These two identified corporeal performances were impetuous attempts to somehow legitimate unequal gender relations through particular practices of sexuality and violence at the local level.

For Groes-Green, then, the two masculine corporeal performances were bifurcated reactions to the inability of these young men to construct and legitimate traditional hegemonic masculinity because of neoliberal-produced poverty-stricken circumstances. Both forms of corporeal performances became an "option to which poor young men in Maputo resort when their hegemony (i.e., their 'taken for granted' authority based on stable jobs and financial abilities) is contested" (296).

Similarly, Chad Broughton (2008) examined how neoliberal globalization in Mexico created a novel northward mass departure from the Mexican southern states by working-age men and women. In particular, Broughton analyzed how economically dislocated southern Mexican men negotiated hegemonic masculinity while confronting extraordinary pressure to migrate as well as the gendered strategies, practices, and identities they adopted during the undertaking.

Following implementation of the North American Free Trade Agreement (NAFTA) on January 1, 1994, numerous trade barriers to foreign investment in Mexico were removed; NAFTA created the conditions for the concentration and acceleration of foreign investment and manufacturing growth at the US-Mexico border, thereby "creating a strong draw for job-hungry, impoverished Mexicans" (Broughton 2008, 570). Moreover, NAFTA opened Mexico's agricultural sector to US agribusiness by increasing trade quotas and decreasing tariffs for major crops (such as corn), necessarily compressing rural economies and boosting northern migration.

Through life-history interviews of sixteen low-income men (eighteen to forty-two years old) who contemplated migrating north from southern Mexico, Broughton found that these men constructed three differing masculinities in reaction to migration pressures in neoliberal Mexico. Drawing on a specific localized hegemonic masculinity that emphasized hierarchical gender relations in the family and vigilant fathering, these men deployed what Broughton labeled "traditionalist," "adventurer," and "breadwinner" masculinities, all of which provided differing gendered responses "to realizing both instrumental and identity goals in a time of rapid and wrenching change" (585).

The *traditionalist* emphasized maintaining the established local hegemonic masculinity and thus unequal gender relations primarily through family cohesion. Viewing the border as a "minefield of moral hazards," the traditionalist decided to endure destitution in the south and refrain from migrating in order to protect his family from such dangers up north. The traditionalist then maintained local hegemonic masculinity in his southern home "in spite of political and economic forces working against the maintenance of such ideals" (577).

For the *adventurer*, the northern border and beyond offered a place to earn considerable money and to "prove" his masculinity in new ways, such as through seeking thrills and breaking free from the inflexibility of rural life. Rejecting the localized notion of hegemonic masculinity, migration to the north presented a progressive, avant-garde means to survive economic disorder by upgrading one's masculine status and assessing his bravery. It proffered a "new and exciting life away from the limitations of a neglected and declining rural Mexico" (585).

Finally, like the adventurer, the *breadwinner* migrated to the north, yet unlike the adventurer, such migration was a reluctant but necessary choice under desperate circumstances—he had to do so to adequately provide for his wife and children. The breadwinner coped with "symbolic indignities" so that he could acquire sufficient economic resources that would conceivably promote social mobility for his entire family. The breadwinner accepted work at or beyond the border "as an inescapable duty" so that his family would enjoy a higher standard of living but in the process constructed unequal gender relations (585).

Broughton's study then demonstrated how low-income Mexican men experiencing economic dislocation intrinsic to neoliberal Mexico negotiated with a specific localized hegemonic masculinity and in the process orchestrated old and new hegemonic and new nonhegemonic masculine configurations. This differing process of masculine identity formation involved much more than simply instrumental calculations; these men had to "make sense of the migration experience as men and arrive at specific and adaptive gendered strategies and decisions regarding northward migration" (586). One of the important aspects of this article was its demonstration of how specific forms of complicity (traditionalist and breadwinner) with, and resistance (adventurer) to, a localized hegemonic masculinity and thus unequal gender relations were constructed under identical neoliberal conditions.

What these studies show is that within countries experiencing the effects of neoliberal globalization, attempts by men at the individual level to maintain localized power relations over women might occur and further display how certain alternative nonhegemonic masculinities might arise under such conditions.

CONCLUSION

The reformulated model of hegemonic masculinity first included certain aspects of the original formulation that empirical evidence over almost two decades of time indicated should be retained, in particular the relational nature of the concept (among hegemonic masculinity, emphasized femininity, and nonhegemonic masculinities) and the idea that this relationship is a pattern of hegemony—not a pattern of simple domination—that legitimates unequal gender relations. Also well supported historically are the foundational ideas that hegemonic masculinity need not be the most powerful and/or the most common pattern of masculinity in a particular setting, and that any formulation of the concept as simply constituting an assemblage of fixed "masculine" character traits should be thoroughly transcended. Second, the reformulated understanding of hegemonic masculinity incorporates a more holistic grasp of gender inequality that recognizes the agency of subordinated groups as much as the power of hegemonic groups and that includes the mutual conditioning or intersectionality of gender with such other social inequalities as class, race, age, sexuality, and nation. Third, the reformulation includes a more sophisticated treatment of embodiment in hegemonic and nonhegemonic masculinities, as well as conceptualizations of how hegemonic masculinity may be challenged, contested, and thus changed. Finally, instead of recognizing simply hegemonic masculinity at only the society-wide level, the reformulated model of hegemonic masculinity suggests that scholars analyze empirically existing hegemonic masculinities at three levels: the local, regional, and global.

Each piece of scholarship discussed above, in its own particular way, broke new ground by concentrating on academic domains that previously had been disregarded (cultivation and contestation) or seemingly deemed incapable of exploration and analysis (globalization). This work inspires additional gender research that further extends our knowledge in similar and/or previously unexplored areas. And the above examples illustrate the academic appropriation of the reformulated model of hegemonic masculinity and the processes involved in gendered knowledge construction. The combined research shows that sundry scholars are demonstrating impressively through their published academic work how specific hierarchical gender relationships between men and women, between masculinity and femininity, and among masculinities are legitimated—in my view, superbly capturing certain of the essential features of the omnipresent reproduction of unequal gender relations. Additionally, these articles reveal in various ways how hegemonic masculinities express models of gender relations that articulate with the practical constitution of masculine and feminine ways of living in everyday circumstances. To the extent they do this, they contribute to our understanding of the legitimation and stabilization of unequal gender relations locally, regionally, and globally.

Finally, although identifying a single society-wide or global "ascendant" hegemonic masculinity may be possible, no one to date has successfully done so. This is probably the case because it is extremely difficult to measure such ascendancy and thereby determine which particular

of hegemonic masculine relations—among the whole variety in the offer-
ing—is indeed *the* ascendant hegemonic masculinity. Until a method is
devised for determining exactly which form of gender hegemony is *the*
hegemonic ascendant, we must speak of hegemonic masculinity—as the
reformulated model suggests and the current evidence documents—
wholly in plural terms, analyzing hegemonic masculini*ties* at the local,
regional, and global levels. Such research will provide a growing expansion of our understanding of the pervasive and omnipresent nature of
how hegemonic masculinity and thus unequal gender relations are legiti-
mized and solidified from the local to the global. And in the next chapter
I contribute to the above research by demonstrating how the reformulated model of hegemonic masculinity has indeed been amplified.

FOUR

Amplification

In chapter 4 I discuss the *amplification* of the reformulated model of hegemonic masculinity. In particular, I examine how recent scholarly work has enlarged upon and contributed to the further conceptualization of hegemonic masculinities. But before turning to these scholarly developments, it is important to point out that certain scholars continue to ignore the core aspect of hegemonic masculinity—the legitimation of unequal gender relations—simply by equating the concept of hegemonic masculinity with fixed masculinity characteristics, and/or they associate the concept solely with certain groups of men (see Flood 2002; Beasley 2008). To illustrate this genre of scholarly work on hegemonic masculinities, I provide an example of each below. Following this, I turn briefly to a number of studies that have pushed the reformulated model of hegemonic masculinity in new directions.

IGNORING UNEQUAL GENDER RELATIONS

Regarding fixed masculinity traits, Trevon Logan (2010) studied gay male escorts occupying the dominant position in the male prostitution industry. Logan was interested in how hegemonic masculinity might be reproduced through the practices of these gay male escorts: how these practices might be dominant in the male prostitution business because they allegedly aligned with a society-wide monolithic hegemonic masculinity that subordinated them. Logan (683) appropriated the concept of hegemonic masculinity by identifying such "masculine" traits (that he claimed defined this monolithic hegemonic masculinity) as drive, ambition, self-reliance, aggressiveness, and physical strength, as well as such bodily traits and practices specific to the hegemonically masculine "sexual arena" as physical appearance (muscularity, body size, body hair, and height) and sexual behaviors (sexual dominance, sexual aggressiveness, and penetrative sexual position).

Using a quantitative online data source that described gay male sex workers, Logan found that muscular men enjoyed a dominant position in the male prostitution market (overweight and thin men faced a penalty) that was "consistent with hegemonic masculinity" because "conformity to hegemonic masculine physical norms is well rewarded in the market" (697). Because muscularity signified maleness and dominance, "the premium attached to muscularity in this market is consistent with hegemonic masculinity" (694). Furthermore, according to Logan, the reward of being a "top" (sexually penetrative position) was substantial, as was the penalty for being a "bottom," and thus this finding allegedly was "consistent with the theory of hegemonic masculinity" (697).

When Logan studied the interaction of these masculine traits with race, he found that black men were positioned at both extremes: they assigned the largest premiums for top behavior and the largest penalties for bottom behavior. Logan argued that the gay community valued black men who conformed to racial stereotypes of sexual behavior and penalized black men who did not. And Logan (698) concluded that gay men who frequented male escorts "adopt and reiterate hegemonic masculine norms among themselves" and that this in turn was reinforced through the idealized "masculine" traits of dominant-gay-male sex escorts.

An example of simply associating hegemonic masculinity with certain groups of men is found in an article written by Elizabeth Gage (2008), who examined the impact that male college athletes' participation in different sports had on their gender attitudes, hegemonic masculinity, sexual behavior, and sexual aggression. Gage (1018) argued that her study offered "an opportunity to refine understanding of what it is about sports participation that leads to hegemonic masculinity and sexual aggression." Unfortunately, this study never formally defined hegemonic masculinity yet created the impression that the concept amounted to specific toxic character traits attached to certain athletes.

By means of a survey, Gage measured the "gender role identification," "attitudes toward women," "hyper-masculinity," and "sexual behavior, sexual aggression, and sexual orientation" of 148 college males, both athletes (football, tennis, and track and field) and nonathletes. Gage found that football players scored significantly higher on hypermasculinity and sexual aggression scales (toxic traits) than did the athletes in the other two sports but scored significantly lower than the same athletes on attitudes-toward-women scales (harmless traits). A similar pattern emerged when football players were compared to nonathletes, but fewer significant differences were noted between nonathletes and tennis and track-and-field athletes.

Despite never actually defining or measuring hegemonic masculinity, Gage (1029) concluded that her research on the role that participation in sports—especially football—had on college males indicated a "more nuanced understanding of the relationship between hegemonic masculinity, attitudes toward women, and violence against women." But the most we can reasonably deduce from this article is that for Gage hegemonic masculinity reduced to such toxic, hypermasculine character traits as "negative attitudes toward women," "violence as manly," and "calloused sex attitudes toward women" that were exclusively embodied in football players.

These two articles are representative examples of how the meaning of the concept continues to be a troubled area in research on hegemonic masculinity. Although these articles are similar in their concentration on "masculine" traits, they differ in the way they associate these traits with hegemonic masculinity: either as constituting alleged *widespread* character traits or as consisting of exclusively specific *toxic* traits consolidated in a particular group of men (football players). Both usages are not solely a matter of individual interpretation of the concept. Within the scholarly area of masculinities studies, there remains a fundamental *collective* tendency by numerous researchers to read hegemonic masculinity as a static character type and/or embodied in certain groups of men, and in the process ignore the whole question of gender relations and the legitimacy of gender inequality. The above two examples unquestionably offer intriguing insight into the adoption of certain "masculine" traits by particular groups of men. Nevertheless, in terms of *hegemony* in unequal gender relations that is explicit in the concept of hegemonic masculinity, their presentation is noticeably abbreviated. That is, they fail to show how a hierarchical *relationship* between masculinity and femininity and among masculinities is legitimated. Their work calls for an additional step to be taken, involving an analysis of the downstream consequences of how the particular "masculine" traits actually legitimate gender inequality and the subordination of women, femininities, and/or nonhegemonic masculinities. Without this necessary relational conceptualization, we simply are left with analyses describing *dominant* rather than *hegemonic* masculinities.

In the following sections I offer selected examples of recent research that overcomes the problems identified above and amplifies the reformulated model of hegemonic masculinity. This research adds to what was noted in chapter 3: the *omnipresent* nature of hegemonic masculinities, from the local to the regional to the global. In other words, this research suggests that hegemonic masculinities are much more common than previously believed—they are ubiquitous throughout society and consequently widely encountered. Despite this pervasiveness, however, hegemonic masculinities often are at once *hidden in plain sight*, operating in a disguised way while concurrently securing an overwhelmingly legitimating influence; that is, hegemonic masculinities are so obvious that people do not actually "see" them—because they are everywhere, they are nowhere—and this social condition signifies bona fide hegemony.

HEGEMONIC AND DOMINANT MASCULINITIES

In chapter 2 and immediately above I discussed inconsistent applications of the concept of hegemonic masculinity, sometimes referring to a fixed type of masculinity, or to "masculine" traits embodied in particular groups of men, or to whatever type of masculinity is dominant at a particular time and place. Christine Beasley (2008) has labeled such inconsistent applications of the concept "slippage," arguing that "dominant" forms of masculinity—such as those that are the most powerful and/or most widespread in particular settings—may actually do little to legitimate men's power over women and, therefore, should not be labeled hegemonic masculinities. And Beasley (89) notes that some scholars continue to equate hegemonic masculinity with particular masculinities that are practiced by certain men—such as politicians, corporate heads, and celebrities—simply because they are in positions of power, ignoring once again questions of gender relations and the legitimation of gender inequality. And Mimi Schippers (2007) has argued that it is essential to distinguish masculinities that legitimate unequal gender relations from those that do not.

An example of what Beasley above labels slippage is found in the work of Richard Howson (2006, 2009), who argued that hegemonic masculinity maintains "hegemonic principles" that shape and sustain its particular historical and situational configuration. Howson designates hegemonic principles as the defining and privileged masculine values, norms, and beliefs of any particular historical time. For Howson, then, contemporary hegemonic masculinity in global North societies can be condensed into three specific principles: heterosexuality, breadwinning, and aggressiveness. However, from the perspective proposed herein, these three "principles" may constitute aspects of a *dominant* form of masculinity in the sense of being widespread throughout contemporary global North societies—and thus dominant at a particular time and place—but such characteristics are not *hegemonic*. In other words, Howson fails to demonstrate how such principles specifically *legitimate* a hierarchical *relationship* between men and women, masculinity and femininity, and among masculinities, and therefore must be considered at best as "dominant principles."

I thus agree with Beasley and Schippers, both of whom seem to be suggesting that the argument put forth in the reformulated model of hegemonic masculinity—which specifically differentiates "hegemonic" from "dominant" masculinities—did not go far enough. Consequently, as early as 2010, I (Messerschmidt 2010) began to take Beasley's and Schippers's arguments seriously and accordingly updated the reformulated model by arguing that to elucidate the significance and salience of hegemonic masculinities, gender scholars *must* meticulously distinguish masculinities that legitimate gender inequality from those that do not. And over the course of various writings, I have carefully differentiated hegemonic from dominant masculinities (Messerschmidt 2010, 2012, 2014, 2016). Most recently in my 2016 book, *Masculinities in the Making*, I define "hegemonic masculinities" as those masculinities constructed locally, regionally, and globally that legitimate an unequal relationship between men and women, masculinity and femininity, and among masculinities. The emphasis here is on hegemonic masculinity as always already constituting an unequal relationship that legitimates gender inequality. Hegemonic masculinities acquire their legitimacy by embodying materially and/or symbolizing discursively culturally supported "superior" gender qualities in relation to the embodiment or symbolization of "inferior" gender qualities (Schippers 2007). That is, certain culturally defined "superior" gendered qualities legitimate unequal gender relations when they are symbolically paired with culturally defined "inferior" qualities attached to femininity (Schippers 2007). In addition, hegemonic masculinities must be culturally ascendant to advance a rationale for social action through consent and compliance—hegemonic masculinities (locally, regionally, and globally) rise to a cultural position of influence. *Dominant masculinities* are not always associated with and linked to gender hegemony but refer to (locally, regionally, and globally) the most celebrated, common, widespread, or current form of masculinity in a particular social setting.

As an example of dominant and hegemonic masculinities constructed by the *same* people, I (Messerschmidt 2016) interviewed fifteen teenage boys who all identified certain boys in their school as notably *dominant*: they were popular, often tough, and renowned as "jocks"; attended parties; participated in heterosexuality; and had many friends. In other words, these dominant boys represented the most *celebrated* form of masculinity in the "clique" structure within schools yet they did not *in and of themselves* legitimate gender inequality. In the past, scholars have mistakenly assumed that such dominant popular boys are simultaneously and exclusively representatives of an in-school hegemonic masculinity (by ignoring gender relations).

Nevertheless, I also found that these same dominant popular boys occasionally construct an in-school localized *hegemonic* masculinity. One way they do this is through the practice of bullying "Other" boys. The victims of such bullying are feminized through verbal and/or physical abuse, especially if they do not respond to the bullying in the way the masculine culture of the school dictates; that is, to physically fight back. In the succinct bullying sequence of events, then, the popular dominant boys construct—what I will discuss more thoroughly later—a localized *fleeting* hegemonic masculinity because in the instance of bullying they embody aggressiveness, invulnerability, and the capacity to engage in physical violence (culturally masculine qualities) while the boys who are bullied embody passivity, vulnerability, and an inability to engage in physical violence (culturally feminine qualities). Unequal masculine and feminine relations then are constructed momentarily within the localized confines of the school. By means of verbal bullying, then, we have the momentary ascendancy of an in-school localized hegemonic masculinity that circulates a legitimating discursive justification for gendered inequality, and is for the most part hidden in plain sight. This example likewise alerts us to the fluidity of masculinities, the movement from dominant to hegemonic and back to dominant masculinities and, thus, how hegemonic masculinities often are contingent and haphazard as well as provisional and temporary. To understand this complex aspect of hegemonic masculinities, then, dominant masculinities must be distinguished from hegemonic masculinities.

A historical example of dominant and hegemonic masculinities constructed in the same localized community by different people is the case of the "Halutzim" in late nineteenth and early twentieth-century Palestine. The Halutzim were young heterosexual Jewish men who worked at manual labor jobs in Palestine, primarily in agriculture. They established collective settlements in Palestine as a "strategy to guarantee the Jewish hold of the land and a monopoly over labor" (Hirsch and Kachtan 2017, 5). Their sense of masculine worth rested on the admiration of the patriarchal "working man," whereby they worked outside the home as breadwinner while their wives were barred from agriculture work and instead "confined to the 'feminine' tasks of childcare, cooking, and cleaning" (6). At home, then, the Halutzim constructed a hegemonic masculinity, yet outside the home they competed with Arab workers for work. In the historical record associated with the Halutzim, Arab workers are "coded" as much more masculine than the Jewish workers: "they are described as more able-bodied, braver, and possessing a stronger ability to endure physical hardships and pain" (6). The Halutzim would attempt to emulate Arab workers by adorning themselves with the clothing of the latter and disregarding the norms of hygiene, which translated into a variety of meanings, such as proletarization, endurance in the face of difficult conditions, native status, and masculinity. To be sure, these practices were described by the Halutzim as explicitly "an attempt to live 'exactly like the Arabs'" (7). In these two different settings, then, we find a fluid construction of dissimilar masculinities based on contrasting gender relations: within the private sphere of the home, a hegemonic masculinity is constructed by the Halutzim, yet in the public realm of work the masculinity of Arab workers was dominant in the sense of being the most celebrated by those purchasing labor as well as by the Halutzim. And in this particular example we see race/ethnicity, nationality, and hegemonic

and dominant masculinity being constituted simultaneously in these localized settings.

There are many examples of present-day dominant masculinities, and
Beasley (2008, 90) provides an excellent illustration in Australia, whereby
a senior manager in the localized setting of a major accounting firm and
his colleagues represent "a dominant masculinity in that he wields a
widely accepted institutional power"; these senior managers most likely
share with each other particular managerial gender qualities that are associated with that dominance, but such managers do not embody the
legitimating relationship required for the construction of hegemonic masculinity. In other words, the managers in an accounting firm clearly exercise considerable authority and power, and are thus celebrated, yet they
do not *in and of themselves* reproduce unequal gender relations (90).

An example of a dominant masculinity at the global level is what
Connell and Wood (2005) labeled "transnational business masculinity."
Connell and Wood interviewed eleven male Australian transnational corporate managers and found that these men operated in a male-dominated corporate world in which they work long hours, they frequently
travel, and therefore their work is extremely intense and stressful. Within
this context, such corporate managers come to treat their lives as an "en-
terprise" through specific embodied practices. As Connell and Wood
(2005, 355) put it: "Treating one's body as a thing to be managed is part of
a larger phenomenon—that is, treating one's life as a thing to be managed." Globalization has heightened their job-related insecurities, yet
their masculinity centers on the attractiveness of high pay and social
power—which involves exercising collective power, institutional power,
and personal authority—as well as distancing themselves from an old-
style bourgeois masculinity involving domestic patriarchy, snobbery, social authority, patriotism, religion, and so on. In fact, this transnational
business masculinity pivots on a global, neoliberal view of transnational
markets as well as simply strategizing and controlling; it has "no deeper
rationale than the 'bottom line'—in fact, no rationale at all except profit
making" (361). Simultaneously, however, these corporate managers are
tolerant of diversity and at least verbally endorse gender equality. What
Connell and Wood, then, are describing here is one type of dominant
masculinity within transnational corporations, and they are quick to
point out that this form of masculinity does not occupy the whole field of
transnational business masculinities and in fact they acknowledge that

hegemony "is by no means firmly established" (362). These men then constitute a global dominant masculinity but not a global hegemonic masculinity because they do not legitimate unequal gender relations.

This emphasis on a distinction between hegemonic and dominant masculinities is significant because it enables a more distinct conceptualization of how hegemonic masculinities are unique—and indeed complex—among the diversity of masculinities. Making a clear distinction between hegemonic and dominant masculinities will not only bring hegemonic masculinities out from hiding, but is bound to enable scholars to now recognize and research various dominant nonhegemonic yet powerful masculinities and how they differ from hegemonic masculinities as well as how they differ among themselves. This then is one of the ways the reformulated model of hegemonic masculinity has been amplified.

DIFFERENCES AMONG HEGEMONIC MASCULINITIES

My recent research also suggests that hegemonic masculinities—at the local, regional, and global levels—are constructed differently. For example, I (Messerschmidt 2016) found and report in the same book mentioned above that hegemonic masculinities vary in the significance and scope of their legitimating influence—the justifying of unequal gender relations by *localized* hegemonic masculinities is limited to the confines of particular institutions, such as schools, whereas *regional* and *global* hegemonic masculinities have respectively a society-wide and worldwide legitimating influence. The power of hegemonic masculinities is dispensed differently depending upon the magnitude and range of their legitimating effect.

I (Messerschmidt 2016) also distinguish between "dominating" and "protective" forms of hegemonic masculinities and accordingly different constructions of gendered power relations. For example, the just mentioned high school popular boys who verbally abuse and feminize "Other" boys consolidate a localized hegemonic masculinity through *dominating* aggressive bullying. In contrast, I uncovered distinct types of hegemonic masculinities—locally and globally—that were established through contrasting forms of benevolent *protection*. For example, at the *local* level I found that in some high school lesbian relationships that are very public, one partner is known to be assertive and confident while the other is recognized as passive and shy. But the former is also compassionately protective, emphasizing caring, guidance, and support. The assertive partner derives her masculine power through the dependent status of her girlfriend; her girlfriend respects, honors, and yields to the caring guidance and support that is offered by her assertive partner. This then is not a dominating and overpowering relationship, but rather the girlfriend submits to the assertive power of her partner and rejoices in the partner's ability to protect. Feminine subordination and gender hegemony then proceeds from the position of compassionate protector, and the relationship centers on clearly defined and enacted "inferior" feminine and "superior" masculine practices and qualities.

At the *global* level, I (Messerschmidt 2016) found in my analysis of foreign policy speeches by US presidents George W. Bush (Bush 43) and Barack Obama that they each metaphorically construct themselves as embodying strength, assertiveness, knowledge, invulnerability, and the ability to protect others (as masculine qualities) through the "global war on terror" while all "Other" people of the world are metaphorically portrayed as passively dependent, innocent, uninformed, vulnerable, and unable to protect themselves from global terrorists (as feminine qualities). Both sets of qualities in global North societies historically and culturally have been associated with men and women respectively, masculinity and femininity respectively, and when these gendered qualities are paired together in a complementary and subordinate way we have the legitimation of gender inequality through the discursive construction of a global hegemonic masculinity. A global protective gendered power relationship then is socially constructed discursively and based on superior/inferior characteristics that legitimated and differentiated unequally hegemonic masculine heroic US presidents and worldwide feminized and possibly victimized men, women, and children.

Furthermore, both Bush 43's and Obama's speeches construct a hero-villain masculine relationship that is based on differing unequal gendered qualities attached to each. In their speeches both Bush 43 and Obama depict themselves as the global compassionate protective hero who is civilized, virtuous, just, and peaceful, whereas Saddam Hussein, the Taliban, Al-Qaeda, and the so-called Islamic State are characterized as uncivilized, cruel, unjust, and violent toxic villains. This pairing signifies an unequal global relationship between two different types of masculinities: one hegemonic and one subordinate. Bush 43's and Obama's gendered qualities were deemed superior in relation to the toxic gendered characteristics attached to Saddam Hussein, the Taliban, Al-Qaeda, and the so-called Islamic State. In this example, then, an overabundance of masculinity is symbolically embodied in the villains and is represented relationally as a form of masculine inadequacy, deficiency, and subordination.

The above identification of "protective" hegemonic masculinities challenges the notion that hegemonic masculinities are exclusively pernicious and toxic, recognizing benevolent and compassionate ways gender hegemonic relations may be practiced. Such hegemonic masculinities are hidden in plain sight because they often are simply uneventful and unexciting, but also misjudged as lacking relations of power. In addition, the first example of a protective hegemonic masculinity corroborates the notion that women and girls occasionally can and do embody hegemonic masculinities.

Finally, I also found and report in the book mentioned above the different ways hegemonic masculinities are constructed: hegemonic masculinities can be fashioned through relational *material* practices—such as physical bullying by dominant popular boys in schools—that have a discursive legitimating influence, whereas hegemonic masculinities can also be constructed through *discursive* practices—such as the speeches by US presidents Bush 43 and Obama that concurrently constituted unequal gender relations linguistically, metaphorically, and thus symbolically. This discursive constitution of hegemonic masculinity is a new development in the field of masculinities studies; it amplifies the reformulated model, and it has also recently been examined by other scholars (for example, see Weitzer and Kubrin 2009; Hatfield 2010, discussed in chapter 3). What this evidence suggests then is that hegemonic masculinities are both materially and discursively hidden in plain sight even as simultaneously they are widespread throughout society and indeed the world.

The analysis here also supports the notion that *local* hegemonic masculinities may have a certain "family resemblance" to regional and global hegemonic masculinities (see chapter 3). In other words, regional and global hegemonic masculinities arguably operate in the localized cultural domain discursively as potential on-hand material to be actualized (or challenged) through practice. For example, in a study of gender hegemony in a US high school, C. J. Pascoe (2011) describes a yearly assembly in which senior boys compete to be named the most popular boy in the school by performing skits. The favored skit involved two white boys proving their local hegemonic masculinity by means of *heroically protect-*

ing and rescuing "helpless" white girls who were kidnapped and thus became the captive *victims* of a gang of racial minority *villainous* "gang-stas."

Although Pascoe's example demonstrates variable constructions of hegemonic masculinity at the local, regional, and global levels linked by a common core of heroic rescue and/or protection, we should not conclude that there exists exclusively one symbolic model of hegemonic masculinity at all three levels. In fact, as at the local level, there exists a diversity of hegemonic masculinities at the regional and global levels. For example, in her work on hegemonic masculinities and multinational corporations, Juanita Elias (2008) shows how certain qualities of this particular hegemonic masculinity—such as rationality and competition—are built into the culture of multinational corporations, and how such a hegemonic masculinity can be understood only in its *relation* to the qualities attached to the femininity of the women workers in these same corporations: docile and diligent nimble-fingered factory "girls." Although the particular masculine and feminine qualities linked to this particular global corporate gendered hegemony differ markedly from those gender qualities articulated by both Bush 43 and Obama in their varying global heroic hegemonic masculine discourses, what unites all three of these contrasting forms of hegemonic masculinity is the regional and global legitimation of a hierarchical relationship between men and women, masculinity and femininity, as well as their collective contribution to the ubiquitous character of hegemonic masculinities that are hidden in plain sight.

HYBRID HEGEMONIC MASCULINITIES

Recent work on hybrid masculinities reveals another layer to the evidence amplifying the reformulated model that hegemonic masculinities are omnipresent yet hidden in plain sight. Hybrid hegemonic masculinities involve the incorporation of subordinated styles and displays (masculine and/or feminine) into certain men's (and women's) identities, and in the process simultaneously secure and obscure their hegemonic power (Bridges and Pascoe 2018). For instance, and as outlined in chapter 2, Demetrakis Demetriou (2001) discussed the increasing cultural visibility of gay masculinities in global North societies and argued that this has made it possible for certain straight men to appropriate particular gay men's styles and practices and construct a new hybrid configuration of gender practice. Demetriou concluded that such an appropriation blurs gender difference but does not undermine gender hegemony.

One of the first scholars to follow Demetriou's lead was Sofia Aboim (2010), who examined the relationship between masculinity and family life. Aboim interviewed sixty Portuguese heterosexual men with three different family types: married/cohabitating couples with children, lone fathers, and blended families. What Aboim found is that these men were involved in a variety of new family practices that challenged traditional notions of patriarchal hegemonic masculinities—there existed a plurality of masculine configurations within the private realm of the family. What united these men were their "new attitudes toward gender equality in family life" and their "day-to-day participation in household and caring tasks" (133). Aboim noted that nevertheless, while adopting such feminine practices, the men did not fall into "excessive feminization" to the point of emasculating themselves. Rather, they experienced a contradiction: enacting femininity while simultaneously rejecting it. The end result was a new configuration of hegemonic masculinity in the family that was orchestrated among these men through subversion; that is, defining themselves as "better" at feminine tasks than women. Aboim's study demonstrated then that the field of possibilities in which to construct masculinities in the family has been transformed and widened, creating in particular "reinventions of hegemony" (135) and thus the amplification of the reformulated model.

Tristan Bridges's (2010, 2014) important work has demonstrated how certain men are able to frame themselves as outside gender hegemony when in fact they align themselves with it and reproduce such inequality. For example, in his study of "Walk a Mile in Her Shoes" marches, Bridges (2010) shows that these marches ask men to wear women's clothing— such as miniskirts, fishnet stockings, and high-heeled shoes—and walk one mile protesting violence against women and pledging support to end it. These men are standing in solidarity with women, actively opposing men's violence, and wearing "feminine" attire and women's shoes—all practices that seem to distance them from and thus challenge hegemonic masculine relations. However, Bridges found that these same march participants reproduced unequal gender relations even as they actively resisted it. For example, participants actually disparaged and subordinated women by joking about wearing in particular women's clothing, about their inability to walk in heels, and they often mocked gay men and same-sex sexual desire, all of which worked to align them with a particularized hegemonic masculinity even as their participation in antiviolence activism distanced them from it.

Kristen Barber (2008, 2016) recently demonstrated how white middle-class heterosexual professional men's embrace of previously feminine-typed consumption of personal beauty grooming actually serves to reproduce hegemonic masculinity. While patronizing hair salons, these men often disparaged women through misogynistic heterosexual discourses while simultaneously subordinating working-class men as "outdated" and "inferior" for frequenting barbershops. The middle-class men also visualized themselves as "classy" because they engaged in "salon talk" with women rather than "barber talk" with men. These white middle-class heterosexual professional men then avoided any notion of feminization by projecting a seemingly progressive, contemporary, stylish, and professional hegemonic masculinity. While their participation in embodied beauty grooming apparently disassociates them from hegemonic masculinity, their situational practices concurrently obscured the reproduction of that particularized and contextualized form of unequal gender relations that simultaneously was constituted by class and sexuality.

Tristan Bridges and C. J. Pascoe (2018) have also shown that the appropriation of subordinated masculine practices into constructions of hegemonic masculinities operates to reproduce unequal gender relations and thereby must be understood as expressions of, rather than challenges to, gender hegemony. They argue that hybrid hegemonic masculinities illustrate some of the changes taking place in reproducing unequal gender relations, demonstrating that experiencing and justifying privilege has transformed, and in the wake of this transformation new "identity projects" are constructed that increase the "elasticity" for, in particular, privileged straight white men. Bridges and Pascoe therefore challenge any claim that hegemonic masculinities are decreasing; rather, they are often changing and new forms are emerging. Bringing to light hybrid hegemonic masculinities then significantly adds to the amplification of the reformulated model of hegemonic masculinity.

The work on hybrid masculinities just discussed concentrates on the global North, yet hybrid hegemonic masculinities also seem to be taking place in some parts of the global South. For example, Christian Groes-Green's (2012) notion of "philogynous masculinities" in Mozambique illustrates this. Philogynous masculinities construct practices that favor women's rights to agency, security, respect, and well-being in gender egalitarian ways. Groes-Green discusses what he labels the *bom pico* (meaning, a good lover) heterosexual form of masculinity, which supports the notion of philogyny through the prioritization of women's sexual pleasure, and it emphasizes caring and attentiveness toward women. Nevertheless, in prioritizing women's sexual pleasure, *bom pico* men reproduce hegemonic notions of virility, potency, and strength and subordinate men who are seen as being "sexually weak" (that is, unable to perform). The *bom pico* then is an example of men who "live up to the ideals of male sexual power vis-à-vis other men and a question of giving pleasure to female partners in order to live up to their expectations of them as men" (99). Men who practice *bom pico* masculinity then are aligning themselves with hegemonic masculinity even as their practices might seem to distance themselves from it and, therefore, they reproduce masculine power over women and "Other" men in a novel way.

Hybrid hegemonic masculinities then work in ways that reproduce unequal gender relations while simultaneously obscuring this process as it happens. Hybrid hegemonic masculinities demonstrate the resilience of gender hegemony, and scholarship continues to document the wide range of sites that hybrid masculinities are constructed, from the metrosexual (de Casanova, Wetzel, and Speice 2016), to Christian hard-core punk (McDowell 2017), to therapeutic boarding schools for privileged young men (Pfaffendorf 2017), to cockfighting in Hawaii (K. M. Young 2017), to US presidents (Messerschmidt 2016), among others. Hybrid masculinities work in ways that amplify the all-pervasive yet disguised nature of assorted contemporary hegemonic masculinities.

FEMININITIES

Research on hegemonic masculinity has now amplified the practices of girls and women and in the process more carefully examined the historical interplay of femininities and masculinities. For example, Mimi Schippers's (2007) important work on "recovering the feminine other" properly places the *relationship* between masculinity and femininity at the center of any conceptualization of the *legitimacy* of gender hegemony. As pointed out earlier, Schippers argues that certain "superior" masculine characteristics legitimate men's power over women when they are symbolically paired with "inferior" qualities attached to femininity (91). In understanding the legitimacy of gender hegemony, then, it is essential to conceptualize in part the relationship between masculinity *and* femininity. What this further means, however, is that gender hegemony can be challenged when girls/women embody masculine qualities—which Schippers labels "pariah femininities" rather than masculinities—because they are "contaminating to the relationship between masculinity and femininity" (95). Pariah femininities tend to center on a refusal to complement hegemonic masculinity, such as expressing sexual desire for girls/women, acting sexually promiscuous, or presenting as authoritarian, physically aggressive, or taking charge.

Given the above, any new configurations of femininities become essential to conceptualizations of hegemonic masculinity and the reproduction of unequal gender relations. For example, recent feminist research suggests that dominant gender constructions by adolescent girls in North America and Europe no longer center on such embodied practices as submissiveness, docility, and passivity. Instead, gender qualities such as self-control, self-entitlement, self-reliance, determination, competition, individual freedom, and athleticism, combined with being attractive and exhibiting heterosexual appeal—the "heterosexy athlete"—form the primary markers signifying dominant adolescent femininity (Adams, Schmitke, and Franklin 2005; Bettis and Adams 2005; Gonick 2006; McRobbie 2009; Ringrose 2007; Budgeon 2014). In other words, the dominant gender construction for adolescent girls today is constituted through a "hybrid femininity," consisting of conventional feminine *and* masculine qualities. This research accordingly raises the question: Does this hybrid femininity challenge gender hegemony? The answer seems to be a resounding no, as a wide range of studies indicate that such hybrid femininities have not resulted in a reorganization or collapse of unequal gender relations (Budgeon 2014, 325). Although this new dominant hybrid femininity displaces for adolescent girls Connell's (1987) notion of "emphasized femininity"—because it requires that girls refrain from practicing a *girly* femininity—it simultaneously requires that girls *must* avoid threatening masculine privilege by rejecting *all* feminine qualities (Budgeon 2014, 327). In other words, hybrid femininities appear to be progressive yet are, as Angela McRobbie (cited in Budgeon 2014, 325) rightly contends, "consummately and reassuringly feminine," and therefore remain a crucial link in the reproduction of gender hegemony. Hybrid femininities then—like hybrid masculinities—promote a gendered dynamic that obscures gender hegemony while concurrently aligning with it and thus represent another example of how gender hegemony is hidden in plain sight.

In a recent study on the differences among femininities and their relation to gender hegemony, Roger Domeneghetti (2017) analyzed 369 newspaper articles that covered the 2016 Wimbledon tennis tournament. The articles were published in the United Kingdom's two best-selling daily newspapers—the *Sun* and the *Daily Mail*—between June 26 and July 11, 2016. Domeneghetti was interested in examining how the British press conveyed notions of femininity among the women competitors in the tournament. And what his discourse analysis revealed was a pattern of racialized femininities in the newspaper coverage that represented the white women players' femininity as reinforcing hegemonic masculinity and the black women players' femininity as contaminating to a particular form of white gender hegemony.

White women players were depicted in ornamental, attractive, and decidedly sexualized ways that "served to trivialize their athletic ability and achievements, instead presenting the female body as a commodity to be enjoyed" (10). For example, the articles featured the white women players in "provocative model shots" wearing solely lingerie or swimwear, and focusing on their legs, buttocks, chest, and face (7). As Domeneghetti (7) argues:

> These photos rendered the players [white women] in passive, "non-active" roles in which they were shorn of their athletic ability and sexualized for the benefit of the male gaze. This had the effect of reinforcing their femininity and trivializing their bodies thus undermining their athleticism and sporting expertise.

In contrast, the articles emphasized the white men players' strength, energy, aggression, and athletic ability. For example, the day after Andy Murray lifted the winning trophy, his victory was proclaimed in the articles as the "Return of the King" and he essentially was portrayed as "royalty." For Domeneghetti (9), then, this obvious discursive distinction between white women and white men players subordinates white femininity to white masculinity and thus "reproduces and re-enforces the dominant hegemonic ideology of masculinity" and, therefore, through both prose and photos, the white women players were portrayed in a "position of weakness within the gendered hierarchy" (7).

Domeneghetti found that differing from the white women players, black women players—in particular, Serena and Venus Williams—were framed in the articles as "natural athletes," two "strong black women," and their bodies were represented "as both sexually grotesque and pornographically erotic" (9–10). For example, the articles expressed "shock" that Serena Williams's nipples were visible in her tight-fitting top and in the same instant she was characterized as a Superwoman figure that highlighted the size and strength of her biceps and thighs as well as her "natural aggressive game" (10). The Williams sisters were depicted as "brutal" against, and who "bludgeoned," their opponents, and they were further stereotyped in the articles as "the naturally able black athlete by employing aggressive language which foregrounded the players' strength" (10). This discursive representation "naturalized" the Williams sisters as outcast, pariah feminine "others" in relation to the "properly" feminine white women players. In short, the prose and photos found in the articles reinforced notions of white hegemonic unequal gender relations, they maintained racialized discourses of inequalities among femininities, and all of this was hidden in plain sight.

A captivating arena for examining femininities and their relation to hegemonic masculinities is in settings that are otherwise perceived as gender neutral. For example, Michelle Wolkomir (2012) examined through participant observation the construction of masculinities and femininities in formally organized poker games at a casino in the American Deep South. On the surface such games can be considered gender neutral because there exist no physical requirements linked to bodily difference (e.g., physical strength), the rules do not favor men, there are no barriers to participation, and men and women directly compete with one another. Wolkomir's analysis, however, revealed that even within this "level-playing field," as men and women play poker they construct hegemonic masculinity and therefore unequal gender relations. Men's participation at the table is invariably aggressive, dominant, and controlling—they were "in command" of the setting and dictated the "action" at the table—and they linked these qualities to masculinity. And not surprising, any poker play that seemed "weak," such as by "folding" when someone raised the bet or when "bluffed," was uniformly labeled feminine. Both men and women players hence could be feminized and thus subordinated if they folded and/or were tricked.

A crucial observation that Wolkomir uncovered was that *none* of the women players attempted to be "in command" at the table, and they did not practice dominance or control during the game. Instead, the women competed by using "deception" and thereby they fit into "traditionally gendered 'slots' available to women within a hegemonic frame," presenting "themselves as passive/submissive, dumb, or sexualized, or some combination of the three" (414). Women poker players then were "doing femininity" as they were doing poker, just as the men were "doing masculinity" as they were doing poker. However, the women used this gendered "deception" as a means to hide their actual game skills "by pretending to fit the men's gendered expectations and then using that perception to manipulate players and win" (422). Their doing of femininity as a game strategy had to remain invisible to be effective, yet this masculine-feminine interaction at the poker table transformed a relatively gender-neutral game into an occasion whereby hegemonic masculinity and thus unequal gender relations were underpinned.

Finally, an impressive study by Kimberly Kay Hoang (2015) examined differing femininities and masculinities among sex workers and their clients in Ho Chi Minh City, Vietnam. Hoang engaged in participant observation of "hostess bars" and observed primarily the interactions between the sex workers and clients who frequented these bars. She details how the intersection of gender, class, sexuality, and nation, as well as the link between global and local, were played out differently in the bars. Each bar maintained varying and unique settings of hegemonic masculinities and specific femininities and thus unequal gender relations, and Hoang describes how each form of gender hegemony reflects and reproduces Vietnam's changing association to globalization. I provide two examples below.

In a "high-end hostess bar," Hoang found that primarily upper-middle-class Vietnamese businessmen frequent this bar and construct a hegemonic masculinity that in part involves successfully attracting foreign investments from Asian business partners. The Vietnamese businessmen entice foreign investors by exhibiting signs of conspicuous consumption in the form of expensive alcohol, ostentatious commodities, unsparing tips, and sexual access to attractive Vietnamese women. The intent here is for the Vietnamese businessmen to demonstrate to prospective investors their elite status in a society that is now a major global player and thus an excellent place to invest capital. The women sex workers reinforce the

Vietnamese businessmen's hegemonic masculinity by practicing feminine deference toward both groups of men in a variety of ways, such as
pouring their drinks, lighting their cigarettes, and feeding them. They
bow when greeting the men, they sit next to them in a submissive way,
and when "clinking" glasses during a toast the women's glass is always
lower than the men's glass. The women also change their bodies through
rhinoplasty and lightening their skin, as well as dieting by eating only
one meal a day that consists of a bowl of noodles and two eggs. Through
all these practices the sex workers in this bar come to embody a subordinate pan-Asian modern erotic femininity influenced by pop culture from
Hong Kong, South Korea, and Japan. As Hoang (2015, 130, 138) puts it,
this particularized femininity "conveys a deliberately exuberant projec-
tion of Vietnam's new position as an emerging economic player within
the globalscape" and assumes "their inferior positions in relation to local
and global men." The ability of Vietnamese businessmen to attract
foreign investment and construct a situational hegemonic masculinity
then hinges on sex workers' well-groomed and practiced feminine bodies—these men contest global North white men's dominance through this
unequal gendered setting. Gender hegemony inside this bar is one small
slice of the local pie that sustains the global economy because it assures
that Vietnam is a vital and enterprising market where return on investment will materialize.

At the time of the study US and European businessmen no longer had
access to such high-end hostess bars, so they patronized "low-end" estab-
lishments. Such hostess bars in Ho Chi Minh City are filled with upper-
strata working- and middle-class global North expatriate men who have
lost their jobs, or maintained failed businesses, in their home country.
Once in Vietnam they accept inferior positions in Vietnamese companies
headed by Vietnamese CEOs. In the evenings the men frequent these
hostess bars in search of gender and sexual interactions that compensate
for their lack of masculine power in the global North and their "inferior"
position in Vietnam. They construct a sentimental hegemonic masculinity
that affirms the superiority of global North white men. Reading this masculine yearning, the sex workers buttress this hegemonic masculinity by
fashioning a "Third World" dependent femininity based on financial
support from global North white men, which in turn satisfies the racialized and sexualized desires of these men. Expatriate men are interested in
developing long-term patriarchal relationships with dark-skinned, tradi-

tionally slim Vietnamese women; they are not interested in sex-for-money exchanges but rather relationships with women "who make them feel desired" (148). The sex workers play on their desire by constructing themselves as virtuous "Third World village girls" who are poor and in need of financial support. They have breast implants rather than rhinoplasty, they wear eye makeup that produces a "smokey-eye effect," and they generally shape their bodies to look "Third World" by wearing cheap, traditional clothing and darken their skin through tanning and/or the use of bronzers. As Hoang (146) puts it: "Altering their skin color was the most notable strategy these women adopted to racialize their bodies in a way that would exaggerate their appearance as poor women in a Third World country." The sex workers then reflected the racialized and sexualized desires of the expatriate men who were in search of an "authentic" experience in Vietnam. They orchestrate "Third World dependent" femininity by portraying Vietnam as a "Third World" nation, inferior to the wealthy global North, and "by presenting themselves as innocent victims of that poverty" (150). The men end up constructing a particularized recuperating white global North hegemonic masculinity by compassionately providing much cash in the form of benevolent remittances to their new "girlfriends" for the purpose of helping them find a morally acceptable trade, escape poverty, and contribute funds to their putative financially strapped families. This relationship of inequality involves improvised "innocent" Third World poor feminine women and financially reliable "rescuer" hegemonically masculine white men that yields a continued flow of cash to both the women and their families as well as to Vietnam generally. In this way foreign direct investment was connected to sex work and unequal gender relations in a different way than in the high-end bar. What this study revealed then is different types of hegemonic masculinities and complementary femininities that intersect with race, class, bodies, and nation. We "see" how the global is linked to the local settings of hostess bars through the construction of unequal gender relations involving particularized femininities.

In short, the studies discussed in this section demonstrate that certain femininities are essential to the continued boundlessness of hegemonic masculinities and how they often are hidden in plain sight. And additional scholarship has confirmed this conclusion (see, for example, Silva 2008; Miller 2004; Schnurr, Zayts, and Hopkins 2016; and Pruitt 2017).

FLEETING HEGEMONIC MASCULINITIES

Hybrids usually are concurrently *fleeting* hegemonic masculinities, which are practiced briefly; they are short lived and momentary, yet they are culturally ascendant despite the fact that they move and pass quickly. And likewise, fleeting hegemonic masculinities are pervasive yet hidden in plain sight. Earlier I referred to popular boys in school who for the most part construct an in-school dominant and celebrated form of non-hegemonic masculinity, yet these same boys now and then temporarily and thus fleetingly fashion an in-school localized hegemonic masculinity through the practice of bullying "Other" boys.

An example of a regional fleeting hegemonic masculinity is a recent General Electric (GE) television advertisement broadcast throughout the United States. In this advertisement we first see a working-class family—father, mother, and young adult son—sitting across from each other in the parents' living room, and it is clear that the son was recently hired at GE. The following dialogue then takes place:

> FATHER, *sitting holding a large sledgehammer.* I'm proud of you, son. GE, a manufacturer. And that's why I dug this out for you. It's your grand-pappy's hammer and he would want you to have it.
> (*The father then belligerently places the hammer on the coffee table right in front of the son.*)
> MOTHER. That hammer meant a lot to him [meaning the grandfather].
> SON. Yes, GE makes powerful machines, but I'll be writing the code that will allow those machines to share information with each other. (*The parents look at each other in a very bewildered way.*) And I'll be changing the way the world—
> FATHER, *interrupting in a hostile way.* You can't pick it up, can you? (*The son looks at his father in an anxious and distressed manner, and he does not attempt to pick up the hammer.*] Go ahead, you can't lift the hammer.
> MOTHER. It's okay, though, you're going to change the world.
> FATHER. Just pick up the hammer.
> SON. I don't need it.
> FATHER. Pick up the hammer. Pick it up.

This advertisement represents an example of a regional fleeting hegemonic masculinity. The advertisement was broadcast society-wide, it lasted only forty-three seconds, yet it personified a working-class father feminizing his soon-to-be middle-class son. The father demonstrated physical strength and superiority (culturally defined masculine qualities) while the son embodied physical weakness and inferiority (culturally defined feminine qualities). By means of this advertisement, then, we have the transitory ascendancy of a regional fleeting hegemonic masculinity that circulates a legitimating discursive justification for unequal gender relations, and it is once again hidden in plain sight.

A second example of a fleeting hegemonic masculinity is a case discussed by Patricia Martin in her important research on practicing gender in transnational corporations. In this work, Martin (2003, 346) reports on an interaction between Tom and Betsy, both vice presidents in a Fortune 100 company, who stood

> talking in a hallway after a meeting. Along the hallway were offices but none was theirs. A phone started to ring in one office and after three or so rings, Tom said to Betsy, "Why don't you get that?" Betsy was surprised by Tom's request but answered the phone anyway and Tom returned to his office.

Afterward, Betsy confronted Tom by stating: "I'm a vice-president too, Tom, and you treated me like a secretary. What were you thinking?" Tom's response was, "I did not even think about it" (346). Although Betsy blames Tom for this incident, they are both equal participants in an instance of a localized, dominating form of fleeting hegemonic masculinity. Tom clearly commanded and controlled the situation by directing Betsy to answer the phone, and Betsy was obedient and complied with Tom's request and answered the phone. What we have then in this momentary situation is the social construction of culturally supported "superior" masculine qualities in unequal relation to culturally supported "inferior" feminine qualities and thus a brief and short-lived contribution to the omnipresence of unequal gender relations that is hidden in plain sight. The overall shape of the unequal encounter was hidden from both contributors: although Betsy quickly recognized the inequality, her actual participation seemingly remained invisible to her, and Tom did not recognize at all what he did until confronted by Betsy.

A final example of fleeting hegemonic masculinities is the case of US president Donald Trump. Certain practices by Trump illustrate the fluid, fluctuating, and temporary nature of hegemonic masculinity and how the transformations of his diverse hegemonic masculinities are highly contingent on context. Permit me to briefly discuss a few examples (this discussion is drawn from Messerschmidt and Bridges 2017).

First, in his speeches and public statements prior to being elected president—and broadcast both regionally and globally—Trump momentarily bullied and subordinated "Other" men by referring to them as "weak," "low energy," or as "losers," or implying they are "inept" or a "wimp." For example, during several Republican presidential debates, Trump consistently labeled Marco Rubio as "little Marco," described Jeb Bush as "low-energy Jeb," implied that John McCain is a "wimp" because he was captured and tortured during the Vietnam War, and suggested that contemporary military veterans battling PTSD are "inept" because they "can't handle" the "horror" they observed in combat. In contrast, Trump consistently referred to himself as, for example, strong, a fighter, and the embodiment of success. In each case, Trump briefly ascribes culturally defined "inferior" subordinate gender qualities to his opponents while imbuing himself with culturally defined "superior" masculine qualities. This pairing signifies an unequal relationship between different masculinities: one both dominating and hegemonic (Trump) and one subordinate (the "Other" men). And because these statements by Trump were broadcast nationwide and indeed globally, each symbolizes a fleeting regional and global illustration of dominating hegemonic masculinity.

A second example of Trump's fluid yet fleeting hegemonic masculinity applies to the way he has discursively depicted himself—again regionally and globally—as *the* heroic masculine "protector" of all Americans. This compassion may appear, at first blush, at odds with the hegemonic masculinity just discussed. For example, in his Republican Convention speech Trump argued that he alone could lead the country back to safety by protecting the American people through the deportation of "dangerous" and "illegal" Mexican and Muslim immigrants and by "sealing the border." In so doing, Trump implied that Americans are *unable* to defend themselves—a fact he used to justify his need to "join the political arena." Trump stated: "I will liberate our citizens from crime and terrorism and lawlessness" by "restoring law and order" throughout the country—"I will fight for you, I will win for you." Here Trump discursively adopts momentarily a position as white hegemonic masculine *protector* of Americans against men of color, instructing all US citizens to entrust their lives to him; in return, he offers safety. Trump depicts himself as aggressive, invulnerable, and able to protect while all remaining US citizens are depicted as dependent and uniquely vulnerable. Trump situates himself as "superior" to "his" "inferior" subjects, which is analogous to the patriarchal masculine protector toward his wife and other members of the patriarchal household. But simultaneously, Trump presents himself as a compassionate, caring, and kindhearted benevolent protector, and thereby constructs a hybrid yet fleeting hegemonic masculinity consisting of both masculine and feminine qualities. Thus we have the construction of a heroic protector and a transitory hybrid hegemonic masculinity both regionally and globally.

Third, in the 2005 interaction between Trump and Billy Bush on the now infamous *Access Hollywood* tour bus, Trump presumes he is entitled to the bodies of women, and (not surprisingly) he admits committing sexual assault against women because, according to him, he has the right. He depicts women as collections of body parts and disregards their desires, needs, expressed preferences, and their consent. Since the video was aired, more women have come forward and accused Trump of sexual harassment and assault. Missed in discussions of this interaction is how that dialogue actually contradicts, and thus reveals, the myth of Trump's *protector* hegemonic masculinity. The brief interaction on the bus demonstrates that Trump is not a "protector" at all; he is a "predator." Yet because of the unequal relational nature of Trump's discourse between predator (Trump) and victims (women), we have here the construction of a predatory fleeting hegemonic (hetero)masculinity.

Trump's various hegemonic masculinities then are fluid, contradictory, situational, and intersectional, and demonstrate the diverse and crisscrossing pillars of support that uphold inequalities worldwide. From different types of hegemonic masculinities, Trump's chameleonic display is part of the contemporary landscape of gender, class, race, age, sexuality, and nationality relations and inequalities. Trump does not construct a consistent form of hegemonic masculinity. Rather, the case of Trump indicates how individuals can oscillate, and in each case his oscillations attempt to overcome the specter of femininity—the fear of being the unmasculine man—through a series of particularized fleeting hegemonic masculinities and therefore the varying constructions of unequal gender relations.

THE INTERNET

Scholarly work on the construction of hegemonic masculinities throughout the internet has been a slow process but has increased and intensified
in the last ten years. One of earliest examinations of this topic was Lori
Kendall's (2000) study of the online forum BlueSky. Kendall documented
the construction of one type of hegemonic masculinity on this forum by
self-described "nerds." As "nerds," participants recognized their lack of
masculine status outside the forum in the "real" world, but through online interaction these "nerds" discursively fashioned unequal gender relations by collectively distancing themselves from women and femininity
while simultaneously dehumanizing women as sexual objects. Although
the vast majority of the young men who participated in this forum identified as heterosexual, they accepted gay and bisexual men within the
group; yet these latter men likewise participated in the sexist banter that
subordinated heterosexual women. Kendall concluded that a form of
"male bonding" occurred whereby the subordination of women "com-
prises a more important component of masculine identity than sexual
distance from men" (271) and thus reproduced gender hegemony in a
unique way.

More recently, Debbie Ging (2017) examined how men's rights activists have migrated to the internet and established a "manosphere,"
which consists of a variety of blogs and forums engaged in the discursive
construction of unequal gender relations. More specifically, Ging investi-
gated the issue of how hegemonic masculinities are amplified locally,
regionally, and globally through the speed, anonymity, and social
(dis)embodiment embedded in manosphere social narratives. What Ging
found is that the internet has greatly magnified the presence of hegemonic masculinities throughout the world, overlapping among local, regional, and global configurations. In addition to this "transnational homogen-
ization," Ging identified "extreme misogyny" as one of the most striking
features of the manosphere. For example, she discovered that it is quite
common for women to be labeled "cumdumpsters," "feminazis," "fem-
tards," and "cunts" throughout the blogs and forums (9). Ging (9) furthermore uncovered an increasing shift away from men's rights activism
toward personal attacks on particular women: "This has been most evident in the proliferation of death and rape threats made by men's rights
advocates to female journalists, game developers, and games journalists."

The narratives today then seemingly have less to do with political action and more to do with "the collective venting of anger" (11).

Similar to Kendall's study, Ging's study shows that the manosphere is generally accepting of gay men, and both gay and straight men profess misogynist views. In other words, the narratives mobilize a pro-gay discourse while simultaneously establishing gender hegemony. This online *hybrid* hegemonic masculinity of the manosphere travels locally, regionally, and globally in primarily an anonymous and disembodied way. As Ging (5) concludes, the omnipresence of hegemonic masculinities and thus unequal gender relations is intensified "by the technological affordances of social media," and the anonymity allows participants to construct certain masculine personas while "liberating them from physical limitations" associated with the body (see also Schmitz and Kazyak 2016).

In a compelling recent article, Nathaniel Burke (2016) examined the relationship between sexuality and masculinity found on a gay adult film industry website that features "str8" films; these films depict sex between two or more men where at least one of the men is heterosexual. Through a content analysis Burke coded the portrayal of the actors as either masculine (e.g., rough, hunk, stud) or feminine (e.g., queen, yummy, small) and as either "bait" (homosexual) or "straight" (heterosexual). The results indicated that "bait" performers possessed mostly feminine characteristics while the "straight" actors had masculine qualities, and the "straight" men were more often penetrators and the "bait" men more often penetrated. In other words, Burke found that the intersection of sexuality, gender, and inequality is constructed through these films: the "straight" performers are intelligible to consumers as heterosexual, masculine, and powerful whereas the "bait" actors are intelligible as homosexual, feminine, and subordinate. Burke (2016, 250) concluded that these films "provide cultural material which reinforces the mechanisms of 'doing' hegemonic and subordinate masculinities at a regional level" that results in the perpetuation of gender hegemony at that level.

Scholarship documents the wide range of websites in which hegemonic masculinities and consequently unequal gender relations are discursively constructed on the internet, such as Facebook pages belonging to the Slut Walk movement (Cook and Hasmath 2014), weight loss forums (Bennett and Gough 2013), dating profiles on Match.com (Walker and Eller 2016), online video games (Fox and Tang 2014), and sport message boards (Kian, Clavio, Vincent, and Shaw 2011).

INTERSECTIONALITY

As pointed out in chapter 1, socialist feminist theorists viewed both capitalism and patriarchy as interacting and co-reproducing each other. Socialist feminist theorists—as the first to attempt an "intersectional" analysis—argued that to understand production relations we must recognize how they interact with reproduction relations, and to understand the latter requires an examination of how they interact with the former. In other words, people's overall life experiences are shaped by the mutual interaction of capitalism and patriarchy. Contemporary studies of "intersectionality" have moved beyond this concentration on the *interaction* of capitalism and patriarchy, encouraging examinations of how gender, class, race/ethnicity, age, sexuality, and nationality mutually *constitute* and thus form and transform each other (Christensen and Jensen 2014; Patil 2013).

Numerous studies previously discussed in this chapter exemplify an intersectional analysis: for example, Barber's (2008, 2016) study examined how hegemonic masculinity is constituted by class and sexuality; Burke (2016) scrutinized how hegemonic masculinity is formed through sexuality; Hirsch and Kachtan (2017) show how a celebrated dominant masculinity is composed by race/ethnicity, class, and nationality; Hoang (2015) demonstrated how differing forms of hegemonic masculinity and their accompanying femininities are constituted by race, class, sexuality, and nationality; and the fleeting hegemonic masculinities—such as the GE advertisement and the various discourses by President Trump—revealed how hegemonic masculinities are constituted by class, race, age, sexuality, and nationality. What these studies demonstrate is that the salience of gender, race, class, age, sexual, and nationality relations is important because each form of inequality is ubiquitous; that is, the significance of each shifts from context to context. For example, in one situation race and sexuality (but not class, age, or nationality) may be important for understanding the construction of hegemonic masculinities; in another, age, class, and nationality but not race and sexuality may be significant; and in still other situations age and sexuality may be more important than race, class, and nationality. In other words, gender, race, class, age, sexuality, and nationality are not absolutes and are not always equally significant in every social setting in which individuals construct unequal gender relations—they *constitute* each other in differing ways depending upon the particular social situation.

Although race, class, age, sexuality, and nationality vary in salience by social situation, these unequal social relations in different ways join us in a common relationship to others: we share gendered, race, class, age, sexual, and nation structural space. Consequently, common or shared blocks of intersecting knowledge about interpersonal practices evolve through interaction in which particular ideals and activities differ in significance. Through such interaction, gender, race, class, age, sexuality, and nationality become institutionalized, permitting, for example, men and women to draw on such existing but previously formed ways of doing or practicing gender, race, class, age, sexuality, and nationality to construct particular strategies for specific settings. The specific criteria of gender, race, class, age, sexuality, and nationality thus are embedded in the social situations and recurrent practices by which such unequal relations are structured. Nevertheless, accountability to race, class, age, sexuality, and nationality is not always, in every social situation, critical to the particular hegemonically masculine interaction. And in my previous work I have emphasized this variable intersectionality (Messerschmidt 2014). Permit me to discuss one historical and one contemporary example of what this varying mutual constitution of intersectionality looks like in practice.

Regarding the historical example, I (Messerschmidt 2014) examined the relationship between large-scale social change and the intersection of race, sexuality, a localized hegemonic masculinity, and lynching during Reconstruction and its immediate aftermath (1865–1900) in the US South. What I found is that Reconstruction created the social context for constructing an alarmist discourse about African American men's sexuality, with the resulting pronounced public mob violence employed by white supremacist men. White supremacist men bonded into lynching mobs that provided arenas for an individual to prove himself a white man among white men. During the economic turbulence of Reconstruction and its immediate aftermath, gender, race, and sexuality became extraordinarily salient, and a particular type of "whiteness" and heterosexual hegemonic masculinity was constituted as one by means of collective practices that subordinated and feminized African American men. White supremacist men, then, simultaneously were doing a specific type of whiteness and hegemonic masculinity as they were doing lynching; the three merged into and thus were constituted as one entity through the same practice (class, age, and nationality were not salient), and a localized white supremacist hegemonic masculinity was reproduced.

Regarding a contemporary example, I turn to one of my life-history studies in which I interviewed a white working-class teenage boy (eighteen years old) whom I called Sam and who ended up sexually assaulting two eight-year-old girls he was babysitting. Sam manipulated both of these girls into fondling him and performing oral sex on him for two years. The sexual violence produced a localized hegemonic masculine/feminine relationship because it inscribed the girls, who embody weakness and vulnerability, as feminine and Sam, who embodies strength and invulnerability, as masculine, thus constructing "inferior" feminine survivors and a "superior" masculine perpetrator. Gender difference and inequality then are established through Sam's heterosexual violent practices. And concurrently gender, age, and sexuality are constituted by each other through the same practice; at once all three were salient to this particular hegemonically masculine practice in this specific social situation, whereas class, race, and nationality were not.

The vast majority of studies on intersectionality and hegemonic masculinities are limited to what Vrushali Patil (2013) labels "domestic intersectionality" because they do not recognize nationality. However, and as demonstrated in the lynching and Sam examples, just as class was not salient to either particular construction of a localized hegemonic masculinity, neither were the dynamics of nationality. In other words, nationality—like other forms of inequality—is not, in every social setting, critical to the constitution of hegemonic masculinities.

Nevertheless, I do agree with Patil that notions of intersectionality and their relation to hegemonic masculinities must be globalized. Through the work of Valerie Orlando (2001), Patil (2013, 856) presents a relevant illustration supporting the significance of "globalized intersectionality":

> Valerie Orlando (2001) points out that French colonial discourse infantilized and emasculated Arab men, constructing them at once as sexual deviants who possessed a "masculine weakness and childlike behavior" (Orlando 2001, 181) and as barbaric in their excessive domination of Arab women. Such discourse authorized "a *carte blanche* for Euro-

peans' tutelage. . . . It was [the French man's] duty to show these Arab despots the way to civilization" (Orlando 2001, 181).

French colonists then constructed a global intersectional hegemonic masculinity and thus unequal gender relations through the mutual constitution of gender, race/ethnicity, and nation. Arab men were deemed "inferior" for allegedly embodying infantile, feminine, and toxic gender qualities while French men were considered "superior" for supposedly embodying gender qualities of authority, control, and tutelage.

Similarly and more recently, during the US military invasion and occupation of Iraq, hegemonic masculinities were constituted through race and nation. For example, Laleh Khalili (2011) studied the relationship between US soldiers and the local Iraqi security forces the soldiers trained to create indigenous police and military forces as proxies for the conquering army. Khalili found that the local Iraqi men joined security forces because it was the only steady form of income under military occupation. During training sessions and interactions with US soldiers, the Iraqi men were "constantly berated, 'effeminised,' called 'women' or 'pussies,' and seen as inadequate and passive enforcers of good order by their trainers" (1484). An unequal masculine relationship then was structured through discourse and based on race and nationality. Moreover, if the Iraqi men refused to "fight" alongside the US soldiers, they were immediately subordinated as inferior and effeminate. For example, during the US military assault on the town of Falluja in which many Iraqi trainees fled the devastation, one US military officer announced, "When are these people going to discover their manhood and stand and fight with us to save their city?" (1484). And other US military personnel often referred to the Iraqi men as a "bunch of women," "pussies," "cowards," and so forth. As Khalili reasons, in the above discourses the US military men are deemed masculine and the Iraqi men feminine and, thus, imperial conquest is considered to be the "natural" expression of masculinity, and those who "fail" to participate in such conquest simply are feminine. Loyalty and military service to the conquering army redeems Iraqi men from femininity. In this setting, then, race and nationality intersect to constitute unequal masculine relations and thereby construct a specific form of global hegemonic masculinity.

In short, intersectionality amplifies and thus contributes significantly to our understanding of the omnipresence of hegemonic masculinities locally, regionally, and globally and how they are simultaneously hidden in plain sight.

THE GLOBAL SOUTH

One of the most recent amplifications of the reformulated model of hegemonic masculinity is research on the construction of hegemonic and non-hegemonic masculinities in the global South. Connell (2016) once again has been at the forefront of this development, arguing that to gain a deeper understanding of hegemonic masculinities we need to learn from both the global North *and* the global South. Academic work on masculinities from the 1950s to the 1990s in the global South added a significant dimension to the notion of hegemonic masculinities by demonstrating the unique relationship among globalization, colonialism, and masculinity (Mernissi 1975; Paz 1950; Nandy 1983; Morrell 1994, 1998, 2001). We learn from this early work that to gain appropriate knowledge about the global South, scholars must begin from a truly historical perspective, examining, for example, how colonialism disrupted gender relations and imposed gender hegemony, such as the suppression of two-spirited people (or the *berdache*) among the indigenous people of North America (Williams 1986). Evelyn Blackwood (1994) documented this change by showing that prior to European intervention, egalitarian gender and sexual systems with third and fourth genders were prevalent in many Native American societies. But by the late nineteenth century such forms of gender equality had all but disappeared because of European colonization and its hegemonic discourse centering on the "superiority" of men, the "inferiority" of women, and the "naturalness" of heterosexuality.

Another example of the disruption of gender relations due to colonization occurred in Peru. In a recent study, Juana R. Vera Delgado and Margreet Zwarteveen (2017) found that in pre-colonial Peru, gender relations were much more equal than those of Europe at the time. Women and men were ascribed different qualities and abilities, yet the binary characteristics were considered equal and complementary. There existed reciprocity between humans and the environment so that even mountains, rivers, and animals were seen as living beings, each with their own gender. Women served as high priestesses in numerous temples, and women were prominent in religious and political affairs. Both men and women had the freedom to choose their partner; they had equal access to land, water, and livestock; and daughters inherited through the maternal line. However, after colonization by Spain—the colonial period was from 1532 to 1821—the linkages between genders of humans and genders of living nature posed a challenge to the Spaniards. In fact, the Spaniards considered the gender relations they encountered in Peru to be "madness, sinful, beastly, and barbarian. Existence of these beliefs even made some of them doubt whether indigenous people were at all human" (Delgado and Zwarteveen 2017, 147). Moreover, the fact that daughters could inherit land through the maternal line and women could choose their future husband led the Spaniards to view indigenous men as weak, effeminate, or not men at all. Consequently, the colonizers began to establish masculine and patriarchal rule in Peru. Priestesses were persecuted, women were forced out of politics and segregated in the home, and men were provided with higher education, all of which were considered part of "civilizing" efforts by the colonizers.

Decolonization is likewise an important part of the historical development in understanding gender hegemony in the global South, such as how liberation movements often mobilized women; yet, after gaining independence gender hegemony often was imposed (Connell 2016). Many postcolonial societies were not, however, well defined in terms of gender and actually constructed quite chaotic gender relations, while for other societies a stable structure of gender hegemony was never achieved but for some gender hegemony was stabilized. In Peru, for example, the postcolonial period extended and deepened the implementation of unequal gender relations established during colonialism (Delgado and Zwarteveen 2017).

Connell (2016) also notes how neoliberal globalization impacted the development of hegemonic masculinities in the global South. I previously discussed examples of neoliberal globalization in chapter 3, as well as the effects neoliberalism has had on the formation of hegemonic masculinities in particular global South countries. Here I add a particularly fascinating study of Kenya by Sanyu A. Mojola (2014) that outlines how hegemonic masculinities can be fashioned in unique ways. Mojola interviewed widowed older women and poor young men who are members of the Luo ethnic group of western Kenya. At the time of the study, the Luo faced the worst HIV/AIDS epidemic in Kenya, which resulted in a large number of widows because of husband death. The Luo practice "widow inheritance," whereby a brother or other adult male relative "inherits" the widow upon the death of her husband. However, many male relatives likewise died from AIDS or simply refused to inherit widows, resulting in an overwhelming number of unaccompanied widows. Simultaneously, Kenya experienced high unemployment rates among young Luo men who now lacked financial resources to construct hegemonic masculinity, which in part involved "the provision of money to girlfriends, bridewealth to a woman's relatives, and a home and land for a wife" (345).

As a result of these particular social conditions, what Mojola found is that many of the young men and older widows joined together to form a domestic relationship that allowed the older women to fulfill the patriarchal obligation of being "inherited" by a man, and the young men were now able to forge a pathway to hegemonic masculinity. Through this relationship a widow actually constructed what was identified earlier as a "hybrid femininity," because the women cooked and cared for the young men and were now "inherited" (traditional feminine practices), but they also sought out a young man, brought him into their home to live symbolically as a "husband," and financially provided for him (traditional masculine practices). In relation to the widows, the young men clearly benefited and were privileged from this arrangement, in the sense that a large number of widows created a "buyer's market" for the young men and thus they could place demands on widows for special types of food to eat, substantial resources, and even an "allowance." The young men took advantage of the widow inheritance tradition and thus enjoyed a leisurely hegemonic masculine life without the bother of traditional husband obligations.

For the older widows and the young men, then, the neoliberal-induced economic crisis, the HIV/AIDS epidemic, and the tradition of widow inheritance resulted in both forging together an unequal gender relationship involving a particular form of hegemonic masculinity. But this distinct partnership had consequences outside the relationship as well. The widows used an unconventional method to meet the social demands of widow inheritance, yet in the process they participated in the widespread preservation of that gender-oppressive system. And the monetary benefits provided to the young men eventually allowed them to leave the "inheritor" position, contract a marriage with a younger woman, and set up an independent (and usually patriarchal) household.

Despite this evidence on the reproduction of gender hegemony in certain global South locales, Connell (2016) further demonstrates that neoliberal regimes have also resulted in egalitarian, rather than hegemonic, gender relations at the local level. Consequently, Connell (2016, 314, 313) concludes that

> the changing structures of imperialism and neoliberal global power are a vital part of our understanding of masculinities. They represent both the structural conditions of hegemonic projects now and the sedimented consequences of gender projects in the past. Hegemony cannot be presumed in the violent and exploitative relations that constitute imperial and transnational gender orders. But hegemony is constantly under construction, renovation, and contestation. . . . The emerging world gender order is far from being a smoothly-running machine. Rather, it is a scene of conflicting hegemonic projects. It has multiple tiers, where different configurations of masculinity are at work, and come into conflict.

This significant history of hegemonic masculinities in the global South—or lack thereof—adds to our knowledge of the omnipresence of hegemonic masculinities worldwide and how globally they often are hidden in plain sight.

CONCLUSION

These few examples of contemporary research—that barely scratch the surface of contemporary scholarship on hegemonic masculinities—amplify the reformulated model and its grasp of multiple hegemonic masculinities. The studies discussed in this chapter enlarge upon the reformulated model and detail new research directions for, and further conceptualizations of, hegemonic masculinities. In particular, they demonstrate the omnipresent nature of hegemonic masculinities, yet simultaneously show how these complex, specific masculinities are essentially hidden in plain sight. What's more, these examples illustrate that particular hierarchical gender relationships between men and women, between masculinity and femininity, and among masculinities are legitimated—remarkably discerning certain of the essential features of the all-pervasive reproduction of unequal gender relations.

The studies further demonstrate the significance of distinguishing between "hegemonic" and "dominant" masculinities, which will of course allow more solid research on when and how both types of masculinities actually are constructed and when they are not. That research question is essential because there has been much confusion among scholars, especially regarding "slippage" and thus wrongly labeling dominant masculinities as actually existing hegemonic masculinities. In addition to this important distinction as part of the amplification of the reformulated model, recognizing the differences among hegemonic masculinities is a major part of the amplification of the concept, especially in terms of local, regional, and global settings, but also in terms of hybrids, dominating versus protective, and material versus discursive. And given the fact that hegemonic masculinities necessarily constitute a relationship, femininities are essential to the amplification of the reformulated model of hegemonic masculinities and thus must be a principal part of future research. The chapter highlighted additional areas that have amplified the reformulated model, such as the recurring nature of fleeting hegemonic masculinities and how they routinely are fluid, contingent, haphazard, provisional, and temporary, the importance of intersectionality and how hegemonic masculinities therefore differ by reason of their constitution with other inequalities, the prominence of the internet and the electronic complexion of hegemonic masculinities, and finally hegemonic masculinities in the global South.

The amplification of the reformulated model then demonstrates that the quotidian prevalence of hegemonic masculinities widely disseminates the cultural knowledge people utilize to guide their gendered social action; the variety of hegemonic masculinities provide models of relations between men and women, between masculinity and femininity, and among masculinities. And because of the ubiquity of hegemonic masculinities, gender inequality often is broadly accepted and unquestioned. Gender hegemony functions to obscure unequal gender relations while effectively permeating public and private life, encouraging all to endorse, unite around, and embody such unequal gender relations. Hegemonic masculinities are expansively distributed as culturally ascendant prototypes of gender relations throughout local, regional, and global levels, they are part of normal, everyday life—they are customary all around us.

The empirical evidence presented in this chapter suggests that hegemonic masculinity must be conceptualized wholly in plural terms. I have explored the omnipresence of hegemonic masculinities at the local, regional, and global levels, how they are hidden in plain sight, the reasons for the continued compliance to and acceptance of unequal gender relations, the variable ways they are constituted by and therefore intersect with other inequalities, and how this plurality establishes gender hegemony as culturally exalted.

Although the hegemonic masculinities just discussed are diverse, the relational practices and discursive meanings are not—each in its unique way legitimates unequal gender relations between men and women, between masculinity and femininity, and among masculinities—they collectively constitute a social structure. These seemingly individual practices of hegemonic masculinity do not occur in a vacuum. Instead, they are situationally influenced by and in turn reproduce the gendered relational and discursive social structures in particular settings. Hegemonic masculinities are configurations of social practice that produce simultaneously particular social relations *and* social meanings, and they are culturally significant because they shape a sense of what is "acceptable" and "unacceptable" gendered behavior for copresent interactants in specific situations. I expand on these ideas in chapter 5 and elaborate a theoretical framework for conceptualizing the social construction of such pervasive hegemonic masculinities and thus unequal gender relations.

FIVE

Theory

In chapter 5 I present a theoretical framework—what I label "structured action theory"—for conceptualizing the amplification of the reformulated model of hegemonic masculinities. To understand the social construction of hegemonic masculinities locally, regionally, and globally, we must first grasp what structured action theory labels "doing" sex, gender, and sexuality. Following this, I discuss how the theory engages with the relationship among hegemonic masculinities and intersectionality, structured action, embodiment, and masculinity challenges.

DOING SEX, GENDER, AND SEXUALITY

Reflecting various theoretical origins (M. S. Archer 2003, 2007, 2012; Connell 1987, 1995; Giddens 1976, 1984; Goffman 1963, 1972, 1979; Kessler and McKenna 1978; Mouzelis 2008; Sartre 1956; West and Fenstermaker 1995; West and Zimmerman 1987), structured action theory emphasizes the reflexive construction of sex, gender, and sexuality as situated social, interactional, and embodied accomplishments. In other words, sex, gender, and sexuality are all social constructions and grow out of embodied social practices in specific social structural settings and serve to inform such practices in reciprocal relation. Understanding each of these is essential to conceptualizing hegemonic masculinities.

Regarding "sex," historical and social conditions shape the character and definition of "sex" (social identification as "male" or "female"). Sex and its meanings are given concrete expression by the specific social relations and historical context in which they are embedded. Historical studies on the definition of sex show its clear association with sexuality, and gender has proved always to be already involved. The work of Thomas Laqueur (1990) is exemplary in this regard, and in his important book *Making Sex*, he shows that for two thousand years a "one-sex model" dominated scientific and popular thought in which male and female bodies were not conceptualized in terms of difference. From antiquity to the beginning of the seventeenth century, male and female bodies were seen as having the same body parts, even in terms of genitalia, with the vagina regarded as an interior penis, the vulva as foreskin, the uterus as scrotum, and the ovaries as testicles. Women thus had the same body as men but the positioning of its parts was different: as one doggerel verse of the period stated, "women are but men turned outside in" (4). In the "one-sex model" the sexes were not seen as different in *kind* but rather in *degree*—woman simply was a lesser form of man. And as Laqueur (8) explains, "*Sex*, or the body, must be understood as the epiphenomenon, while *gender*, what we would take to be a cultural category, was primary or 'real.'" Inequality was imposed on bodies from the outside and seen as God's "marker" of a male and female distinction. To be a man or a woman was to have a specific place in society decreed by God, "not to *be* organically one or the other of two incommensurable sexes. Sex before the seventeenth century, in other words, was still a sociological and not an ontological category" (8).

What emerged after the Enlightenment was a "two-sex model" involving a foundational dichotomy between now two and only two distinct and opposite sexes, as no longer did scientific and popular thought "regard woman as a lesser version of man along a vertical axis of infinite gradations but rather an altogether different creature along a horizontal axis whose middle ground was largely empty" (Laqueur 1990, 148). And Michel Foucault's (1980, vii) well-known discussion of the "hermaphrodite" *Herculine Barbin* (what is referred today as the intersexed), demonstrates that by the mid-1800s there was no allowance for any human being to occupy a "middle ground" through "a mixture of two sexes in a single body," which consequently limited "the free choice of indeterminate individuals" and thus henceforth "everybody was to have one and only one sex." Individuals accepted previously as representatives of the "middle ground" ("hermaphrodites") were now required to submit to expert medical diagnosis to uncover their "true" sex. As Foucault (vii) continues:

> Everybody was to have his or her primary, profound, determined and determining sexual identity; as for the elements of the other sex that might appear, they could only be accidental, superficial, or even quite simply illusory. From the medical point of view, this meant that when confronted with a hermaphrodite, the doctor was no longer concerned with recognizing the presence of the two sexes, juxtaposed or intermingled, or with knowing which of the two prevailed over the other, but rather with deciphering the true sex that was hidden beneath ambiguous appearances.

Arguably, then, under the "two-sex model" it became commonplace to view *the* male sex and *the* female sex as "different in every conceivable aspect of body and soul, in every physical and moral aspect — An anatomy and physiology of incommensurability replaced a metaphysics of hierarchy in the representation of woman in relation to man" (Laqueur 1990, 5–6).

Predictably, these two now fixed, incommensurable, opposite sexes also are conceptualized as *the* source of the political, economic, and cultural lives of men and women (gender and sexuality), since "biology — the stable, ahistorical, sexed body — is understood to be the epistemic foundation for prescriptive claims about the social order" (6). It was now understood as "natural" that women are, for example, passive, submissive, and vulnerable and men are, for example, active, aggressive, and perilous. And given that anatomy is now destiny, a heterosexual instinct to procreate proceeds from the body and is "the natural state of the architecture of two incommensurable opposite sexes" (233).

The shift in thinking to a "two-sex model," consisting now of two different types of humans with complementary heterosexual natures and desires, corresponded to the emergence of the public/private split: It was now "natural" for men to enter the public realm of society, and it was "natural" for women to remain in the private sphere. Explaining these distinct gendered spaces was "resolved by grounding social and cultural differentiation of the sexes in a biology of incommensurability" (Laqueur 1990, 19). In other words, "gender" and "sexuality" became subordinated to "sex," and biology was now primary: *the* foundation of difference and inequality between men and women.

Laqueur makes clear that the change to a two-sex model was not the result of advances in science, inasmuch as the reevaluation of the body as primary occurred approximately one hundred years before alleged supporting scientific discoveries appeared. And although anatomical and physiological differences clearly exist between male and female bodies, what counts as "sex" is determined socially. In short, natural scientists had no interest in "seeing" two distinct sexes at the anatomical and concrete physiological level "until such differences became politically important" and "sex" therefore became "explicable only within the context of battles over gender and power" (10, 11).

The historical work of both Laqueur and Foucault suggests that "sex differences" do not naturally precede "gender and sexual differences" and thus challenge the radical feminist position discussed in chapter 1. As Wendy Cealey Harrison insightfully observes, it is virtually impossible to ever entirely separate the body and our understanding of it from its socially determined milieu. Arguably, what is now necessary is a reconceptualization of "the taken-for-grantedness of 'sex' as a form of categorization for human beings and examining the ways in which such a categorization is built" (2006, 43).

Following this suggestion by Cealey Harrison, it is important to recognize that in an important early work from the 1970s, Suzanne Kessler and Wendy McKenna (1978) argued that social action is constructed through taken-for-granted discourses, or what they call "incorrigible propositions." Our belief in two objectively real, biologically created constant yet opposite sexes is a telling discourse. We assume there are only two sexes; each person is simply an example of one or the other. In other words, we construct a sex dichotomy in which no dichotomy holds biologically, historically, cross-culturally, and contemporaneously (Messerschmidt 2004).

The key process in the social construction of the sex dichotomy is the active way we decide what sex a person is (Kessler and McKenna 1978, 1–20). A significant part of this sex attribution process is the notion that men have penises and women do not. We consider genitals the ultimate criterion in making sex assignments; yet, in our daily interactions we continually make sex attributions with a complete lack of information about others' genitals. Our recognition of another's sex is dependent upon the exhibit of such bodily characteristics as speech, hair, clothing, physical appearance, and other aspects of personal front—through this embodied presentation we "do" *sex*, and it is this doing that becomes a substitute for the concealed genitalia. In short, "sex" is socially constructed; we objectify ourselves as a "sex" object.

Nevertheless, "doing" *gender* (West and Zimmerman 1987) entails considerably more than the "social emblems" representing membership in one of two sex categories. Rather, the social construction of gender involves a situated social, interactional, and embodied accomplishment. Gender grows out of social practices in specific settings and serves to inform such practices in reciprocal relation. Although "sex" defines social identification as "male" or "female," "doing gender" systematically corroborates and qualifies that sex identification and category through embodied social interaction. In effect, there exists a plurality of forms in which gender is constructed: we coordinate our activities to "do" gender in situational ways (West and Zimmerman 1987).

Accordingly, early gender development in childhood occurs through an interactive process between child and parents, other children, and other adults. By reason of this interaction with others—and the social structures this interaction constitutes—children (for the most part) undertake to practice what is being preached, represented, and structured. Raewyn Connell defines the proactive adoption of specific embodied gender practices as the "moment of engagement," the moment when an individual initiates a project of masculinity or femininity as his or her own (1995, 122). The young child has in effect located him- or herself in relation to others within a sexed and gendered structured field (Jackson 2007). Children negotiate the socially structured sexed and gendered practices and their accompanying discourses that are prevalent and attributed as such in their particular milieu(s) and, in so doing, commit themselves to a *fundamental project* of sex and gender self-attribution—for example, "I'm a boy" or "I'm a girl." This fundamental self-attribution as a boy or as a girl is the primary mode by which an agent chooses to relate to the world and to express oneself in it, and thus serves as an important constraint and enabler in the social construction of sex, gender, and sexuality. What makes us human is the fact that we construct ourselves by making reflexive choices that transcend given circumstances and propel us into a future that is defined by the consequences of those choices. Doing sex and gender—normally concurrently—is a continuing process in which agents construct patterns of embodied presentations and practices that suggest a particular sex and gender in specific settings and, consequently, project themselves into a future where new situations are encountered and subsequently new reflexive choices are made (Connell 1995). There exists unity and coherence to one's fundamental sex and gender project in the sense that we tend to embody this particular sexed and gendered self—for example, "I'm a boy" or "I'm a girl"—over time and space.

Nevertheless, and although agents construct a fundamental project as either male or female, the actual accomplishment of gender may vary situationally—that is, gender is renegotiated continuously through social interaction and, therefore, one's gendered self may be fraught with contradictions and diversity in gender strategies and practices. For example, agents may situationally construct a specific fundamental gender project (e.g., masculine) that contradicts their bodily sex category (e.g., female).

Sexuality involves all erotic and nonerotic aspects of social life and social being that relate to bodily attraction or intimate bodily contact between individuals, such as arousal, desire, practice, discourse, interaction, relationship, and identity (see Jackson and Scott 2010). "Doing" sexuality encompasses the same interactional processes discussed above for "doing gender" and therefore likewise involves children initially acquiring knowledge primarily about heterosexuality through structured interaction with mothers, fathers, other children, and other adults. This initial process involves the acquisition of mostly nonerotic forms of heterosexual discursive knowledge, such as male-female marital relationships that suggest this is "where babies come from." However, to adopt such rudimentary heterosexual discursive knowledge, "doing sex" must take primacy. As Stevi Jackson and Sue Scott (2010, 91–92) point out, "We recognize someone as male or female before we make assumptions about heterosexuality or homosexuality; we cannot logically do otherwise." The homosexual/heterosexual socially structured dichotomy hinges on meaningful sexed categories, "on being able to 'see' two men or two women as 'the same' and a man and a woman as 'different'" (92). The notion of two and only two sex categories then establishes the discursive rationale for the homosexual/heterosexual socially structured dichotomy.

Once children begin to develop a sense of the erotic aspects of sexuality—which usually occurs through interaction with peers in secondary school—their sense-making is governed by their embodied sexed and gendered self (Jackson 2007). "Doing" sex, gender, and sexuality intersect here, so that our conceptualization of sex and gender impacts our understanding and practice of sexuality (both the erotic and the nonerotic aspects), and it is through sexual practices (once again both the erotic and the nonerotic) that we validate sex and gender. Agents adopt embodied sexual practices as a "moment of engagement," a moment when the individual begins to affix a specific sexual project to one's fundamental sex and gender project, constructing, for example, heteromasculine and heterofeminine identities. Sex, gender, and sexuality are produced and reproduced by embodied individuals, and interaction with others is essential to one's ability to negotiate and fit in to ongoing and situationally structured patterns of sex, gender, and sexuality.

Crucial to this negotiation and "fitting in" is the notion of "accountability" (West and Zimmerman 1987; Hollander 2013). Accountability—as the cornerstone of social structural reproduction—refers to individuals anticipating assessment of their behavior, and therefore they configure and orchestrate their embodied actions in relation to how such actions may be interpreted by others in the particular social context in which they occur. In other words, in their daily activities agents attempt to be identified bodily as "female" or "male" through sex, gender, and sexual practices. Within socially structured interaction, then, we encourage and expect others to attribute to us a particular sex category—to avoid negative assessments—and we facilitate the ongoing task of accountability through demonstrating that we are male or female by means of concocted practices that may be interpreted accordingly. The specific meanings of sex, gender, and sexuality are defined in social interaction and therefore through personal practice. Doing gender and sexuality renders social action accountable in terms of structurally available gender and sexual practices appropriate to one's sex category in the specific social situation in which one acts. It is the particular structured gender and sexual relations in specific settings that give behavior its sexed, gendered, and sexual meanings.

In this view, then, although we decide quite early in life that we're a boy or a girl and later we adopt an identity as straight, gay, lesbian, bisexual, and so forth, the actual everyday "doing" of sex, gender, and sexuality is accomplished systematically and is never a static or a finished product. Rather, people fashion sex, gender, and sexuality in specific social situations—they are fluid, contingent, provisional, and temporary constructions. People participate in self-regulating conduct whereby they monitor their own and others' embodied social actions, and they respond to and draw from available social structures. This perspective allows for innovation and flexibility in sex, gender, and sexuality construction—and the ongoing potentiality of normative transgression—but also underscores the ever-present possibility of any sexed, gendered, and sexual activity being assessed by copresent interactants. Sex category serves as a resource for the interpretation of situated social conduct, as copresent interactants in each setting attempt to hold accountable behavior as "female" or "male"; that is, socially defined membership in one sex category is used as a means of discrediting or accepting gender and sexual practices. Although we construct ourselves as male or female, we situationally embody gender and sexuality according to our own unique experiences, and accountability attempts to maintain *congruence* among sex, gender, and sexuality; that is, male = masculinity = sexually desires females, and female = femininity = sexually desires males.

Sex, gender, and sexuality construction results from individuals often—but not always—considering the content of their social action and then acting only after internal deliberation about the purpose and consequence of their behavior. *Reflexivity* refers to the capacity to engage in internal conversations with oneself about particular social experiences and then decide how to respond appropriately. In reflexivity we internally mull over specific social events and interactions, we consider how such circumstances make us feel, we prioritize what matters most, and then we plan and decide how to respond (M. S. Archer 2007). Although we internally deliberate and eventually make such reflexive choices to act in particular ways, those choices are based on the situationally socially structured available sex, gender, and sexual practices and discourses. Notwithstanding that sex, gender, and sexuality simply may at specific times be a habitual and routine social practice (Martin 2003), accountability encourages people to deliberate about and then "do" sex, gender, and sexuality appropriate to particular situations. And accountability and thus reflexivity especially come into play when agents are confronted with a unique social situation—such as a challenge to their sex, gender, or sexuality. Nevertheless, the resulting reflexive social action may not actually have been consciously intended to be a sex, gender, or sexuality practice. The social construction of sex, gender, and sexuality is essential to understanding the orchestration of hegemonic masculinities. But before I discuss that, it is important to explore the notion of *social structures* and their relation to social actions.

STRUCTURED ACTION

As the foregoing indicates, although sex, gender, and sexuality are "made," so to speak, through the variable unification of internal deliberations and thus reflexive self-regulated practices, these embodied practices do not occur in a vacuum. Instead, they are influenced by the social structural constraints and enablements we experience in particular social situations. *Social structures,* defined as recurring patterns of social phenomena (practices and discourses) that tend to transcend time and space and thus constrain and enable behavior in specific ways, "only exist as the reproduced conduct of situated actors" (Giddens 1976, 127). In other words, agents draw upon social structures to engage in social action, and in turn, social structures are (usually) reproduced through that same embodied and accountable social action. Social structures require continued acceptance and confirmation to persist. In such duality, structure and action are inseparable as "knowledgeable" human agents of sex, gender, and sexual practices enact social structures by reflexively putting into practice their structured knowledge. Social structures are the "medium" and "outcome" of social action: *medium* because it is through the use of social structures that social action occurs and *outcome* because it is through social action that social structures are reproduced—and sometimes transformed—in time and space (Giddens 1976; Mouzelis 2008). Because agents reflexively "do" sex, gender, and sexuality in specific socially structured situations, they reproduce social structures. And given that agents often reproduce sex, gender, and sexual ideals in socially structured specific practices, there are a variety of ways to do them. Within specific social structural settings, particular forms of sex, gender, and sexual practices are available, encouraged, and permitted. Accordingly, sexed, gendered, and sexual *agency* must be viewed as reflexive and embodied structured action—what people, and therefore bodies, do under specific social structural constraints and enablements (Messerschmidt 1993, 1997, 2000, 2004, 2010, 2012, 2014, 2016).

Although there exists a variety of social structures, two are especially salient for conceptualizing sex, gender, and sexuality and thus hegemonic masculinities: relational and discursive. *Relational* social structures establish through social practice the interconnections and interdependence among individuals in particular social settings and thus define social relationships among people in terms of sex, gender, and sexuality. Relational social structures constrain and enable social action. Examples of relational social structures are the informal yet unequal network of sexed, gendered, and sexual "cliques" in elementary and secondary schools and the sex and gender divisions of labor within workplaces. *Discursive* social structures are representations, ideas, and sign systems (language) that produce culturally significant meanings. Discursive social structures establish through social practice orders of "truth" and what is accepted as "reality" in particular situations. Like relational social structures, discursive social structures constrain and enable the possibilities of social action. Examples of discursive social structures are the notion of "two and only two sexes" mentioned above and social conventions defining styles of dress in terms of sex, gender, and sexuality.

Relational and discursive social structures intersect and work in combination and jointly, but also at times contradictorily. Both relational and discursive social structures are actualized only through particular forms of social action—they have a material base—yet such structured action produces simultaneously particular social relations *and* social meanings that are culturally significant because they shape a sense of what is "acceptable" and "unacceptable" behavior for copresent interactants in specific situations. Through embodied social action, individuals produce relational social structures that concurrently proffer meaningful representations (through embodied appearance and practices) for others as a consequence of their social action. And in turn, through embodied social action individuals also produce discursive social structures that concurrently constitute social relations (through representations, ideas, and sign systems) for others as a consequence of their social action. In other words, discursive social structures often are a part of relational social structures, and the latter often are a component of the former. The intersection of relational and discursive social structures then construct the knowledge we use to engage in particular practices—they recursively constrain and enable social action—and they actualize specific forms of understandings that define what is normal, acceptable, and deviant in particular social situations.

Nevertheless, relational and discursive social structures are not all-encompassing determinants and are not always accepted by agents without question or objection (Mouzelis 2008). Through reflexivity agents actually may distance and separate themselves from particular social structures, clearing the path for improvisation and innovation in social action. For example, when confronting social structures, agents at times engage in reflexive internal deliberations and may decide to break from and analyze, investigate, and possibly resist situational structural constraints and enablements (Mouzelis 2008). As Abby Peterson (2011) shows, it is in reflexivity where we find the mediatory processes whereby structure and action are connected or disconnected. And when such disconnect of agent from structure transpires—and thus *dualism* rather than *duality* occurs—the result often is unique forms of social action.

Furthermore, social action may also be influenced by forms of knowledge as *supplemental* constraints and enablements, which are nonrecurring (because they do not transcend time and space) and thus nonstructural. Examples of supplemental constraints and enablements are specific types of social interaction, such as a one-time intimate conversation with a trusted and influential individual as well as our bodies because the body changes over time and situationally constrains and enables social action. In short, sex, gender, and sexual social action emerges from, and is constrained and enabled by, what is always possible within any particular social situation. We are now in the position to discuss more thoroughly the common yet fluid configuration of hegemonic masculine practices.

HEGEMONIC MASCULINITIES

Power is an important structural feature of sex, gender, and sexual relations. Socially structured power relations among men and women are constructed historically on the bases of sex, gender, and sexual preference. In other words, in specific contexts some men and some women have greater power than other men or other women; some genders have greater power than other genders; some sexualities have greater power than other sexualities; and the capacity to exercise power and do sex, gender, and sexuality is, for the most part, a reflection of one's place in sex, gender, and sexual structured relations of power. Consequently, in general, heterosexual men and women exercise greater power than do gay men, lesbians, and other sexual minorities; upper-class men and women exercise greater power than do working-class men and women; and white men and women exercise greater power than do racial minority men and women. Power, then, is a relationship that structures social interaction not only between men and women but also among men and among women as well as in terms of gender and sexuality. Nevertheless, power is not absolute and at times may actually shift in relation to different axes of power and powerlessness.

Gender hegemony of course involves a power relation, and to recall from earlier chapters, I define "hegemonic masculinity" as those masculinities that *legitimate* an unequal *relationship* between men and women, masculinity and femininity, and among masculinities. The emphasis on *hegemony* and thus legitimation underscores the achievement of hegemonic masculinity through cultural influence and discursive persuasion, encouraging consent and compliance—rather than direct control and commands—to unequal gender relations. The hegemonic masculine configurations of practice that were discussed in previous chapters then construct both relational and discursive social structures because they establish relations of sex and gender inequality and at once signify discursively acceptable understandings of sex and gender relations.

In this regard, I find that Mimi Schippers's (2007) work (mentioned in previous chapters) is significant because it opens an extremely useful approach of conceptualizing how such *legitimacy* in hegemonic masculinity transpires. Schippers (2007, 90) argues that embedded within the meanings of structured gendered relationships are the "qualities members of each gender category should and are assumed to possess"; therefore, it is in "the idealized *quality content* of the categories 'man' and 'woman' that we find the hegemonic significance of masculinity and femininity." For Schippers (91), certain masculine characteristics *legitimate* men's power over women "only when they are symbolically paired with a complementary and inferior quality attached to femininity." The significance of hegemonic forms of masculinity then is found in discursive meanings that legitimate a rationale for structured social relations and that ensure the ascendancy and power of men as well as specific masculinities. What Schippers highlights, therefore, is first the *relationship* between masculinity and femininity and, second, how a certain masculinity is hegemonic only when it articulates discursively particular *gender qualities* that are *complementary* and *hierarchical* in relation to specific feminine qualities. For example, such a complementary and hierarchical relationship might establish masculinity as constituting physical strength, the ability to use interpersonal violence in the face of conflict, and authority, whereas femininity would embrace physical vulnerability, an inability to use violence effectively, and compliance (91). When both masculine and feminine qualities legitimate a complementary and hierarchical relationship between them, we have *hegemonic masculinity*, involving unequal gender relations or the superordinate position of men and subordinate position of women (94).

It is precisely this concentration by Schippers on the *quality content* of masculinity and femininity that describes the examples of hegemonic masculinities in chapters 2, 3, and 4. Moreover, this concentration on *gendered quality content* empirically enables investigating multiple forms of hegemonic masculinity—for example, locally, regionally, and globally, dominating or protective, fleeting—because *whenever a complementary and hierarchical relationship between masculinity and femininity exists, gender hegemony prevails*. To be sure, "gendered quality content" does *not* mean "fixed character traits" but, rather, it signifies changing *relational* attributes in sundry historical and social situations such as those examples discussed in chapters 2, 3, and 4. Through the construction of hegemonic masculinities and thus unequal gender relations, situational notions of "man" and "woman" embody culturally defined "superior" and "inferior" gendered qualities, respectively, that in turn establish consequential masculinities and femininities for copresent interactants.

Where I part from Schippers is in her argument that there exist "neither pariah masculinities nor subordinate masculinities," because "masculinity must always remain superior; it must never be conflated with something undesirable" (96). Schippers makes this point when discussing, *exclusively*, men who embody culturally defined *feminine* qualities (i.e., having erotic desire for men; seemingly weak, ineffectual, and compliant), yet ignoring those men who embody "toxic" masculine qualities, such as those metaphorically represented in US presidents Bush 43's and Obama's discourses (discussed in chapter 4), and those discursively associated with Osama bin Laden, Al-Qaeda, the Taliban, Saddam Hussein, and the Islamic State. In other words, Schippers's perspective fails to account for the "hero-villain" masculine *relationship* based similarly on differing gendered qualities attached to each and that *legitimate* a hierarchical relationship between two different types of masculinities: one heroically hegemonic and one toxically subordinate (in the examples herein). In both presidents' respective discourses, relations among masculinities are articulated and, significantly, just as hegemonic masculinity (hero) in these discourses has no meaning outside its relationship to emphasized femininity (victim), so in the same discourses hegemonic masculinity has no meaning outside its relationship to toxic, subordinate masculinity (villain). Although the application of *quality content* to discern gender hegemony discursively is significant, I extend Schippers's conception of gender hegemony to include *gendered qualities* that establish and legitimate a hierarchical (but not necessarily complementary) relationship to nonhegemonic masculinities.

Hegemonic masculinities form a relational and discursive social structure that has cultural influence but do not determine social action. Hegemonic masculinities often—but not always—underpin the conventions applied in the enactment and reproduction of masculinities (and femininities)—the lived embodied patterns of meanings, which as they are experienced as practice, appear as reciprocally confirming. Hegemonic masculinities relationally and discursively shape a sense of "reality" for men and women in specific situations and are continually renewed, re-created, defended, and modified through social action. And yet they are at times resisted, limited, altered, and challenged (see chapter 6).

The diversity and wide variety of hegemonic masculinities outlined in chapters 2, 3, and 4 operate as components of this social structure, constituting recurring "on-hand" meaningful practices and discourses that are culturally influential and thus available to be actualized into social action in a range of different circumstances. Gender hegemony then is essentially *decentered*; there exist not one or a few hegemonic masculinities but, rather, hegemonic masculinities that are multifarious and found in a whole variety of settings—locally, regionally, and globally. Hegemonic masculinities do not discriminate in terms of race/ethnicity, class, age, sexuality, and nationality, and hegemonic masculinities do not represent a certain *type* of man but, rather, they personify and symbolize an unequal *relationship* between men and women, masculinity and femininity, and among masculinities that is widely dispersed and operates intimately and diffusely. And these copious hegemonic masculinities provide a conceptual framework that is materialized in the design of daily practices, interactions, and discourses. As individuals construct hegemonic masculinities they simultaneously present those unequal gender relations as culturally significant for others as a consequence of their embodied social action. Gendered power, then, is both "top down" and "disciplinary" (Foucault 1979), and constituted through acceptance of, and consent to, hegemonically masculine forms of meanings, knowledge, and practice that are ubiquitous locally, regionally, and globally, yet simultaneously they are hidden in plain sight—this is indeed bona fide hegemony.

In addition to the above, the relationship between hegemonic masculinity and emphasized femininity underpins what has become known as *heteronormativity*, or the legal, cultural, organizational, and interpersonal practices that derive from and reinforce the discursive structure that there are two and only two naturally opposite and complementary sexes (male and female), that gender is a natural manifestation of sex (masculinity and femininity), and that it is natural for the two opposite and complementary sexes to be sexually attracted to each other (heterosexuality). In other words, the social construction of sex differences intersects with the assumption of gender and sexual complementarity, or the notion that men's and women's bodies are naturally compatible and thus "made for each other"—*the* "natural" sex act allegedly involves vaginal penetration by a penis (Jackson and Scott 2010). Heterosexuality is understood culturally as the natural erotic attraction to sex/gender difference, as well as a natural practice of male active dominance and female passive receptivity, and thus this notion of "natural attraction and practice" reinforces hegemonic masculinity and emphasized femininity as innate, complementary, and hierarchical opposites (Schippers 2007). Heteronormativity, therefore, refers to "the myriad ways in which heterosexuality is produced as a natural, unproblematic, taken-for-granted, ordinary phenomenon" (Kitzinger 2005, 478).

Accordingly, there is nothing "natural" about heterosexuality, and indeed the term "heterosexuality" actually did not appear until the 1890s, and then it was used to specifically designate an identity based not on procreation but rather on sexual desire for the opposite sex. Heterosexuality became disconnected from procreation, and "normal" sexuality was henceforth defined as heterosexual attraction; "abnormal" sexuality was homosexual attraction. The concept of heterosexuality was defined in terms of its relationship to the concept of homosexuality, both terms categorizing a sexual desire unrelated to procreation, and individuals now began to define their sexual identity according to whether they were attracted to the same or the opposite sex. And Steven Seidman (2010, 158) articulates well the historically constructed close connection between gender and heterosexuality:

There can be no norm of heterosexuality, indeed no notion of heterosexuality, without assuming two genders that are coherent as a relationship of opposition and unity. If there were no fixed categories of
gender, if there were no "men" and "women," there could be no concept of heterosexuality! So, heterosexuality is anchored by maintaining
a gender order through either celebrating and idealizing gender or by
stigmatizing and polluting gender nonconformity.

Gender hegemony and sexual hegemony intersect so that both masculinity and heterosexuality are deemed superior, and femininity and homosexuality (and alternative sexualities) are judged to be inferior. The social
construction of men and women as naturally different, complementary,
and hierarchical sanctions heterosexuality as *the* normal and natural form
of sexuality and masculine men and feminine women as *the* normal and
natural gender presentation; any sexual or gender construction outside of
these dichotomies is considered problematic.

Heteronormativity then reproduces a sexual social structure based on
an unequal sexual binary—heterosexuality and homosexuality—and that
is dependent upon the alleged natural sexual attraction of two and only
two opposite and complementary sexes that in turn constructs heteromasculine and heterofeminine difference. Nevertheless, some heterosexual practices are more powerful than other heterosexual practices; that is,
normative heterosexuality determines its own social structure and thus
internal boundaries as well as marginalizing and sanctioning sexualities
outside those boundaries.

In addition to sexuality, and as discussed earlier in this chapter, structured action theory emphasizes the construction of race, class, age, and
nationality as situated social, interactional, variable, and embodied accomplishments that are coconstituted with hegemonic masculinities. In
other words, race, class, age, and nationality grow out of embodied social
practices in specific unequal structural settings and serve to inform such
practices episodically in reciprocal relation. The key to understanding the
maintenance of existing race, class, age, and nationality social inequalities—and as intersecting with hegemonic masculinities—is the accomplishment of such practices through reflexive embodied social interaction. Social actors perpetuate and sometimes transform inequalities and
structures through their social action, and these inequalities and structures constrain and enable race, class, age, nationality, and hegemonically
masculine social actions. The result is the ongoing social construction of

hegemonic masculinities as variably constituted by unequal race, class, age, and nationality relations. In other words, the significance of each accomplishment to particular hegemonic masculinities is socially situated and thus intermittent.

NONHEGEMONIC MASCULINITIES AND FEMININITIES

In addition to variable intersection of hegemonic masculinities with race, class, age, sexuality, and nationality, structured action theory identifies distinct nonhegemonic masculinities: dominant, dominating, subordinate, and positive. To review (from chapter 4) and to add femininities to the theoretical picture, *dominant* masculinities and femininities differ from hegemonic masculinities and emphasized femininities in that they are not always associated with and linked to gender hegemony but refer fundamentally to the most celebrated, common, or current form of masculinity and femininity in a particular social setting. *Dominating* masculinities and femininities are similar to dominant masculinities and femininities but differ in the sense that they involve commanding and controlling specific interactions and exercising power and control over people and events—"calling the shots" and "running the show." Dominant and dominating masculinities and femininities do not necessarily legitimate a hierarchical relationship between men and women, masculinity and femininity. Although hegemonic masculinities and emphasized femininities at times may also be dominant or dominating, dominant and dominating masculinities and femininities are never hegemonic or emphasized if they fail culturally to *legitimate* unequal gender relations; in this latter scenario, dominant and dominating masculinities/femininities are thereby constructed *outside* relations of gender hegemony. However, dominant and dominating masculinities and femininities necessarily acquire meaning only in relation to other masculinities and femininities (Messerschmidt 2008, 2010, 2012, 2014, 2016).

Dominant and dominating masculinities and femininities exhibit different logics and degrees of power. For masculinities in particular, dominant masculinities may construct, for instance, celebratory power while dominating masculinities fashion commanding and controlling power; neither in and of themselves orchestrate hegemonic masculine power. Although it is true that hegemonic masculinities may not always be dominant and dominating in the above sense, the reverse also holds true: In addition to their legitimating influence (which is essential), hegemonic masculinities may concurrently be socially dominant and/or dominating. It is crucial, therefore, to leave open investigative room for empirical exploration as to when, how, and under what particular social conditions hegemonic masculinities are simultaneously dominant and/or dominating, and when they are not.

Subordinate masculinities and femininities refer to those masculinities and femininities situationally constructed as lesser than or aberrant and deviant to hegemonic masculinity or emphasized femininity as well as dominant/dominating masculinities and femininities. Depending upon the particular context, such subordination can be conceptualized in terms of, for example, race, class, age, sexualities, or nationality. Although homophobia has likely diminished somewhat in recent years in global North societies, it clearly has not disappeared. And given the discussion above in this chapter, it should be obvious that a form of subordination is that of gay boys/men and lesbian girls/women—still today, frequently the former are culturally feminized and the latter culturally masculinized. In a gender and heteronormative hegemonic culture, then, gayness continues to be socially defined in many contexts as the embodiment of whatever is expelled from hegemonic masculinity, and lesbianism is the embodiment of whatever is expelled from emphasized femininity.

Related to this, a second form of subordination usually occurs if there exists *incongruence* within the sex-gender-heterosexuality interconnection. For example, girls and women perceived as female who construct "incongruent" bodily practices defined as masculine—such as expressing sexual desire for girls ("dyke"), acting sexually promiscuous ("slut"), and/or presenting as authoritarian, physically aggressive, or take charge ("bitch")—are viewed as polluting "normal" and "natural" hegemonic gender and sexual relations and often are verbally, socially, and physically subordinated (Schippers 2007). Similarly, individuals perceived as male but who construct "incongruent" bodily practices defined as feminine—such as sexually desiring boys or simply practicing celibacy ("fag"), being passive, compliant, or shy ("sissy"), and/or being physically weak or unadventurous ("wimp")—likewise are seen as polluting "normal" and "natural" hegemonic gender and sexual relations and often are verbally, socially, and physically subordinated. Social structures that actualize unequal gender and sexual relations then are sustained in part through the subordination of the above genders and sexualities.

Finally, subordination can also occur among individuals who construct situationally accountable masculinities and femininities. For example, the masculinity of a son may be judged to be subordinate to the *dominant* masculinity of his father, and the femininity of a daughter may be considered subordinate to the *dominant* femininity of her mother. Both of these are subordinate primarily by reason of age, not because of any incongruence between sex and gender, and usually are established and thus practiced independent of gender hegemony.

Positive masculinities and femininities are those that legitimate an egalitarian relationship between men and women, between masculinity and femininity, and among masculinities and femininities, and therefore are constructed exterior to gender hegemonic relational and discursive structures in any particular setting. Such masculinities and femininities do not assume a normal and natural relationship to sex and sexuality, usually are not constructed as naturally complementary, and will be further discussed in chapter 6.

Structured action theory permits investigation of the different ways men and women experience their everyday worlds from their particular positions in society and how they relate to other men and women; the embodied hegemonic practices variably intersect and are constituted by race, class, age, sexuality, and nationality, and are associated with the specific context of individual action and are for the most part self-regulated—through reflexivity—within that context; social actors self-regulate their behavior and make specific reflexive choices in specific socially structured contexts. In this way, then, men and women construct varieties of hegemonic masculinities and thus unequal gender relations through specific embodied practices. And by emphasizing diversity in hegemonic masculine construction, we achieve a more fluid and situated approach to our understanding of embodied gender hegemony.

EMBODIMENT

As I have emphasized, constructing sex, gender, and sexuality entails *embodied* social practices—reflexive structured action. Only through our bodies do we experience the social world, and the very possibility of a social world rests upon our embodiment (Crossley 2001). As Iris Marion Young (1990, 147–48) long ago pointed out:

It is the body in its orientation toward and action upon and within its surroundings that constitutes the initial meaning-given act. The body is the first locus of intentionality, as pure presence to the world and openness upon its possibilities. The most primordial intentional act is the motion of the body orienting itself with respect to and moving within its surroundings.

We understand the world from our embodied place in it and our perceptual awareness of situational surrounding space. The body is a sensuous being—it perceives, it touches, and it feels; it is a lived body, and given that consciousness consists of perceptual sensations, it is therefore part of the body and not a separate substance (Crossley 2001). The mind and the body are inseparably linked—a binary divide is a fiction— and live together as one in the social construction of hegemonic masculinities. In this conceptualization, then, the body forms the whole of our being and, therefore, one's reflexive self is located in the body, which in turn acts, and is acted upon, within a social environment. And in contemporary industrialized societies the body is central to the social construction of self (Giddens 1991). A proficient and able body is necessary for social action and, therefore, embodied discipline is fundamental to the competent social agent: "It is integral to the very nature both of agency and of being accepted (trusted) by others as competent" (Giddens 1991, 100).

Related to the above is Pat Martin's (2003) differentiation between "gender practices" and "practicing gender." The term "gender practices" refers to forms of embodied behavior that are structurally "available" in specific social settings for individuals "to enact in an encounter or situation in accord with (or in violation of) the gender institution" (354). In other words, these are potential, situationally available embodied structured actions and discourses "that people know about and have the capacity or agency to do, assert, perform, or mobilize" (354). The term "practicing gender" entails actually "doing" the situationally available gendered practices and is usually reflexively accomplished with copresent interactants. To do gender reflexively, individuals must "carefully consider the content of one's actions and act only after careful consideration of the intent, content, and effects of one's behavior" (356). Although we make reflexive choices to act in particular ways, that reflexivity is based on the situationally embodied gender practices associated with contextual relational and discursive social structures.

Through embodied social action, then, individuals "do" hegemonic masculinities while simultaneously reproducing structures and presenting such practices as resources for others as a consequence of their embodiment. The social situations in which embodied actions are oriented "are populated by others and it is these others, in part, towards whom the actions are oriented. Action is other oriented" (Crossley 1995, 141). Embodied social action is embedded within the specific social structural context of the agent, so that what we actually conceptualize are social situations that require specific "practical accommodation from our action" (p. 136) —we reflexively respect, acknowledge, reproduce, and sometimes resist structured embodied practices. And as Goffman (1979, 6) acutely observes, such embodied actions are situational forms of "social portraiture" in which individuals discursively convey information that "the others in the gathering will need in order to manage their own courses of action —which knowledgeability he [sic] in turn must count on in carrying out his [sic] own designs." Doing hegemonic masculinity, therefore, is necessarily both reflexive and physical; it is intelligent, meaningful, and embodied.

Bodies are active in the production and transmission of social structures as well as embodied social actions, and are based on the reaction of others to our embodiment —whether or not it is judged accountable is important to our sense of self. Embodied accountability is vital to an individual's situational recognition as a competent social agent. If one's embodied appearance and practice are categorized by others as "failed," that degradation may result in a spoiled self-concept and identity (Goffman 1968). Consequently, adequate participation in social life depends upon the successful presenting, monitoring, and interpreting of bodies.

Goffman helps us understand how doing hegemonic masculinities are socially structured in the sense that we accomplish each bodily and in a manner that is accountable to situationally populated others. Individuals exhibit embodied hegemonic masculine competence through their appearance and by producing situationally appropriate "behavioral styles" that respond properly to the styles produced by others. In other words, "competent" individuals develop an embodied capacity to provide and to read structured depictions of hegemonic masculinities in particular settings, and appropriate body management is crucial to the smooth flow of interaction essential to satisfactory attribution and accountability by others. To be "read" by others as male, female, masculine, feminine, straight, gay, lesbian, and so forth, individuals must ensure that their proffered selves are maintained through situationally appropriate display and behavior—the body is social and social settings are created through intercorporeality.

But in addition, properly accountable bodies construct relational and discursive social structures, and they signal and facilitate through their appearance and action the maintenance of hegemonic masculine power dynamics. Suitably adorned and comported bodies constitute the "shadow and the substance" of unequal gender relations (Goffman 1979, 6): "The expression of subordination and domination through the swarm of situational means is more than a mere tracing of symbol or ritualistic affirmation of social hierarchy. These expressions considerably constitute the hierarchy; they are the shadow and the substance." Individuals produce (and at times challenge) hegemonically masculine relations through their embodied appearance and actions.

The body is an essential part of hegemonically masculine construction in which we fashion appearance and actions to create properly and situationally adorned and performed bodies. The body is an inescapable and integral part of doing gender hegemony, entailing social practice that constantly refers to bodies and what bodies do; it is not social practice reduced to the body (Connell 2000). Constructing hegemonic masculinities involves a dialectical relationship in which practice deals with the biological characteristics of bodies: "It gives them a social determination. The connection between social and natural structures is one of practical relevance, not causation" (Connell 1987, 78). In the social construction of hegemonic masculinities, then, bodily similarities between men and women are negated and suppressed, whereas bodily differences are exaggerated. The body is essential to, for example, the discourse of "two and only two sexes" in the sense that "men have penises and women do not." The body is significant for our fundamental projects discussed at the beginning of this chapter, our sense of self that we subjectively sustain through time and space. Bodies impact our recurring self-attributions and thus one's identity as male or female, masculine or feminine, straight or gay, and so forth. Because "sex" is associated with genitalia, there is likely to be a degree of social standardization of individual lives—we recursively construct ourselves as, for example, a "boy/man" or as a "girl/woman" with a particular sexual orientation, and thus such identities constrain and enable our social action. For most people sex is the primary claimed identity that is relatively solid and unchanging while gender and sexuality are qualifiers to sex (Paechter 2006). Nevertheless, some turn this on its head—such as certain transgender people—whereby sex is the qualifier and gender is the primary mode in which one relates to the world (Paechter 2006, 259).

Bodies participate in social action by delineating courses of social conduct: bodies are agents of social practice and, given the context, will do certain things and not others; our bodies are *supplemental* constraints and enablers of social action and therefore they situationally mediate and influence social practices (Connell 1995). The body often is lived in terms of what it can "do," and the "consequence of bodily practice is historicity: the creation and transformation of situations. Bodies are drawn into history and history is constituted through bodies" (Connell 1998, 7). In short, the body is a participant in the shaping and generating of hegemonically masculine social practice and thus unequal gender relations—it is impossible to consider human agency without taking sexed, gendered, and sexual embodiment into account.

CHALLENGES

Nevertheless, certain occasions present themselves as more effectively intimidating for demonstrating and affirming embodied gender. In certain situations individuals may experience body betrayal and be identified by others as embodying gender "failure." The constitution of hegemonic masculinities through bodily appearance and performance means that sex and gender accountability are vulnerable when the situationally and socially structured appropriate appearance and performance are not (for whatever reason) sustained. Because the taken-for-granted sex and gender of individuals can be challenged in certain contexts, each may become particularly salient. They are, as David Morgan (1992, 47) would put it, "more or less explicitly put on the line," and the responding social action can generate an intensified reflexivity and a distinct type of gender construction. Such challenges are contextually embodied interactions that result in, for example, sex, gender, or sexual degradation—the individual is constructed as a "deviant" member of society. Such challenges arise from interactional threats and insults from peers, teachers, parents, or workmates and from situationally and bodily defined expectations that are not achievable. Challenges, then, in various ways, proclaim a man or boy or a woman or girl subordinate in contextually defined embodied terms. Such challenges may motivate social action toward specific situationally embodied practices that attempt to correct the subordinating social situation (Messerschmidt 1993, 1997, 2000, 2004, 2010, 2012, 2014, 2016). Given that such interactions question, undermine, and/or threaten one's sex, gender, or sexuality, only contextually "appropriate" embodied practices can help overcome the challenge. The existence of challenges alerts us to the transitory and fleeting nature of sex and gender construction—including hegemonic masculinities—and to how particular forms of social action may arise as gendered practices when they are regularly threatened and contested.

CONCLUSION

Social action is never simply an autonomous event but is amalgamated into larger assemblages—what is labeled here as socially structured embodied actions. The socially structured situational practices encourage specific lines of social action, and relational and discursive social structures shape the capacities from which social actions are constructed over time. Men and boys and women and girls negotiate the situations that face them in everyday life and in the process pursue, for example, a sex, gender, and sexuality project. From this perspective, then, social action is often—but not always—designed with an eye to one's sex, gender, and sexual accountability individually, bodily, situationally, and structurally. Structured action theory, then, permits us to explore how and in what respects hegemonically masculine embodied practices and thus unequal gender relations are constituted in certain settings at certain times. To understand the multifarious hegemonic masculinities discussed herein, we must appreciate how structure and action are woven inextricably into the ongoing reflexive activities of constructing embodied unequal gender relations.

This chapter then has concentrated on how hegemonic masculinities are recurrently reconstructed, re-created, supported, justified, and refashioned through structured social action. In chapter 6 I turn to how hegemonic masculinities are at times opposed, restricted, changed, contested, and dismantled.

SIX

Prospects

Throughout this book my argument has been that contemporary hegemonic masculinities are decentered, fluid, contingent, provisional, and omnipresent locally, regionally, and globally; they are hidden in plain sight; and they collectively constitute a social structure that relationally and discursively *legitimates* unequal gender *relations* between men and women, masculinities and femininities, and among masculinities. If my perspective is correct, this requires novel strategies to challenge and resist gender hegemony. The hegemonic masculine social structure consists of different types of power relations—that have been detailed throughout this book—and therefore is continually and pervasively renewed, re-created, defended, and modified through social action. And it is this reproduction of hegemonic masculinities within everyday life that makes gender social change so difficult. Yet it is within the multiple sites and locations whereby hegemonic masculinities are fashioned that we find the seeds necessary for that structure to be resisted, limited, altered, challenged, and dismantled.

Hegemonic masculinities are always already constructed relationally, and thus the key to gendered social change is *not* to concentrate exclusively on "changing men." This solitary strategy is what Connell (1995, 220–24) referred to as "exit politics," or "refusing to be a man"; that is, escaping from masculinity rather than conducting a dissident politics within it. Nevertheless, individual men can positively impact social change by concentrating on the relational nature of hegemonic masculinity, building new egalitarian relationships between men and women, masculinity and femininity, and among masculinities. And this political action necessarily involves girls, women, and femininities as well.

Some masculinities scholars, however, have argued we no longer need to consider social change because recent developments in the social construction of masculinities in global North societies have resulted in hegemonic masculinities being supplanted by egalitarian "inclusive masculinities." For inclusive masculinity scholars, young men in global North countries are now accomplishing inclusive masculinities and, thus, gender and sexual equality has been achieved by this genre of men. In this final chapter, I first consider the validity of this argument by inclusive masculinity scholars. Following this, I briefly discuss a few concrete examples of counterhegemonic practices that move beyond alleged inclusive masculinities and actually present a challenge to the *relational* nature of hegemonic masculinities. These examples then provide promising prospects for gendered social change.

INCLUSIVE MASCULINITY

Erik Anderson (2009), Mark McCormack (2012), and numerous followers have studied primarily adolescent, middle-class, white, sporty, heterosexual men in England and the US. From the evidence produced in these studies, they argue that the masculinity of these young men is characterized today by "inclusivity" rather than "exclusivity." In other words, there allegedly has been a cultural shift in global North societies involving a substantial decrease in what is labeled "homohysteria," or the fear by heterosexual men of being homosexualized, empowering such men to construct masculinities that are completely accepting of sexual diversity and include numerous feminine qualities—such as friendships based on emotional openness, increased peer tactility, and softened and accepting interaction—without the fear of being perceived as gay.

Anderson (2009) proposed "inclusive masculinity theory" (IMT) to explain this alleged new masculine configuration among adolescent males, arguing that global North societies have advanced through three "zeitgeists" in sequential progression from "elevated," to "diminishing," and finally to "diminished" homohysteria. In elevated homohysteria, hegemonic masculinity predominates and is culturally significant. Homophobic discourse polices masculinity and reproduces hegemonic masculinity, and young men act aggressively, maintain homophobic attitudes, are emotionally distant from one another, and boast about their heterosexual exploits. In such a zeitgeist, young men who display physical and sexual intimacy with other young men "are socially homosexualized and consequently stripped of their perceived masculinity" (8).

As homohysteria abates culturally over time, two dominant forms of masculinity appear: one conservative and one inclusive. According to Anderson, hegemonic masculinity is no longer applicable because it has now been replaced by a conservative dominant masculinity he labels "orthodox." Men who practice this type of masculinity remain homohysterical and are tactilely and emotionally distant. In contrast, "inclusive" masculinity emerges and is a competing dominant masculinity alongside orthodox masculinity, emphasizing emotional and physical homosocial closeness. In this "diminishing" stage of masculine development, "men who value orthodox masculinity might use homophobic discourse with specific intent to demonize homosexuals, while inclusive acting men may use homophobic discourse but without intent to degrade homosexuals" (8).

In the final "diminished" zeitgeist, homohysteria has all but disappeared and therefore intentional homophobia ceases to exist. The result is social inclusion of those masculinities previously subordinated by hegemonic masculinity. In such settings, multiple masculinities—including inclusive masculinities—proliferate horizontally and young men begin to encounter a variety of acceptable nonhegemonic heteromasculine practices in which homophobic discourses and behaviors are subordinated.

For Anderson, then, hegemonic masculinity is solely prevalent in times of "elevated" homohysteria, becoming increasingly irrelevant during "diminishing" and "diminished" zeitgeists. Anderson maintains that global North societies currently are at the "diminishing" or "diminished" stages and thus inclusive masculinities, rather than hegemonic masculinities, have become widespread. As Anderson puts it, the "theory of hegemonic masculinity" is no longer pertinent because the documented changes in masculine constructions he and others have uncovered are "not accounted for with hegemonic masculinity theory. Times have changed, and this requires new ways of thinking about gender" (32).

I have no reason to question Anderson's, McCormack's, and other IMT scholars' findings; in fact, we should support men being emotionally open, tactile, and softened in their interaction with one another. What I initially contest is Anderson's (and most other IMT scholars') failure to

properly consider Connell's original formulation of hegemonic masculinity (see chapter 2) as well as Anderson's (and most other IMT scholars')
disregard of the reformulation of the concept (see chapter 3). To reiterate,
Connell's initial conceptual formulation concentrated on how hegemonic
masculinity in a given historical and society-wide setting legitimates unequal gender relations between men and women, masculinity and femininity, and among masculinities. Both the *relational* and *legitimation* features were central to her argument, involving a particular form of masculinity in unequal relation to a certain form of femininity—that is, "emphasized femininity," which is practiced in a complementary, compliant, and
accommodating subordinate relationship with hegemonic masculinity—
and to certain forms of nonhegemonic masculinities. The achievement of
hegemonic masculinity occurs largely through discursive legitimation (or
justification), encouraging all to consent to, unite around, and embody
such unequal gender relations.

As outlined in chapter 3, the reformulation of the concept involved a
number of changes to Connell's original formulation, but most important
for the discussion here is that instead of conceptualizing hegemonic masculinity at only the society-wide level, the reformulated concept recognized empirically existing hegemonic masculini*ties* at three levels—local,
regional, and global—and links among the three levels exist: global hegemonic masculinities pressure regional and local hegemonic masculinities,
and regional hegemonic masculinities provide cultural materials adopted
or reworked in global arenas and utilized in local gender dynamics.

Anderson (2009, 30–31) initially agreed with Connell's original formulation of the concept, stating: "Hegemonic masculinity is not an archetype" but instead involves "a social process of subordination and stratification." Nevertheless, in the same breath he peculiarly conceals hegemonic masculinities by adopting in their place what he labels "orthodox
masculinity" as an archetype (31): "In order to avoid confusing hegemonic masculinity as a social process from hegemonic masculinity as an
archetype, I do not use 'hegemonic masculinity' as a categorical label;
instead, I use the archetype of 'orthodox masculinity.'" Anderson therefore substitutes orthodox masculinity for hegemonic masculinity and in
the process describes orthodox and inclusive masculinities as distinct and
competing categories of archetypes. Through this cunning sleight of
hand, hegemonic masculinity vanishes from theoretical and empirical
consideration and its replacement—orthodox masculinity—becomes a

fixed character type, as does inclusive masculinity. For Anderson, orthodox and inclusive masculinities are static character types embodied by
certain men and/or groups of men. The result is that Anderson ignores
the whole question of gender relations and the legitimacy of gender inequality—that is, *the* foundation of hegemonic masculinities—and
through fiat concurrently conceals them from view.

Given that hegemonic masculinity is *not* operationalized and thus *not*
measured by Anderson (and other IMT scholars), it is disingenuous for
Anderson to claim that under "diminishing" and "diminished" homohysteria, hegemonic masculinities are no longer current and therefore
"hegemonic masculinity theory" is decidedly irrelevant. Inclusive masculinity scholars spuriously *assume* rather than empirically *demonstrate* the
alleged declining presence of hegemonic masculinities in global North
societies. Undeniably, the evidence presented throughout this book documents the persistence and omnipresence of hegemonic masculinities locally, regionally, and globally, yet needless to say they are "hidden in
plain sight" from inclusive masculinity scholars. I have detailed herein
that the hegemonic masculine social structure is an unbounded nexus of
practices and discourses that legitimate unequal gender relations. And in
view of the fact that the reformulated model of hegemonic masculinity is
different from Connell's original formulation—specifically in the sense of
recognizing multiple hegemonic masculinities at the local, regional, and
global levels—it is additionally scandalous for Anderson (2009, 93) to
declare that Connell argues there exists "only one hegemonic archetype
of masculinity." Anderson and other IMT scholars utterly erase gender
relations and sexual politics from consideration. As Rachel O'Neill (2015,
109) put it, for IMT scholars "sexual political matters are not simply ignored but are instead presented as *already settled*, or *in the process of being
settled*," and thus global North societies are seen as simply predisposed to
gender and sexual equality.

We cannot deny the increasing visibility and acceptance of gay masculinities and sexualities in global North societies, and Anderson, McCormack, and other IMT researchers have demonstrated that this change has
made it possible for certain straight men to appropriate aspects of gay
masculinities into their specific and situational configurations of masculinities. Nevertheless, and as discussed in chapter 4, work by masculinities scholars on hybrid hegemonic masculinities has likewise captured
this change, demonstrating the flexibility, adaptability, and fluidity of

hegemonic masculinities, by contextually incorporating certain features of gay masculinities and in the process blurring gender difference yet not undermining unequal gender relations. As Sam de Boise (2015, 324) has pointed out, inclusive masculinities may therefore represent quite simply "another hegemonic strategy for some heterosexual, white, middle-class men to legitimately maintain economic, social, and political power in the wake of gay rights." In fact, Nicola Ingram and Richard Waller found this to be the case. These authors studied middle-class undergraduate men in England and discovered that these young men "play" with different forms of masculinity, including hegemonic masculinity. As Ingram and Waller (2014, 48) point out, "playing" with masculinities involved these middle-class men constructing hegemonic masculinities "whilst adapting to the requirements to assume a veneer of inclusivity or present a liberal attitude on issues such as homophobia and gender inequalities." Ingram and Waller go on to argue that IMT is unsatisfactory in accounting for their findings and that the masculinities of the young men do not represent "a genuine engagement in the erosion of inequalities. IMT therefore can be seen as a blunt tool for analyzing masculinities as it fails to excavate power relations and uncover the continuance of gender related inequalities" (48).

De Boise (2015) additionally argues that although today it may be the case that homophobia is less essential to the construction of gender hegemony within certain contexts, this actually does little to disrupt different patterns of unequal gender relations. Arguably, the vast majority of studies discussed in chapter 4 that document (only partially) the amplification of the reformulated model of hegemonic masculinity—from the differences among hegemonic masculinities, to hybrid hegemonic masculinities, to fleeting hegemonic masculinities, to hegemonic masculinities on the internet, to the role intersectionality plays in hegemonic masculinities, and to hegemonic masculinities in the global South—do not center on homophobia. The common theme among these examples of diverse hegemonic masculinities is that subordination occurs through the contradistinction of hegemonic masculine qualities with feminine and toxic qualities.

Although gay men clearly constitute a subordinate masculinity within the context of gender hegemony, such subordination is associated with the historical and cultural construction of gay men as effeminate and feminine. Homophobia among straight boys and men does not necessarily concern a fear about with whom one has sex, but rather involves a disdain for "the symbolic blurring with femininity and men perceivably acting 'like women.' The fear of homosexuality . . . is often more about distancing from the feminine due to the perceived object of desire being that 'natural' to women than the fear of being homosexualized" (de Boise 2015, 329).

Along with coauthors Steven Roberts and Rory Magrath, one of Anderson's (Magrath, Anderson, and Roberts 2015; Roberts, Anderson, and Magrath 2017) most recent studies has concentrated on interviews with English football players who lived together at a football club academy and exemplifies two additional enduring problems with IMT—ignoring fluidity and women. The sample consisted of twenty-two male teenage working-class and heterosexual elite football players. The results indicated that these athletes are unanimously supportive of gay footballers coming out on their team and they are unconcerned about sharing a room with a gay player, changing with gay members in locker rooms, or relating to them on a social and emotional level. In addition, among themselves the heterosexual footballers engaged in positive emotional closeness, enhanced physical tactility, and practiced bantering not as a mechanism of ridicule but as a way to strengthen closeness and togetherness.

Despite the encouraging gender qualities among the teenage footballers identified by Anderson, Roberts, and Magrath, I am troubled by the lack of empirical investigation into the fluidity of masculine construction by these *heterosexual* footballers. For example, the authors report that the adolescent footballers enjoyed discussing with each other relational dynamics "about their romantic interests, including relationship troubles," yet we learn nothing about such discussions or their heterosexual relationships outside the academy. What is the relationship between these young men and young women in settings external to the academy? Given the emphasis in this book on the fluidity of masculine construction, to truly conceptualize the masculinity of these footballers one must investigate the possible changing masculine constructions in the different situations they interact. Do they engage in egalitarian or inegalitarian relations in their heterosexual romances? Accordingly, both the fluidity of masculine constructions and the relationship between men and women and masculinity and femininity are invisible in the vast majority of inclusive masculinity studies—indeed, women pass from sight—and this study is a typical example of this genre.

The adolescent footballers furthermore indicated in the interviews that they were more open with friends "back home" than with their teammates at the academy—what then is the difference between these contrasting settings? How do these footballers interact with their friends "back home"? Do they practice positive emotional closeness and enhanced physical tactility in this differing setting? Or do they interact in dissimilar ways?

Finally, considering Anderson's emphasis (in so-called "diminished" homohysteria) on the existence of multiple masculinities horizontally, it is surprising that these footballers seemingly are all constructing the identical masculinity within the academy; apparently, there exists exclusively one and only one style of masculinity in this setting. Can this be true? If so, it flies in the face of one of Anderson's theoretical principles as well as thirty years of research by masculinity scholars generally.

In contrast, consider a recent study by Tim Lomas and colleagues (2016) that demonstrates how crucial it is to examine multiple sites in order to secure a full and accurate understanding of masculine constructions. Briefly, these researchers interviewed thirty men who were participants at a meditation-based center, examining the men's masculinities both "inside" and "outside" the center. Inside the center, the men were encouraged to adopt new ideas and behaviors—that collectively constituted a new way of doing masculinity—which fell into three broad areas: (1) *physical intimacy* (e.g., being emotionally open, sharing feelings, being more caring); (2) *abstinence* (e.g., reduced alcohol and/or drug use); and (3) *spirituality* (e.g., physical-emotional experiences, adoption of Buddhist ideologies). Although the men reported the value of embracing these new masculine practices, many of the men found doing so to be challenging, both inside and outside the center.

Inside the center the men encountered hierarchical notions of masculinity that are emphasized alongside the new attention to intimacy, abstinence, and spirituality. For example, the center underscored a ranking among participants based on meditation skills, and thus moving up the hierarchy was a "coveted marker of spiritual progress" (Lomas et al. 2016, 300). Inherent in the hierarchy was competitiveness among the participants, which created a drive for achievement and status, as well as rivalry among the meditators. Subordination was consequently attached to those who "failed" to attain the meditation goals featured by the center. On that account, then, the men experienced a contradiction inside the center whereby they were situationally encouraged to adopt both "new" *and* "old" masculine practices that seemingly constructed differing masculinities among a variety of "winners" and "losers."

Outside the center, the men found it difficult to practice the new aspects of masculinity emphasized by the center. For example, socializing with friends who frequently consumed alcohol and drugs made it extremely difficult to pursue abstinence outside the center. The men also reported difficulties with physical intimacy and emotional openness with friends on the outside. One of the meditators reported to the researchers that inside the center he was "quite tactile" but in outside settings with his friends "I'm not, because I'm not sure how people will take it" (301). And the men further detailed encountering hostility by outside friends to their own developing sense of spirituality.

In short, although new ways of constructing masculinity were encouraged in the meditation center, actually practicing this new masculinity was difficult both inside and outside the center. Inside the center dominant and subordinate masculinities seemingly were orchestrated, and the "new" masculinity did not translate to the outside as the men experienced censure, ostracism, and conflict with friends. As Lomas and colleagues (2016, 303) conclude, local masculinities "that appear positive at first glance are not entirely positive on deeper examination."

This study furthers our understanding of how masculine constructions are fluid and thus impacted by the social structures of particular settings; unfortunately, the studies by Roberts, Anderson, and Magrath do not. The Lomas and colleagues study suggests that the latter studies are noticeably abbreviated and incomplete. That is, Anderson and colleagues fail to show the construction of masculinities in "outside" arenas by the adolescent footballers—they miss this additional and essential step in researching this population. And as seems to be typical among IMT scholars, Roberts, Anderson, and Magrath steer clear of any intellectual concern about unequal gender relations and the gendered power and privilege these footballers benefit from regardless of their inclusiveness within the academy setting. To be inclusive among each other in one setting does not automatically free one from participation in unequal gender relations within other settings.

IMT scholars' concentration is on "new" individual masculine constructions and interactions *among men* within particular singular social settings. In this sense, then, IMT insufficiently contributes to challenging or dismantling of the hegemonic masculine social structure. In other words, alongside the construction of inclusive masculinities lurks the ever-present and ubiquitous hegemonic masculinities documented in this book.

In the following section, I present a few examples of scholarship that recognize and highlight counterhegemonic practices that actually oppose, challenge, question, and in some cases dismantle unequal gender relations.

COUNTERHEGEMONIC PRACTICES

Although I do not claim to possess a firm and concrete answer to the problem of gender hegemony—especially given its omnipresence and complex structure—we do know that hegemonic masculinities can be contested and undermined through alternative practices that do not support unequal gender relations; in particular, counterhegemonic practices that critique, challenge, or actually dismantle hegemonic masculinities. Studying the diversity of masculinities helps us to gain some grasp as to where energy should be directed to promote gendered social change; that is, those social situations where counterhegemonic practices are particularly possible or likely to materialize. One place to begin is with what I refer to as *positive masculinities and femininities*, or those gender constructions (locally, regionally, and globally) that contribute to legitimating egalitarian *relations* between men and women, masculinity and femininity, and among masculinities. Such masculinities and femininities are counterhegemonic because they actually are, or they have the means to become, culturally conceptualized as legitimate and authentic alternatives to gender hegemonic relations. A number of scholars have uncovered that such "positive" masculinities and femininities usually are constructed outside the realm of gender hegemonic relations yet often in turn they contribute to legitimating egalitarian gender relations (Swain 2006; Haywood and Mac an Ghaill 2012; Messerschmidt 2016; Schippers 2000, 2007). In this section, then, I discuss a variety of these counterhegemonic practices and I begin with a consideration of adolescent boys.

Adolescent Boys

Jon Swain's (2006) study of ten-to-eleven-year-old boys in three schools in the United Kingdom builds on Connell's original scheme of multiple masculinities by showing that although some boys are hegemonic, complicit, and subordinate, certain boys construct personalized masculinities that transcend the available masculinities in the sphere of hegemonic relations at school. These boys have no desire to practice in-school hegemonic or dominant masculinities, and they are not subordinated nor do they subordinate others (boys or girls). In fact, their masculinities are rather positive in the sense of being practiced in small groups of boys with similar interests (e.g., computers, theater, band), they are inclusive and egalitarian, and they are nonhierarchical without any clearly identified leader. This study then demonstrates the variety of masculinities in one particular setting, their specific relationality, and that the very presence of positive personalized masculinities suggests they have the means to become counterhegemonic.

Similarly, I (Messerschmidt 2016) found in my research such positive nonhegemonic masculinities constructed by certain teenage boys, who frequently reported, for example, hanging out with unpopular groups at school that included both boys *and* girls who were inclusive and nonviolent, they did not emphasize heterosexuality and accepted celibacy, the boys were not misogynist, they embraced diversity in bodies and sexuality, they were nonhierarchical, and they had no desire to be popular. Members of such groups viewed themselves as different from rather than inferior to the dominant boys and girls. Such positive masculinities were not constructed in a structural relationship of gender and sexual inequality, they did not legitimate unequal gender and sexual relations, and they were practiced in settings situated outside stable unequal gender relations. Like the boys in Swain's study, these boys were positioned as embodying counterhegemonic practices in their particular context.

The boys in Swain's and in my study constructed what is usually considered to be atypical masculine behavior by boys outside the social situation of the dominant popular group. For these boys, the accountable way to construct masculinity is to signify one's embodied disassociation from unequal gender relations. Such egalitarian gendered behavior is normalized within the unpopular group—it is encouraged, permitted, and privileged by both boys and girls—and therefore within that setting it does not call into question their "maleness." These boys are engaging in such positive masculinities authentically as boys—they are not feminized by others, they are not perceived as engaging in femininity, and they are not "refusing to be a man." The boys underscored through their social action how equality and masculinity are not mutually exclusive but rather are lived practices of particular contextual realities and gender relations. The boys aimed to be seen as boys as well as egalitarian in their gender relations, thus disrupting gender difference by redefining what it means to be a boy through the orchestration of positive masculinities.

In addition to the above, one aspect of the nonviolent boys' positive masculinities in my study involved their response to frequently being bullied by the dominant popular boys. Some nonviolent boys responded to such bullying in a particular way—they simply employed the counter-hegemonic personal practice of "walking away" from the bullying without acknowledging the bully or the verbal abuse. In other words, this particular practice re-embodies boys who are "feminized" through bullying by constructing a self-assertive, tenacious, and immovable form of masculinity that challenges the masculine culture of the school to physically fight back. "Walking away" effectively upends hegemonic masculine relations because the alleged effeminate boy is instead transformed into a courageous, audacious (bold), and brave "man" with the "guts" it takes to reject gender hegemony—in the process, masculinity is constructed in a new and positive way. These boys then were practicing dissident politics within a particular personalized masculine construction.

Permit me to briefly summarize one of the life stories from my study, which demonstrates an example of the social process leading to engagement in the positive masculinities identified above. I named this boy Jerry.

The Case of Jerry

Jerry was a tall, slightly overweight, working-class seventeen-year-old. When Jerry was young, he lived alone with his mother, who had separated from his father because of his alcohol abuse. To make ends meet, Jerry's mother worked two jobs in the unskilled-labor market. While his mother worked, Jerry was cared for by several different couples who were friends of the family. Around the age of six Jerry met his biological father for the first time. Jerry and his father had a wonderful time together; they went for a walk in the park and spent the entire afternoon side by side as one. And it was not long after this first meeting with his father that Jerry's parents actually reconciled and all three began living under the same roof.

Jerry's father owned a small business in the unskilled manual-labor market, and when not working he spent much "quality time" with Jerry, who in turn referred to his father as "my hero." This closeness with his father nourished Jerry's idea of future labor-force participation: Jerry drew from the relationally and discursively socially structured practices at home that emphasized the binary construction of sex and he thus saw himself as one side of that binary—a boy—who wants to have a similar business after finishing high school and work hard like his father. Drawing from these social structures of work Jerry mapped out a future work plan for himself. Because Jerry's father was contributing economically to the household, his mother was able to quit one of her two jobs and had time to pursue other interests.

Despite these positive developments, Jerry's parents seemed unable to get along with each other. Although the arguments between his mother and father constituted one of the most distressing events in Jerry's family life, his parents always protected Jerry from responsibility for their problems. In fact, Jerry and his parents were very "connected." And regardless of the frequent arguments, Jerry described his parents as warm and affectionate toward him and who maintained an extremely egalitarian relationship. Jerry then grew up within, drew from, and successfully actualized through his in-home masculine social actions the gender egalitarian relational and discursive social structures at home.

Although his father worked at a "masculine" job and his mother at a "feminine" job, at home Jerry observed and participated in both "masculine" and "feminine" forms of domestic labor—from emptying the garbage and cutting the lawn to helping with the cooking and cleaning. Jerry clearly identified first and foremost with his father, yet Jerry's mother also had a significant influence on him. Both parents were equal participants in the household labor—as well as repudiating interpersonal physical violence—and such practices constructed relational and discursive social structures that defined for him a specific form of masculinity. Jerry's father and mother respectively embodied a localized gender equal relationship, and Jerry seemed to adopt what was offered. Jerry turned to the structured gender equality at home to engage in social action, and he in turn reproduced this social structure through this same social action.

And it is in this setting where Jerry began to take up a project of this type of masculinity as his own; his fundamental gender project was to be like "Dad." In the particular setting of the home, then, Jerry identified as a boy who embodied an accountably nonviolent positive masculinity through his gender practices.

The social setting of the school, however, was not as congenial a place for Jerry as home. In particular, from elementary school through high school Jerry was the consistent target of the dominant popular boys' verbal bullying for being an overweight "wimp." Jerry found himself confronting a new and combined relational and discursive social structure at school, and Jerry reflexively responded by internally mulling over the bullying by the popular dominant boys at school. Ultimately Jerry decided to avoid interacting in public as much as possible because actually he accepted the characterization of his body by the popular dominant boys.

Jerry revealed here the institutionalization of masculine structured relations in his school—the informal "clique" relational and discursive social structures—and his reflexive response. We "see" through this interaction the construction of a fleeting hegemonic masculinity whereby Jerry is positioned in a subordinate relationship to the dominant boys through verbal bullying about the "wimpish" shape of his body and for not fighting back as the masculine culture of the school dictated. And he is placed in this masculine subordinate position without his own choice or purposeful undertaking but rather exclusively through the discursive practices of the dominant popular boys. Jerry reflexively deliberates about this positioning at school and initially decides simply to refrain as much as possible from being seen in public.

Jerry, however, was unable to escape the negative impact every time this fleeting hegemonic masculinity incorporated him into this oppressive gender relation, and he continued to internally develop the same reflexive response: Jerry developed a painful lack of masculine self-esteem at school because of the acute distress over the verbal bullying and subordinating comments about his "wimpish" body and being physically unable to "fight back." Ultimately, in third grade—after further reflexivity—Jerry decided to draw on the acceptable masculine practice in the school to "fight back" when bullied, and consequently Jerry became involved in a number of "fistfights" at school. These fights were simply part of what Jerry labeled "playground business," which he defined as "some kid does something and the other kid takes it as he has insulted him, so he goes up and hits the kid for insulting him. That's how kids in my grade school handled business on the playground." The bullying by the dominant boys compelled Jerry to internally feel subordinate, insecure, and small at school. So during his internal deliberations about this masculine insecurity he decided he would respond according to the playground practice of appropriately handling "playground business." If Jerry did not bully or fight back, he would invariably be labeled a "wimp." Jerry reflexively decided that he wanted to be "tough" in front of the other kids, so he got into eight fights that year.

In the social setting of the school, then, Jerry found himself embedded in different gender relations than what he experienced at home. The verbal bullying and fleeting hegemonic masculinity constructed a gender challenge for Jerry at school, as he was now defined as subordinate in relation to the popular dominant bullies. And Jerry reflexively decided to respond in a way that the particular masculine culture of the school emphasized—that is, with physical violence—which initially negated the subordination and allowed Jerry to construct an in-school dominant masculinity. Through reflexivity, then, Jerry decided to align with the masculine culture at school to engage in accountable social action that reproduced the unequal masculine relations. Jerry was now accountably masculine, there was congruence between sex and gender, and the duality of structure and action transpired.

Because of Jerry's close relationship with his parents, he discussed the bullying and fighting with them, and they emphasized that he should never "fight back" when bullied and instead should simply "walk away" from the bullies. At first Jerry reflexively decided not to accept his parents' suggestion, and he chose to continue to respond in a physically violent way at school. Jerry explained that he internally determined he could not simply "walk away" because "you have to show kids you're not afraid to do it. My mom and dad didn't understand what it was like." Here we "see" Jerry reflexively negotiating a contradictory social situation: on the one hand he is confronted with the culturally significant masculine culture of the school that emphasized "handling playground business" by fighting back, and on the other hand he is challenged through a supplemental constraint and enabler in the form of intimate conversations with people he highly respects—his parents—who stressed turning his back to the bullies and walking away. After further discussion with his parents, eventually Jerry reflexively broke from the masculine culture of the school by accepting a nonviolent response to the discursive bullying challenges. Jerry decided to try his parents' suggestion, and "if a kid started saying stuff I would just walk away. And that's when it really started to sink in. It was nice, and I'd come home and say to my parents, 'Hey, you guys are right.'"

Distancing himself from the influential masculine culture, Jerry drew on the intimate conversations with his parents that eventually constrained Jerry from "fighting back" and enabled him to resolve the contradiction by practicing an alternative response—to simply "walk away." Jerry determined through his conversations with his parents that "walking away" was actually a more compelling form of masculinity than was fighting back.

Despite the fact that Jerry continued to be the victim of bullying, these discussions with his parents convinced him to never again respond by fighting. Instead, he reflexively decided to simply walk away: "Usually it resolves itself. You just walk away and the kid doesn't even say anything to you because he can't get a rise out of you." Jerry reflexively concluded that this is the best way to handle such a situation. Although Jerry continued to be defined as subordinate in relation to the dominant masculine boys at school, he now felt confident responding this way because, although the bullying continues "as you're walking away, later it's like you just don't even acknowledge that he's there." Jerry successfully opposed the in-school attempt by the dominant popular boys to subordinate him. Through his practice of "walking away," Jerry both challenged his position as "subordinate" in the "clique" masculine social structural relations and he refused to reproduce these structural relations; instead, through reflexivity Jerry decided to break from both the relational and discursive social structures and practice an alternative nonviolent positive masculinity. Jerry reflexively distanced himself from and successfully challenged these structures through a novel form of dissident masculine social action.

The bullying persisted in high school, but Jerry reflexively chose to never respond in a violent way. The "walking away" reaction continued to work in the sense that the verbal bullying did not disturb or trouble him in any way and he felt comfortable engaging in this particular practice. The most frequent verbal bullying Jerry experienced in high school was being "called a fag a lot, and queer, and anything pertaining to being homosexual. So I just shrug it off. I could yell at the kid or something, but there's no point. He is just going to be narrow-minded about it. So I just turn my back on it instead of putting up the dukes."

And accordingly, this counterhegemonic practice in high school led Jerry to become a practicing member of the "laid-back" crowd while continually orchestrating an alternative masculine response through the personalized practice of walking away. In this third social setting now in the peer group, Jerry's positive masculinity was thoroughly welcomed and embraced. The "laid-back" crowd included both boys and girls who refrained from any bullying about the shape and size of bodies, and all members of this group never engaged in violent behavior. This laid-back group accepted gender and sexual diversity, and they were not misogynist, homophobic, or hierarchical, and there was no emphasis in this group on constructing hegemonic, dominant, or dominating masculinities. The laid-back group seemed to celebrate their difference from the dominant boys and girls in the school. In other words, this laid-back group constructed egalitarian gender relations at school, and Jerry actualized these relations by engaging in similar forms of social action that collectively composed his positive masculinity.

From a structured action perspective, Jerry drew upon relational and discursive social structures in three different locales—home, school, and peer group—to engage in masculine social action, and in turn he reproduced (at home) and challenged (at school) and reproduced (in the peer group) specific social structures through distinct practices—Jerry's masculine identity is fluid through time and place. At home Jerry's embodied practices articulated a positive masculinity that contributed to reproducing in-home egalitarian gender relations; he was a masculine conformist at home; yet at school, Jerry was labeled a masculine deviant by the dominant popular boys. The distress from this continued label became unbearable and led Jerry to reflexively decide to "handle playground business" in the situationally "appropriate" masculine way: that is, to physically "fight back." Jerry resolved to exhibit a "tough" masculine persona, and he decided his tall body could facilitate such masculine agency. So Jerry engaged in numerous playground fights, but the bullying continued unabated. Here we "see" Jerry's body actually participating in his reflexive agency by suggesting a possible course of action, which Jerry embraced. But his parents eventually pointed to a new direction as to how he should use his body in bullying incidents—they advised him to "walk away." Jerry adopted this dissident personalized practice, and his body then became the object of a new reflexive masculine social action. Electing to "walk away" rather than "fight back" was an attempt at validation by embodying a specific masculine self for his audience and for himself—it was an attempt to reduce/offset the subordinating interactions and feelings produced at school, yet simultaneously it constructed a new nonviolent positive form of masculinity within the setting of the school. By "walking away" Jerry was not "refusing to be a man," but rather he orchestrated the embodiment of a powerfully peaceful impartial masculinity in the eyes of others. And although the derogatory bullying continued, it no longer reinforced feelings of masculine inadequacy because "walking away" secured a stronger masculine response than that presented by the bullies. This new nonviolent positive masculine agency was additionally supported and fully recognized by his new friends in the social setting of the "laid-back" group—he was now a masculine conformist in a different way in this third milieu. Jerry practiced a re-embodiment of new gender relations through his participation in the "laid-back" group as well as by "walking away." Such display and practice opposed hegemonic masculine bodily relations through its emphasis on nonviolence and the celebration of bodily difference.

Offshore Oil Rig Workers

The examples of uniting with an alternative "laid-back" group and "walking away" from bullies embody *reflexive* counterhegemonic practices to combat subordination and oppressive gender relations. However, counterhegemonic practices can appear in the form of an *unanticipated* consequence to certain policy changes, without any conscious reflexive strategy devised. For example, a fascinating study by Matthew Filteau (2014) of offshore oil rig workers in the US found that hegemonic masculinity actually was fortuitously replaced by a positive dominant masculinity in one notable worksite. The particular oil rig Filteau examined traditionally excluded women (only men worked there), and a hegemonic/subordinate masculine relationship endured for years, whereby hegemonic masculinity was characterized by such gender qualities as bravado, toughness, competitiveness, and little concern for one's own safety. Committing oneself to safety signified weakness, a quality associated with subordinate masculinity, and therefore men who deviated from hegemonic notions of masculinity were feminized and stigmatized as "sissies" for not being brave or tough, and for worrying about their safety.

As shifting economic, environmental, and political climates emerged, this forced the oil rig industry to enforce stricter safety policies to avoid lawsuits and to maximize profits. Filteau found that because of the policy change, workers actually began to praise the new safety standards and in turn unintentionally changed their masculine practices at work—they condemned so-called brave, tough, reckless, unsafe behaviors and conformed to the new safety guidelines. Filteau discovered that feminizing "Other" men likewise became nonexistent, and workers began to value a collective performance of safety, all of which became the defining qualities of a socially dominant nonhegemonic masculinity at this particular oil rig. Workers now cooperate and work together to reinforce this new dominant positive masculinity and, in turn, they subordinate men who work unsafely and feminize other men. In other words, workers denounce traditionally hegemonic masculine practices and relations as deviant and incongruent with the new dominant positive masculinity. Filteau concluded that the reorganization of the workplace unintentionally created opportunities for men to constitute new nonhegemonic masculine relations and thus practice a positive yet dominant masculinity.

These examples of counterhegemonic practices—one conscious (Jerry) and the other coincidental (oil rig workers)—destabilized gender hegemony or the superior/inferior binary qualities and relations upon which hegemonic masculinity is based. The examples demonstrate how the coexistence of hegemonic and nonhegemonic masculinities can possibly lead to more humane and less oppressive ways of being a boy or a man. In these cases, practices that previously were identified as feminine behavior became recognized and established as positive masculine behavior and thus challenged gender hegemony. Boys and men participate in hegemonic masculinities within certain contexts, but these same boys and men distance themselves from hegemonic masculinity in other situations and construct positive egalitarian masculinities.

Both studies, therefore, demonstrate the significance of investigating difference settings of masculine construction. Jerry practiced a positive masculinity at home, but at school he was labeled a "wimp" and overcame this label by constructing a situationally specific counterhegemonic masculinity at school and in the social setting of the "laid-back" group. Filteau's research demonstrated the opposite as he examined the oil workers' masculinities at both the workplace and the home. As we have seen, in the workplace the workers fashioned a dominant positive masculinity, but at home they continued to practice hegemonic masculinity. In comparing the two sites, Filteau (2014, 409) found that the new positive dominant masculinity at work "reinforces each man's ability to fulfill hegemonic masculinity in other contexts: safe work practices promote hegemonic masculinity in the domestic sphere through breadwinning." To be sure, *every* participant in the study expressed to Filteau that being a man meant providing economically for his family and, therefore, men *must* practice safety at work or face termination. Filteau's study then alerts us to how the masculinity in one context that *challenges* unequal gender relations can impact the masculinity in a separate setting that *reproduces* unequal gender relations.

Adolescent Competitive Swimmers

Similarly, in a study of eight-to-ten-year-old boys and girls who participated on a Southern California youth swim team, Michela Musto (2014) found gender "spill over" from one context to another. Musto examined two main contexts that organized gender relations at the pool: formally focused time actually swimming in the pool and unfocused free time on the deck. In the former, the coach instructed the boys and girls to share swim lanes, race one another, and compare times. Swimmers "worked out" formally together in the pool, and thus they experienced athletic parity between boys and girls who interacted as genderless individuals—swimmers were recognized as "boys" and "girls," yet gender equality was constructed because gender was not salient to the formal interactions. In the latter, gender became more prominent during the swimmers' informal free time on the deck; boys and girls interacted apart in sexed groups, they affirmed opposite gendered boundaries, and accordingly awareness of gender similarity was obscured. In this context, then, gender difference was emphasized.

What is particularly striking about Musto's study is that in neither context were unequal gender relations constructed and thus boys were never deemed superior to girls. Although the binary of "boys" and "girls" was prevalent throughout both contexts, the athletic equivalence in the pool made it difficult to sustain any notion of unequal gender relations, and on the deck gender difference was further highlighted but not gender inequality. Musto (2014, 376) explained the lack of hierarchical unequal gender relations in the context of the deck in the following way: "If individuals enact more equitable gender relations in one context, aspects of these gender relations may 'spill over' into other settings within daily life." For example, the girls embodied strength and confidence in the pool, and this allowed for self-assurance and assertiveness on the deck; the boys' experiences of losing to girls in swim races "helped create a baseline of respect for the girls outside the pool" (376). The result was that the gender equality in the pool—and thus the "undoing" of gender in this particular setting (see Deutsch 2007 and Risman 2009)—transferred in some measure to the deck in the sense of creating a differing circumstance encompassing a quest for gender difference with equality.

Alternative Rock Musicians

Most studies of counterhegemonic practices concentrate on boys, men, and masculinities. Given that hegemonic masculinities are always already relational—and as the above study of adolescent competitive swimmers demonstrates—girls, women, and femininities are equally essential to conceptualizing the possibilities of dismantling hegemonic masculinities. In a compelling participant observation study of an alternative rock music group, Mimi Schippers (2000) reported that the members of this group—in particular the women—incorporated counterhegemonic practices into their interactions. Specifically, the women practiced intersectionality by challenging heterosexism as a means to counter gender hegemony. For example, Schippers detailed an interaction that involved several people attempting to decide what to do that particular evening. One of the women (Maddie) said to the group, "Come on you guys, could you just make up your minds. Let's go" (Schippers 2000, 755). The men "totally" ignored this request, so Maddie stated specifically to Dan, "Get your thumb out of your ass, and let's do something." Dan turned to Maddie and declared, "Why do you have to be such a dyke all the time?" Maddie then responded, "Thanks for the compliment. See ya . . ." and left (755).

All the participants in this interaction were heterosexual, so the use of the word "dyke" did not necessarily refer to same-sex sexuality but rather to the fact that Maddie was being assertive. Dan attempted to reinforce unequal gender relations through a fleeting hegemonic masculinity by subordinating Maddie as a "dyke," yet she would have no part of it and refashioned that attempt into a compliment. And that redefinition "made

explicit her refusal to enact femininity in a way that reproduced hegemonic gender relations" and "illustrates how a positive deployment of
the identity *dyke* made gender resistance possible" (755). Thus, sexuality
and gender were constituted through the same practice that challenged
and disallowed unequal gender relations.

In another example, Maddie and Schippers walked by Colleen and a
man talking, and Colleen said jokingly to the man that Maddie was a
"lesbian" and a "bitch." Maddie and Colleen then both laughed, hugged
each other, and engaged in playful banter. When Maddie and Schippers
began to move away from the interaction, Colleen said to Schippers,
"Now be careful, she's a lesbian" (756). Maddie then responded, "She
knows. She's my girlfriend. Jealous?" Colleen then laughed and pro-
fessed, "Yeah, but I have my own girlfriend. He [referring to the man she
was talking with] is really a she!" (756).

Schippers (757) insightfully argues that the use of "lesbian" and
"bitch" in this dialogue mocks these terms through their verbal competition of who really is a "lesbian" or a "bitch": "This shifted the meaning of
those labels to positive attributes, which worked as gender resistance
because the femininities associated with both challenged hegemonic femininity." Moreover, subversive gender relations were constructed during
the dialogue by labeling the man as "girlfriend" of Colleen. As Schippers
(757) puts it:

> Colleen constructed the social roles in the interaction in a way that
> subverted male dominant power relations—after all, the gender order
> does not confer masculine power to "girlfriends." In this interaction,
> queering sexuality and destabilizing gender subverted both hegemonic
> gender and sexual relations.

Accordingly, at the local level these interactions involved fashioning dissident politics within particular positive feminine practices that destabilized the attempted formulation of unequal gender relations.

Fair Heterosexual Couples

In Barbara Risman's (1998) classic text *Gender Vertigo: American Families in Transition*, she documents how some heterosexual couples are challenging gender hegemony by constructing equitable gender relations.
That is, "fair heterosexual couples" are "those in which husbands and
wives occupy breadwinner and nurturer roles equally" (93). The fifteen

couples interviewed by Risman were highly educated and devoted an equal number of hours to paid work as well as to household labor. They were all dual-career couples and held egalitarian values. They balanced family and career priorities and equally shared parenting. Each husband and wife articulated that "a fulfilling life involves both paid and family work," and they "adopted the culturally available feminist view on equality as their own taken-for-granted reality" (107). And they did not organize household labor in terms of traditional gender expectations as each did their fair share of housework. The couples were likewise dual nurturers in the sense of organizing work schedules to maximize equal time with children, and thus for the majority "this looked like a home with two mothers" (110). Regarding authority and coercion, Risman interviewed the couples about decision-making as to where to live, how to discipline children, how to organize housework, and how to allocate leisure time. For the majority, equal power in decision-making existed; in fact, "in no couple did the husband seem to hold more power than the wife" (117).

These couples then successfully established egalitarian gender relations as both husband and wife were equal in social and economic status and neither were solely responsible for earning a living or caring for children. The women were found to be forthright, assertive, and task oriented; none were quiet, passive, or dependent; and "none use their domestic skills to help define them as real women or to do gender" (126). The husbands similarly challenged traditional notions of masculinity by adopting "ideological commitments to equality and begun to invent a version of masculinity that integrates strength, warmth, and nurturance" (126). Although both the women and men challenged unequal gender relations in the home through their communal practice of equality, Risman (127) interestingly concludes that

> it is perhaps the men who are the most atypical here, who are secure enough to challenge the patriarchal version of masculinity that permeates our culture. They are creating a version of masculinity with an umbrella large enough to cover competition at work and concern with material success, along with domesticity, emotional supportiveness, and nurturance.

In short, the "fair heterosexual couples" established through interaction particular counterhegemonic practices that fashioned egalitarian gender relations, and both the men and the women orchestrated positive masculinities and femininities respectively (see further, Deutsch 1999; Lorber 2005).

Antiviolence Activists

Michael Flood recently detailed a different type of positive nonhegemonic masculinity: men who become activists in preventing violence against women. As Flood (2014, 35) states, "Men's antiviolence activism is a clear instance of counterhegemonic practice" because it directly challenges a type of unequal gender relations and thus hegemonic masculinity: men's violence against women. Participation by men in antiviolence activism is the most widespread and publicly visible form of pro-feminist work by men today, and some of the common themes as to why certain men become dedicated to this practice include witnessing or having personal experience with sexual and/or domestic violence, inspiration and encouragement from peers and/or women mentors, and as part of one's social justice ideals. Many of these activists also report feeling "compelled to action" (e.g., doing nothing contributes to the problem), they proclaim a change in their own point of view (e.g., violence is a concerning issue for the women they care for), and such work allows them to "join with others" (e.g., it helps to build connections with like-minded men and serves as a means to foster community and mutual support) (41). Men's antiviolence activism then is an example of a positive masculinity because it involves the arrangement of "gender-equitable forms of identity and behavior" accompanied by progressive personal change (48).

Nevertheless, Flood points out that some of these men reproduce hegemonic masculinity as they participate in antiviolence activism. He writes that these men do this by (47)

> using their newfound knowledge to do power to women, claiming to be better feminists than women, playing off one women's group against another, or taking over women's spaces. Men and women learn to relate in ways that advantage men as a group and disadvantage women as a group, because of wider gender inequalities and gender norms.

In other words, some men construct a *hybrid hegemonic masculinity*—rather than a *positive masculinity*—through their involvement in antiviolence activism (see chapter 4). Arguably, then, it is essential to distinguish genuine positive masculinities from deceptive hybrid hegemonic masculinities when discussing antiviolence activism as well as other progressive masculine practices by men.

Michael Messner, Max Greenberg, and Tal Peretz (2015) recently added an important historical dimension to our understanding of antiviolence activism: examining certain men's engagements with progressive gender politics from the 1970s to the present, particularly efforts by these men to prevent sexual and domestic violence against women. Their analysis demonstrates how the intersection of race, class, and gender shaped which men engage in political action with feminist women at particular historical moments, and also how these men and women strategize to counteract this type of violence. For men who engaged in this activist work in the 1970s and 1980s, for example, they were found to be disproportionately white (often Jewish), college educated, and attracted to anti-rape and anti-domestic-violence work by their immersion in feminist and other radical social movements of the era. Today, men seem to be drawn to this type of antiviolence work in a different way: white, middle-class men commonly begin through university-based activism, women's studies courses, and volunteer or paid work in feminist community nonprofits, while men of color attempt to prevent violence against women by working with boys and young men in poor communities around youth gang violence, substance abuse programs, and prison reform. Either way, the research by Messner, Greenberg, and Peretz is valuable in the sense of recognizing and pinpointing certain historically positive masculine practices that challenge unequal gender relations and have crucial implications for social policy.

CONCLUSION

Judith Lorber (1994) noted more than twenty years ago that the "prime paradox" of gender is that in order to dismantle unequal gender relations we must first make them visible. Through a conception of hegemonic masculinity as decentered, fluid, contingent, provisional, yet omnipresent locally, regionally, and globally, I am hopeful this book has contributed to making unequal gender relations more perceptible and thus visible. Multifarious hegemonic masculinities constitute a social structure that legitimates unequal gender relations between men and women, masculinity and femininity, and among masculinities. Hegemonic masculin-

ities are always already constructed *relationally*; they are not something
certain men (and women) or groups of men (and women) exclusively
possess. Concentrating on "exit politics" or encouraging men to "refuse
to be a man"—that is, escaping from masculinity altogether—therefore
has limited validity in dismantling hegemonic masculinities.

In this chapter I offered a critique of IMT that was based on a misunderstanding of hegemonic masculinity and the ignoring of gender
fluidity, women, unequal gender relations, and sexual politics. I then
proffered some positive examples of counterhegemonic personalized
practices that actually present a challenge to the relational quintessence
of hegemonic masculinities. Each of the examples discussed above provides evidence of the differing ways unequal gender relations are or have
been resisted, challenged, and at times actually dismantled. These examples—obviously neither exhaustive nor comprehensive—argue persua-
sively that gendered social change indeed is possible. And by participating in more egalitarian gender relations, both men and women are re-
embodied, constructing new, different, and positive masculinities and
femininities. The goal is not a simplistic androgyny in which everyone is
the same, but *difference with relational equality*—not only between men and
women but among men and among women as well.

The urgency of "difference with relational equality" horrifyingly came
to light when Donald J. Trump was elected the forty-fifth president of the
United States. I will not go into specifics as I have previously (in chapter
4) discussed Trump's fluid and fleeting hegemonic masculinities and
subsequent policies—undeniably a terrifying and alarming election. As I
completed writing this final chapter, however, Trump presented his first
address to the United Nations General Assembly on September 19, 2017,
and in that speech he emphasized that if the United States is "forced to
defend itself or its allies, we will have no choice but to totally destroy
North Korea. Rocket Man is on a suicide mission for himself and for his
regime." Trump's masculine practices and communicative social actions
should now seem all too familiar and predictable to those who have read
this book. If "difference with relational equality" is indeed a critical part
of the response to this madness—and I believe it is—we can ill afford to
wait another day before demanding its embrace.

References

Aboim, S. 2010. *Plural Masculinities: The Remaking of the Self in Private Life.* Burlington, VT: Ashgate.

Acker, J. 1989a. "Making Gender Visible." In *Feminism and Sociological Theory,* edited by R. A. Wallace. Newbury Park, CA: Sage.

———. 1989b. "The Problem with Patriarchy." *Sociology* 23, no. 2: 235–40.

Adams, N., A. Schmitke, and A. Franklin. 2005. "Tomboys, Dykes, and Girly Girls: Interrogating the Subjectivities of Adolescent Female Athletes." *Women's Studies Quarterly* 33, nos. 1/2: 73–91.

Altman, D. 1972. *Homosexual: Oppression and Liberation.* Sydney: Angus and Robertson.

Anderson, E. 2009. *Inclusive Masculinity: The Changing Nature of Masculinities.* New York: Routledge.

Archer, L. 2001. "'Muslim Brothers, Black Lads, Traditional Asians': British Muslim Young Men's Constructions of Race, Religion and Masculinity." *Feminism & Psychology* 11, no. 1: 79–105.

Archer, M. S. 2003. *Structure, Agency, and the Internal Conversation.* New York: Cambridge University Press.

———. 2007. *Making Our Way through the World: Human Reflexivity and Human Mobility.* New York: Cambridge University Press.

———. 2012. *The Reflexive Imperative in Late Modernity.* New York: Cambridge University Press.

Baca Zinn, M. 1982. "Chicano Men and Masculinity." *Journal of Ethnic Studies* 10, no. 2: 29–44.

Barber, K. 2008. "The Well-Coiffed Man: Class, Race, and Heterosexual Masculinity in the Hair Salon." *Gender & Society* 22: 455–76.

———. 2016. *Styling Masculinity: Gender, Class, and Inequality in the Men's Grooming Industry.* New Brunswick, NJ: Rutgers University Press.

Barrett, F. J. 1996. "The Organizational Construction of Hegemonic Masculinity: The Case of the U.S. Navy." *Gender, Work and Organization* 3, no. 3: 129–42.

Beasley, C. 2008. "Re-thinking Hegemonic Masculinity in a Globalizing World." *Men and Masculinities* 11, no. 1: 86–103.

Beechey, V. 1987. *Unequal Work.* London: Verso.

Belton, R. J. 1995. *The Beribboned Bomb: The Image of Woman in Male Surrealist Art.* Calgary: University of Calgary Press.

Bennett, E., and B. Gough. 2013. "In Pursuit of Leanness: The Management of Appearance, Affect and Masculinities within a Men's Weight Loss Forum." *Health* 17, no. 3: 284–99.

Benston, M. 1969. "The Political Economy of Women's Liberation." *Monthly Review* 21, no. 4: 13–27.

Berg, L. D. 1994. "Masculinity, Place and a Binary Discourse of 'Theory' and 'Empirical Investigation' in the Human Geography of Aotearoa/New Zealand." *Gender, Place and Culture* 1, no. 2: 245–60.

Bettis, P., and N. Adams, eds. 2005. *Geographies of Girlhood: Identities In-Between*. Mahwah, NJ: Lawrence Erlbaum.

Bird, S. R. 1996. "Welcome to the Men's Club: Homosociality and the Maintenance of Hegemonic Masculinity." *Gender & Society* 10, no. 2: 120–32.

Blackwood, E. 1994. "Sexuality and Gender in Certain Native American Tribes: The Case of Cross-Gender Females." In *Theorizing Feminism*, edited by A. C. Hermann and A. J. Stewart. Boulder, CO: Westview.

Bourdieu, P. 2001. *Masculine Domination*. Stanford, CA: Stanford University Press.

Brannon, R. 1976. "The Male Sex Role: Our Culture's Blueprint of Manhood, and What It's Done for Us Lately." In *The Forty-Nine Percent Majority: The Male Sex Role*, edited by D. S. David and R. Brannon. Reading, MA: Addison-Wesley.

Bridges, T. 2010. "Men Just Weren't Made to Do This: Performances of Drag at 'Walk a Mile in Her Shoes' Marches." *Gender & Society* 24, no. 1: 5–30.

———. 2014. "A Very 'Gay' Straight? Hybrid Masculinities, Sexual Aesthetics, and the Changing Relationship between Masculinity and Homophobia." *Gender & Society* 28, no. 1: 58–82.

Bridges, T., and C. J. Pascoe. 2018. "On the Elasticity of Gender Hegemony: Why Hybrid Masculinities Fail to Undermine Gender and Sexual Inequality." In *Gender Reckonings: New Social Theory and Research*, edited by J. W. Messerschmidt, P. Martin, M. Messner, and R. Connell. New York: New York University Press.

Brod, H. 1987. *The Making of Masculinities: The New Men's Studies*. Boston: Allen & Unwin.

———. 1994. "Some Thoughts on Some Histories of Some Masculinities: Jews and Other Others." In *Theorizing Masculinities*, edited by D. S. David and R. Bannon. Thousand Oaks, CA: Sage.

Broker, M. 1976. "'I May Be a Queer, but at Least I Am a Man': Male Hegemony and Ascribed versus Achieved Gender." In *Sexual Divisions and Society*, edited by D. Leonard Barker and S. Allen. London: Tavistock.

Broughton, C. 2008. "Migration as Engendered Practice: Mexican Men, Masculinity, and Northward Migration." *Gender & Society* 22, no. 5: 568–89.

Brown, B. 1988. "Review of *Capitalism, Patriarchy, and Crime*." *International Journal of the Sociology of Law* 16, no. 3: 408–12.

Brown, D. 1999. "Complicity and Reproduction in Teaching Physical Education." *Sport, Education and Society* 4, no. 2: 143–59.

Brownmiller, S. 1975. *Against Our Will*. New York: Simon & Schuster.

Budgeon, S. 2014. "The Dynamics of Gender Hegemony." *Sociology* 48: 317–34.

———. 2015. "Theorizing Subjectivity and Feminine Embodiment: Feminist Approaches and Debates." In *Handbook of Children and Youth Studies*, edited by J. Wyn and H. Cahill. New York: Springer.

Bufkin, J. L. 1999. "Bias Crime as Gendered Behavior." *Social Justice* 26, no. 1: 155–76.

Burke, N. B. 2016. "Straight-Acting: Gay Pornography, Heterosexuality, and Hegemonic Masculinity." *Porn Studies* 3, no. 3: 238–54.

Campbell, A. 1991. *The Girls in the Gang*. 2nd ed. Cambridge, MA: Basil Blackwell.

Campbell, H. 2000. "The Glass Phallus: Pub(lic) Masculinity and Drinking in Rural New Zealand." *Rural Sociology* 65, no. 4: 562–81.

Carrigan, T., R. W. Connell, and J. Lee. 1985. "Toward a New Sociology of Masculinity." *Theory and Society* 14, no. 5: 551–604.

———. 1987. "Hard and Heavy: Toward a New Sociology of Masculinity." In *Beyond Patriarchy*, edited by M. Kaufman. New York: Oxford University Press.

Cavender, G. 1999. "Detecting Masculinity." In *Making Trouble: Cultural Constructions of Crime, Deviance and Control*, edited by J. Ferrell and N. Websdale. New York: Aldine de Gruyter.

Cealey Harrison, W. 2006. "The Shadow and the Substance: The Sex/Gender Debate." In *Handbook of Gender and Women's Studies*, edited by K. Davis, M. Evans, and J. Lorber, 35–52. Thousand Oaks, CA: Sage.

Cheng, C. 1996. "'We Choose Not to Compete': The 'Merit' Discourse in the Selection Process, and Asian and Asian American Men and Their Masculinity." In *Masculinities in Organizations*, edited by C. Cheng. Thousand Oaks, CA: Sage.

Christensen, A. D., and S. Q. Jensen. 2014. "Combining Hegemonic Masculinity and Intersectionality." *NORMA: International Journal for Masculinity Studies* 9, nos. 1/2: 60–75.

Cockburn, C. 1983. *Brothers: Male Dominance and Technological Change*. London: Pluto.

———. 1991. *In The Way of Men: Men's Resistance to Sex Equality in Organizations*. London: Macmillan.

Cohn, C., and C. Enloe. 2003. "A Conversation with Cynthia Enloe: Feminists Look at Masculinity and the Men Who Wage War." *Signs* 28, no. 4: 1187–1207.

Collier, R. 1998. *Masculinities, Crime and Criminology: Men, Heterosexuality and the Criminal(ised) Other*. London: Sage.

Collinson, D., and J. Hearn. 2005. "Men and Masculinities in Work, Organizations, and Management." In *Handbook of Studies on Men & Masculinities*, edited by M. S. Kimmel, J. Hearn, and R. W. Connell. Thousand Oaks, CA: Sage.

Collinson, D., D. Knights, and M. Collinson. 1990. *Managing to Discriminate*. London: Routledge.

Connell, R. 1977. *Ruling Class, Ruling Culture*. Cambridge: Cambridge University Press.

———. 1982. "Class, Patriarchy, and Sartre's Theory of Practice." *Theory and Society* 11: 305–20.

———. 1983. *Which Way Is Up? Essays on Sex, Class and Culture*. Sydney: Allen & Unwin.

———. 1985. "Theorizing Gender." *Sociology* 19, no. 2: 260–72.

———. 1987. *Gender and Power*. Sydney: Allen & Unwin.

———. 1990. "An Iron Man: The Body and Some Contradictions of Hegemonic Masculinity." In *Sport, Men and the Gender Order*, edited by M. Messner and D. Sabo. Champaign, IL: Human Kinetics Books.

———. 1995. *Masculinities*. Cambridge, UK: Polity.

———. 1998. "Masculinities and Globalization." *Men and Masculinities* 1, no. 1: 3–23.

———. 2000. *The Men and the Boys*. Sydney: Allen & Unwin.

———. 2003. "Masculinities, Change and Conflict in Global Society: Thinking about the Future of Men's Studies." *Journal of Men's Studies* 11, no. 3: 249–66.

———. 2005. "Globalization, Imperialism, and Masculinities." In *Handbook of Studies on Men & Masculinities*, edited by M. S. Kimmel, J. Hearn, and R. Connell. Thousand Oaks, CA: Sage.

———. 2009. *Gender*. 2nd ed. Cambridge, UK: Polity.

———. 2016. "Masculinities in Global Perspective: Hegemony, Contestation, and Changing Structures of Power." *Theory and Society* 45: 303–18.

Connell, R., D. J. Ashenden, S. Kessler, and G. W. Dowsett. 1982. *Making the Difference: Schools, Families and Social Division.* Sydney: Allen & Unwin.

Connell, R., and J. W. Messerschmidt. 2005. "Hegemonic Masculinity: Rethinking the Concept." *Gender & Society* 19: 829–59.

Connell, R., and J. Wood. 2005. "Globalization and Business Masculinities." *Men and Masculinities* 7, no. 4: 347–64.

Consalvo, M. 2003. "The Monsters Next Door: Media Constructions of Boys and Masculinity." *Feminist Media Studies* 3, no. 1: 27–46.

Cook, J., and R. Hasmath. 2014. "The Discursive Construction and Performance of Gendered Identity on Social Media." *Current Sociology* 62, no. 7: 975–93.

Cott, N. F. 1979. "Passionlessness: An Interpretation of Victorian Sexual Ideology, 1790–1850." In *A Heritage of Her Own,* edited by N. F. Cott and E. H. Pleck. New York: Simon & Schuster.

Crenshaw, K. 1989. "Demarginalizing the Intersection of Race and Sex: A Black Feminist Critique of Antidiscrimination Doctrine, Feminist Theory, and Anti-racist Politics." *University of Chicago Legal Forum* 1989, no. 1: 139–67.

Crompton, R., and K. Sanderson. 1990. *Gendered Jobs and Social Change.* Boston: Unwin Hyman.

Crossley, N. 1995. "Body Techniques, Agency and Intercorporeality: On Goffman's *Relations in Public.*" *Sociology* 29, no. 1: 133–49.

———. 2001. *The Social Body: Habit, Identity and Desire.* Thousand Oaks, CA: Sage.

Dasgupta, R. 2000. "Performing Masculinities? The 'Salaryman' at Work and Play." *Japanese Studies* 20, no. 2: 189–200.

Davis, A. 1983. *Women, Race, and Class.* New York: Vintage.

de Beauvoir, S. (1949) 1972. *The Second Sex.* New York: Penguin.

de Boise, S. 2015. "I'm Not Homophobic, 'I've Got Gay Friends': Evaluating the Validity of Inclusive Masculinity." *Men and Masculinities* 18, no. 3: 318–39.

de Casanova, E. M., E. E. Wetzel, and T. D. Speice. 2016. "Looking at the Label: White-Collar Men and the Meanings of 'Metrosexual.'" *Sexualities* 19: 64–82.

Delgado, J. R. V., and M. Zwarteveen. 2017. "Queering Engineers? Using History to Re-think the Associations between Masculinity and Irrigation Engineering in Peru." *Engineering Studies* 9, no. 2: 140–60.

D'Emilio, J., and E. B. Freedman. 1988. *Intimate Matters: A History of Sexuality in America.* New York: Harper & Row.

Demetriou, D. 2001. "Connell's Concept of Hegemonic Masculinity: A Critique." *Theory and Society* 30, no. 3: 337–61.

Denborough, D. 1996. "Step by Step: Developing Respectful and Effective Ways of Working with Young Men to Reduce Violence." In *Men's Ways of Being,* edited by C. McLean, M. Carey, and C. White. Boulder, CO: Westview.

Deutsch, F. 1999. *Halving It All: How Equally Shared Parenting Works.* Cambridge, MA: Harvard University Press.

———. 2007. "Undoing Gender." *Gender & Society* 21, no. 1: 106–27.

Dill, B. T. 1988. "Our Mothers' Grief: Racial Ethnic Women and the Maintenance of Families." *Journal of Family History* 13, no. 1: 415–31.

Domeneghetti, R. 2017. "'The Other Side of the Net': (Re)presentations of (Emphasised) Femininity during Wimbledon 2016." *Journal of Policy Research in Tourism, Leisure and Events,* November 2017, 1–13.

Donaldson, M. 1991. *Time of Our Lives: Labor and Love in the Working Class*. Sydney: Allen & Unwin.

———. 1993. "What Is Hegemonic Masculinity?" *Theory and Society* 22: 643–57.

Donaldson, M., and S. Poynting. 2004. "The Time of Their Lives: Time, Work and Leisure in the Daily Lives of Ruling-Class Men." In *Ruling Australia: The Power, Privilege & Politics of the New Ruling Class*, edited by N. Hollier. Melbourne: Australian Scholarly.

Duncanson, C. 2009. "Forces for Good? Narratives of Military Masculinity as Peacekeeping Operations." *International Feminist Journal of Politics* 11, no. 1: 63–80.

Dworkin, A. 1979. *Pornography: Men Possessing Women*. New York: Plume.

———. 1980a. "Pornography and Grief." In *Take Back the Night*, edited by L. Lederer. New York: William Morrow.

———. 1980b. "Why So-Called Radical Men Love and Need Pornography." In *Take Back the Night*, edited by L. Lederer. New York: William Morrow.

———. 1987. *Intercourse*. New York: Free Press.

Echols, A. 1989. *Daring to Be Bad: Radical Feminism in America, 1967–1975*. Minneapolis: University of Minnesota Press.

Eisenstein, H. 1983. *Contemporary Feminist Thought*. Boston: G. K. Hall.

Eisenstein, Z. R. 1979. *Capitalist Patriarchy and the Case for Socialist Feminism*. New York: Monthly Review Press.

Elias, J. 2008. "Hegemonic Masculinities, the Multinational Corporation, and the Developmental State: Constructing Gender in 'Progressive' Firms." *Men and Masculinities* 10, no. 4: 405–21.

Engels, F. (1884) 1942. *The Origin of the Family, Private Property, and the State*. New York: International.

Ferguson, H. 2001. "Men and Masculinities in Late-Modern Ireland." In *A Man's World? Changing Men's Practices in a Globalized World*, edited by B. Pease and K. Pringle. London: Zed Books.

Filteau, M. R. 2014. "Who Are Those Guys? Constructing the Oilfield's *New* Dominant Masculinity." *Men and Masculinities* 17, no. 4: 396–416.

Firestone, S. 1970. *The Dialectic of Sex*. New York: William Morrow.

Fishman, L. 1993. "Slave Women, Resistance and Criminality: A Prelude to Future Accommodation." Paper presented at the Annual Meeting of the American Society of Criminology, Phoenix, Arizona, October 29.

Flood, M. 2002. "Between Men and Masculinity: An Assessment of the Term 'Masculinity' in Recent Scholarship on Men." In *Manning the Next Millennium: Studies in Masculinities*, edited by S. Pearce and V. Muller. Chicago: Black Swan.

———. 2014. "Men's Antiviolence Activism and the Construction of Gender-Equitable Masculinities." In *Alternative Masculinities for a Changing World*, edited by A. Carabi and J. M. Armengol. New York: Palgrave Macmillan.

Foucault, M. 1979. *Discipline and Punish: The Birth of the Prison*. New York: Vintage.

———. 1980. *Herculine Barbin*. New York: Vintage.

Fox, J., and W. Y. Tang. 2014. "Sexism in Online Video Games: The Role of Conformity to Masculine Norms and Social Dominance Orientation." *Computers in Human Behavior* 33: 314–20.

Fox-Genovese, E. 1988. *Within the Plantation Household*. Chapel Hill: University of North Carolina Press.

Freud, S. (1917) 1955. *From the History of an Infantile Neurosis. Complete Psychological Works, Standard Edition*, vol. 17. London: Hogarth.

Friedman, R. M., and L. Lerner. 1986. "Toward a New Psychology of Men: Psychoanalytic and Social Perspectives." *Psychoanalytic Review* 73, no. 4: 10–23.

Gage, E. A. 2008. "Gender Attitudes and Sexual Behaviors: Comparing Center and Marginal Athletes and Nonathletes in a Collegiate Setting." *Violence against Women* 14, no. 9: 1014–32.

Gerschick, T. J., and A. S. Miller. 1994. "Gender Identities at the Crossroads of Masculinity and Physical Disability." *Masculinities* 2, no. 1: 34–55.

Giddens, A. 1976. *New Rules of Sociological Method: A Positive Critique of Interpretive Sociologies.* New York: Basic Books.

———. 1984. *The Constitution of Society.* Berkeley: University of California Press.

———. 1991. *Modernity and Self Identity.* Stanford, CA: Stanford University Press.

Ging, D. 2017. "Alphas, Betas, and Incels: Theorizing the Masculinities of the Manosphere." *Men and Masculinities*, May 2017.

Goffman, E. 1963. *Behavior in Public Places.* New York: Free Press.

———. 1968. *Stigma.* Englewood Cliffs, NJ: Prentice Hall.

———. 1972. *Relations in Public.* New York: Harper & Row.

———. 1979. *Gender Advertisements.* New York: Harper & Row.

Gonick, M. 2006. "Between 'Girl Power' and 'Reviving Ophelia': Constituting the Neoliberal Girl Subject." *NWSA Journal* 18, no. 2: 1–22.

Goode, W. 1982. "Why Men Resist." In *Rethinking the Family: Some Feminist Questions*, edited by B. Thorne and M. Yalom. New York: Longman.

Groes-Green, C. 2009. "Hegemonic and Subordinated Masculinities: Class, Violence and Sexual Performance among Young Mozambican Men." *Nordic Journal of African Studies* 18, no. 4: 286–304.

———. 2012. "Philogynous Masculinities: Contextualizing Alternative Manhood in Mozambique." *Men and Masculinities* 15: 91–111.

Gutmann, M. C. 1996. *The Meanings of Macho: Being a Man in Mexico City.* Berkeley: University of California Press.

Hacker, H. M. 1957. "The New Burdens of Masculinity." *Marriage and Family Living* 19, no. 3: 227–33.

Halberstam, J. 1998. *Female Masculinity.* Durham, NC: Duke University Press.

Hanke, R. 1992. "Redesigning Men: Hegemonic Masculinity in Transition." In *Men, Masculinity, and the Media*, edited by S. Craig. Newbury Park, CA: Sage.

Hartmann, H. 1981. "The Unhappy Marriage of Marxism and Feminism: Toward a More Progressive Union." In *Women and Revolution*, edited by L. Sargent. Boston: South End.

Hatfield, E. F. 2010. "'What It Means to Be a Man': Examining Hegemonic Masculinity in *Two and a Half Men.*" *Communication, Culture & Critique* 3: 526–48.

Hawkesworth, M. 1997. "Confounding Gender." *Signs* 22, no. 3: 649–85.

Haywood, C., and M. Mac an Ghaill. 2012. "What's Next for Masculinity? Reflexive Directions for Theory and Research on Masculinity and Education." *Gender and Education* 24, no. 6: 577–92.

Hearn, J. 1996. "Is Masculinity Dead? A Critique of the Concept of Masculinity/Masculinities." In *Understanding Masculinities: Social Relations and Cultural Arenas*, edited by M. Mac an Ghaill. Buckingham, UK: Open University Press.

———. 2004. "From Hegemonic Masculinity to the Hegemony of Men." *Feminist Theory* 5, no. 1: 49–72.

———. 2006. "From Masculinities Back to Men: Tracing Diverse Psychological, Social and Political Threads." *Psychology of Women Section Review* 8, no. 1: 38–51.

Herdt, G. H. 1981. *Guardians of the Flutes: Idioms of Masculinity*. New York: McGraw-Hill.

Heyn, D. 1992. *The Erotic Silence of the American Wife*. New York: Random House.

Higate, P. R. 2003. *Military Masculinities: Identity and the State*. London: Praeger.

Hirsch, D., and D. G. Kachtan. 2017. "Is 'Hegemonic Masculinity' Hegemonic *as* Masculinity? Two Israeli Case Studies." *Men and Masculinities*.

Hoang, K. K. 2015. *Dealing in Desire: Asian Ascendancy, Western Decline, and the Hidden Currencies of Global Sex Work*. Berkeley: University of California Press.

Hochschild, A. 1989. *The Second Shift: Working Parents and the Revolution at Home*. New York: Viking.

Hollander, J. A. 2013. "'I Demand More of People': Accountability, Interaction, and Gender Change." *Gender & Society* 27, no. 1: 5–29.

Hollway, W. 1984. "Women's Power in Heterosexual Sex." *Women's Studies International Forum* 7, no. 1: 63–68.

Holter, Ø. G. 1997. *Gender, Patriarchy and Capitalism: A Social Forms Analysis*. Oslo: University of Oslo.

———. 2003. *Can Men Do It? Men and Gender Equality—The Nordic Experience*. Copenhagen: Nordic Council of Ministers.

hooks, b. 1984. *Feminist Theory: From Margin to Center*. Boston: South End.

Hooper, C. 1998. "Masculinist Practices and Gender Politics: The Operation of Multiple Masculinities in International Relations." In *The "Man" Question in International Relations*, edited by M. Zalewski and J. Parpart. Boulder, CO: Westview.

———. 2000. "Masculinities in Transition: The Case of Globalization." In *Gender and Global Restructuring*, edited by M. H. Marchand and A. S. Runyan. London: Routledge.

———. 2001. *Manly States: Masculinities, International Relations, and Gender Politics*. New York: Columbia University Press.

Howson, R. 2006. *Challenging Hegemonic Masculinity*. New York: Routledge.

———. 2009. "Deconstructing Hegemonic Masculinity: Contradiction, Hegemony and Dislocation." *Nordic Journal for Masculinity Studies* 4, no. 1: 6–24.

Hunt, P. 1980. *Gender and Class Consciousness*. London: Macmillan.

Ingram, N., and R. Waller. 2014. "Degrees of Masculinity: Working- and Middle-Class Undergraduate Students' Construction of Masculine Identities." In *Debating Modern Masculinities: Change, Continuity, Crisis?*, edited by S. Roberts. New York: Palgrave Macmillan.

Irvine, L., and J. Vermilya. 2010. "Gender Work in a Feminized Profession: The Case of Veterinary Medicine." *Gender & Society* 24, no. 1: 56–82.

Ishii-Kuntz, M. 2003. "Balancing Fatherhood and Work: Emergence of Diverse Masculinities in Contemporary Japan." In *Men and Masculinities in Contemporary Japan*, edited by J. E. Roberson and N. Suzuki. London: RoutledgeCurzon.

Jackson, S. 2007. "The Sexual Self in Late Modernity." In *The Sexual Self*, edited by M. Kimmel, 3–15. Nashville, TN: Vanderbilt University Press.

Jackson, S., and S. Scott. 2010. *Theorizing Sexuality*. New York: McGraw-Hill.

Jaggar, A. 1983. *Feminist Politics and Human Nature*. Totowa, NJ: Rowman & Littlefield.

Jaggar, A., and W. McBride. 1985. "'Reproduction' as Male Ideology." *Women's Studies International Forum* 8, no. 3: 185–96.

Jansen, S. C., and D. Sabo. 1994. "The Sport-War Metaphor: Hegemonic Masculinity, the Persian-Gulf War, and the New World Order." *Sociology of Sport Journal* 11, no. 1: 1–17.

Jefferson, T. 1994. "Theorizing Masculine Subjectivity." In *Just Boys Doing Business? Men, Masculinities and Crime*, edited by T. Newburn and E. A. Stanko. London: Routledge.

———. 2002. "Subordinating Hegemonic Masculinity." *Theoretical Criminology* 6, no. 1: 63–88.

Kendall, L. 2000. "'Oh No! I'm a Nerd!' Hegemonic Masculinity on an Online Forum." *Gender & Society* 14, no. 2: 256–74.

Kessler, S. J., and W. McKenna. 1978. *Gender: An Ethnomethodological Approach*. New York: Wiley.

Kessler, S. J., D. J. Ashenden, R. W. Connell, and G. W. Dowsett. 1982. *Ockers and Disco-Maniacs*. Sydney: Inner City Education Center.

Khalili, L. 2011. "Gendered Practices of Counterinsurgency." *Review of International Studies* 37: 1471–91.

Kian, E. M., G. Clavio, J. Vincent, and S. Shaw. 2011. "Homophobic and Sexist Yet Uncontested: Examining Football Fan Postings on Internet Message Boards." *Journal of Homosexuality* 58, no. 5: 680–99.

Kimmel, M. S. 1987. "Rethinking 'Masculinity': New Directions in Research." In *Changing Men: New Directions in Research on Men and Masculinity*, edited by M. S. Kimmel. Newbury Park, CA: Sage.

———. 2005. "Globalization and Its Mal(e)contents: The Gendered Moral and Political Economy of Terrorism." In *Handbook of Studies on Men & Masculinities*, edited by M. S. Kimmel, J. Hearn, and R. W. Connell. Thousand Oaks, CA: Sage.

Kimmel, M. S., and M. Mahler. 2003. "Adolescent Masculinity, Homophobia, and Violence: Random School Shootings, 1982–2001." *American Behavioral Scientist* 46, no. 10: 1439–58.

Kimmel, M. S., and T. E. Mosmiller. 1992. *Against the Tide*. Boston: Beacon.

King, D. K. 1988. "Multiple Jeopardy, Multiple Consciousness: The Context of Black Feminist Ideology." *Signs* 14, no. 1: 42–72.

Kitzinger, C. 2005. "Heteronormativity in Action: Reproducing the Heterosexual Nuclear Family in After-Hours Medical Calls." *Social Problems* 52, no. 4: 477–98.

Koedt, A. 1973. "The Myth of the Vaginal Orgasm." In *Radical Feminism*, edited by A. Koedt, E. Levine, and A. Rapone. New York: Quadrangle Books.

Kupers, T. A. 1993. *Revisioning Men's Lives: Gender, Intimacy, and Power*. New York: Guilford.

Laqueur, T. 1990. *Making Sex: Body and Gender from the Greeks to Freud*. Cambridge, MA: Harvard University Press.

Lea, S., and T. Auburn. 2001. "The Social Construction of Rape in the Talk of a Convicted Rapist." *Feminism & Psychology* 11, no. 1: 11–33.

Liddle, A. M. 1989. "Feminist Contributions to an Understanding of Violence against Women: Three Steps Forward, Two Steps Back." *Canadian Review of Sociology and Anthropology* 26, no. 5: 759–75.

Light, R. 2007. "Re-examining Hegemonic Masculinity in High School Rugby: The Body, Compliance and Resistance." *Quest* 59: 323–38.

Lindemann, B. S. 1984. "'To Ravish and Carnally Know': Rape in Eighteenth-Century Massachusetts." *Signs* 10, no. 1: 63–82.

Logan, T. D. 2010. "Personal Characteristics, Sexual Behaviors, and Male Sex Work: A Quantitative Approach." *American Sociological Review* 75, no. 5: 679–704.

Lomas, T., T. Cartwright, T. Edginton, and D. Ridge. 2016. "New Ways of Being a Man: 'Positive' Hegemonic Masculinity in Meditation-Based Communities of Practice." *Men and Masculinities* 19, no. 3 (March): 289–310.

Lopata, H., and B. Thorne. 1978. "On the Term 'Sex Roles.'" *Signs* 3: 718–21.

Lorber, J. 1994. *Paradoxes of Gender*. New Haven, CT: Yale University Press.

———. 2005. *Breaking the Bowls*. New York: Norton.

Mac an Ghaill, M. 1994. *The Making of Men: Masculinities, Sexualities and Schooling*. Buckingham, UK: Open University Press.

MacInnes, J. 1998. *The End of Masculinity: The Confusion of Sexual Genesis and Sexual Difference in Modern Society*. Buckingham, UK: Open University Press.

MacKinnon, C. 1989. *Toward a Feminist Theory of the State*. Cambridge, MA: Harvard University Press.

Magrath, R., E. Anderson, and S. Roberts. 2015. "On the Doorstep of Equality: Attitudes toward Gay Athletes among Academy-Level Footballers." *International Review for the Sociology of Sport* 50, no. 7: 804–21.

Martin, P. Y. 1998. "Why Can't a Man Be More Like a Woman? Reflections on Connell's Masculinities." *Gender & Society* 12, no. 4: 472–74.

———. 2001. "'Mobilizing Masculinities': Women's Experiences of Men at Work." *Organizations* 8, no. 4: 587–618.

———. 2003. "'Said and Done' versus 'Saying and Doing': Gendering Practices, Practicing Gender at Work." *Gender & Society* 17: 342–66.

Martino, W. 1995. "Boys and Literacy: Exploring the Construction of Hegemonic Masculinities and the Formation of Literate Capacities for Boys in the English Classroom." *English in Australia* 112: 11–24.

McCormack, M. 2012. *The Declining Significance of Homophobia: How Teenage Boys Are Redefining Masculinity and Heterosexuality*. New York: Oxford University Press.

McDowell, A. D. 2017. "Aggressive and Loving Men: Gender Hegemony in Christian Hardcore Punk." *Gender & Society* 31, no. 2: 223–44.

McMahon, A. 1993. "Male Readings of Feminist Theory: The Psychologization of Sexual Politics in the Masculinity Literature." *Theory and Society* 22, no. 5: 675–95.

McRobbie, A. 2009. *The Aftermath of Feminism: Gender, Culture and Social Change*. London: Sage.

Mernissi, F. 1975. *Beyond the Veil: Male-Female Dynamics in Modern Muslim Society*. London: Saqi Books.

Messerschmidt, J. W. 1993. *Masculinities and Crime: Critique and Reconceptualization of Theory*. Lanham, MD: Rowman & Littlefield.

———. 1995. "Managing to Kill: Masculinities and the Space Shuttle Challenger Explosion." *Masculinities* 3, no. 4: 1–22.

———. 1997. *Crime as Structured Action: Gender, Race, Class and Crime in the Making*. Thousand Oaks, CA: Sage.

———. 2000. *Nine Lives: Adolescent Masculinities, the Body, and Violence*. Boulder, CO: Westview.

———. 2004. *Flesh & Blood: Adolescent Gender Diversity and Violence*. Lanham, MD: Rowman & Littlefield.

———. 2005. "Men, Masculinities, and Crime." In *Handbook of Studies on Men & Masculinities*, edited by M. S. Kimmel, J. Hearn, and R. W. Connell. Thousand Oaks, CA: Sage.

———. 2008. "And Now, the Rest of the Story . . ." *Men and Masculinities* 11, no. 1: 104–8.

————. 2010. *Hegemonic Masculinities and Camouflaged Politics*. Boulder, CO: Paradigm.

————. 2012. *Gender, Heterosexuality, and Youth Violence*. Lanham, MD: Rowman & Littlefield.

————. 2014. *Crime as Structured Action*. 2nd ed. Lanham, MD: Rowman & Littlefield.

————. 2016. *Masculinities in the Making: From the Local to the Global*. Lanham, MD: Rowman & Littlefield.

Messerschmidt, J. W., and T. Bridges. 2017. "Trump and the Politics of Fluid Masculinities." *Feminist Reflections: The Society Pages*, July 17, 2017. https://thesocietypages.org/feminist/2017/07/17/trump-and-the-politics-of-fluid-masculinities/.

Messner, M. A. 1992. *Power at Play: Sports and the Problem of Masculinity*. Boston: Beacon.

Messner, M. A., M. A. Greenberg, and T. Peretz. 2015. *Some Men: Feminist Allies and the Movement to End Violence against Women*. New York: Oxford University Press.

Messner, M. A., and D. Sabo, eds. 1990. *Sport, Men, and the Gender Order: Critical Feminist Perspectives*. Champaign, IL: Human Kinetics Books.

Meuser, M. 2001. "'This Doesn't Really Mean She's Holding a Whip': Transformation of the Gender Order and the Contradictory Modernization of Masculinity." *Diskurs* 1: 44–50.

————. 2003. "Modernized Masculinities? Continuities, Challenges and Changes in Men's Lives." In *Among Men: Moulding Masculinities*, edited by S. Ervø and T. Johansson. Aldershot, UK: Ashgate.

Meuser, M., and C. Behnke. 1998. "Tausendeine männlichkeit? Männlichkeitsmuster un sozialstrukturelle einbindungen." *Widersprüche* 67: 7–25.

Mieli, M. 1980. *Homosexuality and Liberation: Elements of a Gay Critique*. Translated by D. Fernbach. London: Gay Men's Press.

Miller, G. E. 2004. "Frontier Masculinity in the Oil Industry: The Experience of Women Engineers." *Gender, Work and Organization* 11, no. 1: 47–73.

Millett, K. 1970. *Sexual Politics*. New York: Doubleday.

Mitchell, J. 1966. "Women: The Longest Revolution." *New Left Review* 40: 11–37.

Mittelman, J. H. 2004. *Whither Globalization? The Vortex of Knowledge and Ideology*. London: Routledge.

Mohanty, C. T. 1988. "Under Western Eyes: Feminist Scholarship and Colonial Discourse." *Feminist Review* 30: 61–88.

Mojola, S. A. 2014. "Providing Women, Kept Men: Doing Masculinity in the Wake of the African HIV/AIDS Pandemic." *Signs* 39, no. 2: 341–63.

Morgan, D. 1992. *Discovering Men*. New York: Routledge.

Morgan, R. 1978. *Going Too Far*. New York: Random House.

Morin, S. F., and E. M. Garfinkle. 1978. "Male Homophobia." *Journal of Social Issues* 34, no. 1: 29–47.

Morrell, R. 1994. "Masculinity and the White Boys' Boarding Schools of Natal, 1880–1930." *Perspectives in Education* 15: 27–52.

————. 1998. "Of Boys and Men: Masculinity and Gender in Southern African Studies." *Journal of Southern African Studies* 24: 605–30.

————, ed. 2001. *Changing Men in Southern Africa*. London: Zed Books.

Morrell, R., and S. Swart. 2005. "Men in the Third World: Postcolonial Perspectives on Masculinity." In *Handbook of Studies on Men & Masculinities*, edited by M. S. Kimmel, J. Hearn, and R. W. Connell. Thousand Oaks, CA: Sage.

Morris, C., and N. Evans. 2001. "'Cheese Makers Are Always Women': Gendered Representations of Farm Life in the Agricultural Press." *Gender, Place and Culture* 8, no. 4: 375–90.

Morris, E. W. 2008. "'Rednecks,' 'Rutters,' and 'Rithmetic': Social Class, Masculinity, and Schooling in a Rural Context." *Gender & Society* 22, no. 6: 728–51.

Mosher, D. L., and S. S. Tomkins. 1988. "Scripting the Macho Man: Hypermasculine Socialization and Enculturation." *Journal of Sex Research* 25, no. 1: 60–84.

Mouzelis, N. P. 2008. *Modern and Postmodern Theorizing: Bridging the Divide.* New York: Cambridge University Press.

Musto, M. 2014. "Athletes in the Pool, Girls and Boys on the Deck: The Contextual Construction of Gender in Co-ed Youth Swimming." *Gender & Society* 28: 359–80.

Namaste, V. K. 2000. *Invisible Lives: The Erasure of Transsexual and Transgendered People.* Chicago: University of Chicago Press.

Nandy, A. 1983. *The Intimate Enemy: Loss and Recovery of Self under Colonialism.* New York: Oxford University Press.

Newburn, T., and E. A. Stanko. 1994. *Just Boys Doing Business? Men, Masculinities, and Crime.* New York: Routledge.

Oakley, A. 1972. *Sex, Gender, and Society.* San Francisco: Harper & Row.

O'Neill, R. 2015. "Whither Critical Masculinity Studies? Notes on Inclusive Masculinity Theory, Postfeminism, and Sexual Politics." *Men and Masculinities* 18, no. 1: 100–120.

Orlando, V. 2001. "Transposing the Political and the Aesthetic: Eugene Fromentin's Contributions to Oriental Stereotypes of North Africa." In *Images of Africa: Stereotypes and Realities,* edited by Daniel M. Mengara. Trenton, NJ: Africa World.

Ozyegin, G. 2018. "Rethinking Patriarchy through Unpatriarchal Male Desires." In *Gender Reckonings: New Social Theory and Research,* edited by J. W. Messerschmidt, P. Martin, M. Messner, and R. Connell. New York: New York University Press.

Paechter, C. 2006. "Masculine Femininities/Feminine Masculinities: Power, Identities, and Gender." *Gender and Education* 18, no. 3: 253–63.

Pascoe, C. J. 2011. *Dude You're a Fag.* Berkeley: University of California Press.

Patil, V. 2013. "From Patriarchy to Intersectionality: A Transnational Feminist Assessment of How Far We've Really Come." *Signs* 38, no. 4: 847–67.

Paz, O. 1950. *The Labyrinth of Solitude.* New York: Penguin.

Pease, B., and K. Pringle, eds. 2001. *A Man's World? Changing Men's Practices in a Globalized World.* London: Zed Books.

Peterson, A. 1998. *Unmasking the Masculine: 'Men' and 'Identity' in a Sceptical Age.* London: Sage.

———. 2003. "Research on Men and Masculinities: Some Implications of Recent Theory for Future Work." *Men and Masculinities* 6, no. 1: 54–69.

———. 2011. "The 'Long Winding Road' to Adulthood: A Risk-Filled Journey for Young People in Stockholm's Marginalized Periphery." *Young* 19, no. 3: 271–89.

Pfaffendorf, J. 2017. "Sensitive Cowboys: Privileged Young Men and the Mobilization of Hybrid Masculinities in a Therapeutic Boarding School." *Gender & Society* 31, no. 2: 197–222.

Pleck, J. 1981. *The Myth of Masculinity.* Cambridge, MA: MIT Press.

Plummer, K., ed. 1981. *The Making of the Modern Homosexual.* London: Macmillan.

Porter, R. 1986. "Rape—Does It Have a Historical Meaning?" In *Rape,* edited by S. Tomaselli and R. Porter. New York: Basil Blackwell.

Prieur, A. 1990. "The Male Role and Sexual Assault." In *Gender, Sexuality, and Social Control*, edited by B. Rolston and M. Tomlinson. Bristol, UK: European Group for the Study of Deviance.

Pruitt, A. S. 2017. "Redoing Gender: How Women in the Funeral Industry Use Essentialism for Equality." *Gender, Work and Organization*, September 2017, 1–15.

Rich, A. 1976. *Of Woman Born*. New York: Norton.

Ringrose, J. 2007. "Successful Girls? Complicating Post-feminist, Neoliberal Discourses of Education Achievement and Gender Equality." *Gender and Education* 19, no. 4: 471–89.

Risman, B. 1998. *Gender Vertigo: American Families in Transition*. New Haven, CT: Yale University Press.

———. 2009. "From Doing to Undoing: Gender as We Know It." *Gender & Society* 23, no. 1: 81–84.

Roberts, P. 1993. "Social Control and the Censure(s) of Sex." *Crime, Law and Social Change* 19, no. 2: 171–86.

Roberts, S., E. Anderson, and R. Magrath. 2017. "Continuity, Change and Complexity in the Performance of Masculinity among Elite Young Footballers in England." *British Journal of Sociology* 68, no. 2: 336–57.

Roper, M. 1994. *Masculinity and the British Organization Man since 1945*. Oxford: Oxford University Press.

Roper, M., and J. Tosh. 1991. Introduction to *Manful Assertions*, edited by M. Roper and J. Tosh. New York: Routledge.

Rowbotham, S. 1973. *Women's Consciousness, Man's World*. New York: Penguin.

———. 1981. "The Trouble with 'Patriarchy.'" In *People's History and Socialist Theory*, edited by S. Raphael. Boston: Routledge & Kegan Paul.

Rubin, H. 2003. *Self-Made Men: Identity and Embodiment among Transsexual Men*. Nashville, TN: Vanderbilt University Press.

Sabo, D., and D. F. Gordon, eds. 1995. *Men's Health and Illness: Gender, Power and the Body*. Thousand Oaks, CA: Sage.

Sabo, D., and S. C. Jansen. 1992. "Images of Men in Sport Media: The Social Reproduction of Gender Order." In *Men, Masculinity, and the Media*, edited by S. Craig. Newbury Park, CA: Sage.

Salisbury, J., and D. Jackson. 1996. *Challenging Macho Values: Practical Ways of Working with Adolescent Boys*. Washington, DC: Falmer.

Sartre, J.-P. 1956. *Being and Nothingness*. New York: Washington Square.

Schippers, M. 2000. "The Social Organization of Sexuality and Gender in Alternative Hard Rock: An Analysis of Intersectionality." *Gender & Society* 14, no. 6: 747–64.

———. 2007. "Recovering the Feminine Other: Masculinity, Femininity, and Gender Hegemony." *Theory & Society* 36, no. 1: 85–102.

Schmitz, R. M., and E. Kazyak. 2016. "Masculinities in Cyberspace: An Analysis of Portrayals of Manhood in Men's Rights Activist Websites." *Social Sciences* 5, no. 18: 1–16.

Schnurr, S., O. Zayts, and C. Hopkins. 2016. "Challenging Hegemonic Femininities? The Discourse of Trailing Spouses in Hong Kong." *Language in Society* 45: 533–55.

Schwalbe, M. 1992. "Male Supremacy and the Narrowing of the Moral Self." *Berkeley Journal of Sociology* 37: 29–54.

Scott, J. W. 1997. "Comment on Hawkesworth's 'Confounding Gender.'" *Signs* 22, no. 3: 697–702.

Seccombe, W. 1973. "The Housewife and Her Labour under Capitalism." *New Left Review* 83, no. 1: 3–24.

Segal, L. 1988. *Is the Future Female? Troubled Thoughts on Contemporary Feminism*. New York: Peter Bedrick Books.

———. 1990. *Slow Motion: Changing Masculinities, Changing Men*. London: Virago.

Seidman, S. 2010. *The Social Construction of Sexuality*. 2nd ed. New York: Norton.

Silva, J. M. 2008. "A New Generation of Women? How Female ROTC Cadets Negotiate the Tension between Masculine Military Culture and Traditional Femininity." *Social Forces* 87, no. 2: 937–60.

Skelton, A. 1993. "On Becoming a Male Physical Education Teacher: The Informal Culture of Students and the Construction of Hegemonic Masculinity." *Gender and Education* 5, no. 3: 289–303.

Smart, C. 1987. "Review of *Capitalism, Patriarchy, and Crime*." *Contemporary Crises* 11, no. 3: 327–29.

———. 1989. *Feminism and the Power of Law*. New York: Routledge.

Snodgrass, J., ed. 1977. *For Men against Sexism: A Book of Readings*. Albion, CA: Times Change.

Spellman, E. V. 1988. *Inessential Woman: Problems of Exclusion in Feminist Thought*. Boston: Beacon.

Stoller, R. J. 1968. *Sex and Gender: On the Development of Masculinity and Femininity*. New York: Science House.

Swain, J. 2006. "Reflections on Patterns of Masculinity in School Settings." *Men and Masculinities* 8, no. 3: 331–49.

Taga, F. 2003. "Rethinking Male Socialization: Life Histories of Japanese Male Youth." In *Asian Masculinities*, edited by K. Louie and M. Low. London: RoutledgeCurzon.

Talbot, K., and M. Quayle. 2010. "The Perils of Being a Nice Guy: Contextual Variation in Five Young Women's Constructions of Acceptable Hegemonic and Alternative Masculinities." *Men and Masculinities* 13, no. 2: 255–78.

Thompson, S. 1990. "'Drastic Entertainments': Teenage Mothers' Signifying Narratives." In *Uncertain Terms: Negotiating Gender in American Culture*, edited by F. Ginsburg and A. L. Tsing. Boston: Beacon.

Thorne, B. 1993. *Gender Play*. New Brunswick, NJ: Rutgers University Press.

Thornton, M. 1989. "Hegemonic Masculinity and the Academy." *International Journal of the Sociology of Law* 17: 115–30.

Tolson, A. 1977. *The Limits of Masculinity*. London: Tavistock.

Tomsen, S. 2002. *Hatred, Murder and Male Honour: Anti-homosexual Homicides in New South Wales, 1980–2000*. Canberra: Australian Institute of Criminology.

Tong, R. 1989. *Feminist Thought*. Boulder, CO: Westview.

Ulrich, L. T. 1983. *Goodwives*. New York: Knopf.

Valdés, T., and J. Olavarría. 1998. "Ser hombre en Santiago de Chile: A pesar de todo, un mismo modelo." In *Masculinidades y equidad de género en América Latina*, edited by T. Valdés and J. Olavarría. Santiago, Chile: FLACSO/UNFPA.

Wajcman, J. 1999. *Managing Like a Man: Women and Men in Corporate Management*. Sydney: Allen & Unwin.

Walby, S. 1986. *Patriarchy at Work*. Minneapolis: University of Minnesota Press.

———. 1997. *Gender Transformations*. London: Routledge.

Walker, L., and J. Eller. 2016. "Raising Capital: Claims of Masculinity among Men on Match.com." *Men and Masculinities* 19, no. 1: 42–63.

Warren, S. 1997. "Who Do These Boys Think They Are? An Investigation into the Construction of Masculinities in a Primary Classroom." *International Journal of Inclusive Education* 1, no. 2: 207–22.

Weitzer, R., and C. E. Kubrin. 2009. "Misogyny in Rap Music: A Content Analysis of Prevalence and Meanings." *Men and Masculinities* 12, no. 1: 3–29.

West, C., and S. Fenstermaker. 1995. "Doing Difference." *Gender & Society* 9: 8–37.

West, C., and D. Zimmerman. 1987. "Doing Gender." *Gender & Society* 1, no. 2: 125–51.

Wetherell, M., and N. Edley. 1999. "Negotiating Hegemonic Masculinity: Imaginary Positions and Psycho-discursive Practices." *Feminism and Psychology* 9, no. 3: 335–56.

Whitehead, S. M. 1998. "Hegemonic Masculinity Revisited." *Gender, Work, and Organization* 6, no. 1: 58–62.

———. 2002. *Men and Masculinities: Key Themes and New Directions*. Cambridge, UK: Polity.

Williams, W. L. 1986. *The Spirit and the Flesh: Sexual Diversity in American Indian Culture*. Boston: Beacon.

Willis, P. 1977. *Learning to Labor: How Working Class Kids Get Working Class Jobs*. Farnborough, UK: Saxon House.

Wolkomir, M. 2012. "'You Fold Like a Little Girl': (Hetero)Gender Framing and Competitive Strategies of Men and Women in No Limit Texas Hold 'Em Poker Games." *Qualitative Sociology* 35: 407–26.

Young, I. M. 1990. *Throwing Like a Girl and Other Essays in Feminist Philosophy and Social Theory*. Bloomington: Indiana University Press.

Young, K. M. 2017. "Masculine Compensation and Masculine Balance: Notes on the Hawaiian Cockfight." *Social Forces* 95, no. 4 (June): 1341–70.

Zalewski, M., and J. Parpart, eds. 1998. *The "Man" Question in International Relations*. Boulder, CO: Westview.

Zaretsky, E. 1975. "Male Supremacy and the Unconscious." *Socialist Revolution* 4: 7–55.

Index

About the Author

James W. Messerschmidt is professor of sociology and chair of the Department of Criminology at the University of Southern Maine. In addition to more than sixty-five articles and book chapters, he has authored thirteen books, with the most recent being *Gender Reckonings: New Social Theory and Research*, coedited with Patricia Martin, Michael Messner, and Raewyn Connell (2018), and *Masculinities and Crime: A Quarter Century of Theory and Research*, 25th Anniversary Edition (Lanham, MD: Rowman & Littlefield, 2018). In 2011 he received the Outstanding Feminist Faculty Award from the Women and Gender Studies Program at the University of Southern Maine for his notable contributions to scholarship in gender studies, and in 2012 he received the Outstanding Alumni Award from San Diego State University for his distinguished scholarly contributions to criminology. He is also an adjunct faculty member at the School of Justice, Faculty of Law, Queensland University of Technology, Brisbane, Australia.